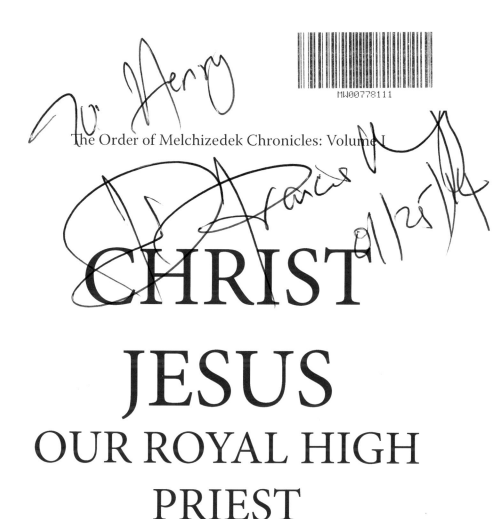

The Order of Melchizedek Chronicles: Volume I

CHRIST
JESUS
OUR ROYAL HIGH
PRIEST

A Christian's Guide to Understanding the Book of Hebrews and the
Inner Workings of Yeshua Ha-Mashiach's Melchizedek Priesthood!

By

Dr. Francis Myles

Christ Jesus: Our Royal High Priest

Published by: The Order of Melchizedek Leadership Initiative, P.O Box 528, Higley, AZ 85236

Unless otherwise indicated, all scriptural quotations are from the King James Version.

Cover Design by Workinperkins Media

ACKNOWLEDGEMENTS

WHAT we become in God is a sum total of the divine encounters we have had, the people we have met, the experiences that we have had and the books we have read. The saying "No man is an Island" is certainly true in the context of the authoring of this wonderful book. I want to acknowledge the impact that the following men and women of God have had on my life: Dr. Jonathan David (my father in the faith), Daniel and Ester Mbepa (my beloved parents), Dr. John P. Kelly (who commissioned me as an apostle), Bishop Robert Smith (who taught me about the One New Man), Kyle and Tari Newton, Danny Seay, Prophet Richard Eberiga, Prophet Kevin Leal, Dr. G.E. Bradshaw and Dr. Bruce Cook (my covenant brothers), Apostle Cheryl Fortson, Apostle Guillermo Maldonado and Sid Roth. Their teachings and personal conversations with me have added to the richness of this book.

While much of the material in this book is original, I have included a few quotes that have been taken from the published works of other notable Christian authors. Wherever such quotes have been used, I have given complete credit for the quote to the original author by referencing the name of the author, the name of their book, the year it was published, the name of the publisher and the exact page number where the quote is found.

DEDICATION

This book is dedicated to:

- The Kingdom of God that is advancing into every sphere of human enterprise.

- To Senior Pastors of Churches who are looking for a more "excellent way" to disciple their congregations into the deep things of the Kingdom of God.

- To born again believers who have long desired to understand the book of Hebrews and the Melchizedek priesthood of Yeshua.

- To all the Josephs and Daniels in the Marketplace who have been looking for a more excellent way of manifesting their marketplace mantles.

- To all disfranchised Christians who know intuitively that there is more to God's Kingdom than what they have seen in most traditional churches.

- To the faithful members of my congregation, "Royal Priesthood Fellowship Church" who have chosen to sow their lives into the apostolic vision that God has placed on my life to transform nations.

AUTHORS
HALL OF APPRECIATION

The Lord gave the word: **great was the company** *of those that published it.*

Psalm 68:11

IT has been said that great projects are never the work of one man, but the collective effort of a team that shares a common destiny. I want to give a heartfelt God bless you to the following brothers and sisters for making the publishing of this book a reality. May God give you a tremendous harvest for every person who will be transformed by the truths contained in this book.

- My dear wife and best friend, Carmela Real Myles.

- To Minister Linda Reiter and LaWanda Whyte for laboring to edit this book so I could present a masterpiece to the world. I love you both.

- To my dear friend, Prophet Jesse Bielby for your prophetic inspiration.

- To Jamie and Angie Bokelmann, my spiritual children, who exemplify the transforming power of the Melchizedek Priesthood.

- To the members of Royal Priesthood Fellowship Church.

- To Ventures 7000 and TFF for your ongoing financial support.

- To Fred and Lisa Simila for being tireless at managing my finances in a spirit of excellence!

- To my dear friends, Kyle and Tari Newton, for all the little major things that you do.

- To my mother in law, "Mommy Avelina Real" and to May, Nick and Katie. I love you guys.

ENDORSEMENTS

IF If the book of Hebrews was taken out of the entire Bible, the Body of Christ would never come into the full understanding and revelation of the Eternal Priesthood of our Lord Jesus Christ. In this powerful exegesis of the book of Hebrews, my husband, like an archeologist, will uncover one of the most important mysteries of all ages that have been hidden from the Body of Christ for a long time. It has always been there so this book will give you powerful insight that will help you re-dig this ancient well of revelation regarding the Order of our Lord's Eternal Priesthood.

If Jesus Christ is our head and He is under the Order of Melchizedek then we, His body, should also be operating under this Order. So why is it that even as of this writing, a major part of the Body of Christ, including pastors, has limited understanding or have not even heard of Melchizedek? According to the Apostle Paul in Hebrews 5:10-15, he had many things to say about Melchizedek but was not able to because certain believers were just content with milk and were not ready for this strong meat. However, I believe that we have entered a season in which the Body of Christ is ready and hungry for this revelation. It makes sense that a time will come when His body has to be realigned with His Head and there is only one direction to go. My husband and I have traveled throughout the United States and the nations of the world and have met many believers with the same cry, "We need something different, there's got to be something more". I have seen the same people come alive as they were awakened to this revelation and their testimonies are off the chart. It is time!

So I challenge you to open your heart and mind and allow the Holy Spirit to flood the heart of your understanding with His light with the revelation in this book to be magnified in your very being. Proverbs 25:2 states that it is the glory of God to conceal a matter but it is the glory of the kings to search them out. It is time to awaken the king inside of you and let this revelation be your glory. I promise you that you will never be the same.

This book will not only give you a solid foundation in your Christian walk, but it will also give you an eternal revelation of the Order of Priesthood in which you should be operating. This revelation is one of the keys that will unlock your breakthrough to converge you with your destiny. It will transform your mindset and will transcend you beyond time to know your place and position from before the foundation of this world.

— Carmela Real Myles

— 🌿 —

Dr. Francis Myles provides a clear and profound exegesis on the book of Hebrews. His specific detail to the importance of Christ's Melchizedek Priesthood and its inner workings particularly written to a Jewish audience is made plain to all who read.

Doctor Francis Myles' sensitivity in the understandings of Christ Melchizedek Priesthood and its relevant applications for today's believer's walk, challenges the Church to re-examine its Traditional Doctrine with regard to Christology

— Apostle Brinson, *Chicago, IL*

— 🌿 —

The truth revealed in The Order of Melchizedek Chronicles: Volume I, Christ Jesus: Our Royal High Priest is a teaching for this season. Understanding the Order of Melchizedek is foundational for the advancement of the Kingdom of God within the market place, local churches, and the Nations. It is vital that the church understand its position within the Order of Melchizedek with Jesus Christ as our Royal High Priest. Dr. Myles, as God's archeologist, has uncovered the ancient truth of the Order of Melchizedek in an enlightening exegetical exploration of the Bible. This book will transform your life! Every believer needs to have this invaluable book within arms reach.

— Rev. Ty McGehee, *Lead Pastor/ Founder, Kingdom International, Mesa, AZ*

God raises those in every generation who will trumpet a clarion call to bring the Church closer to fulfillment of His eternal purposes. Dr. Francis Myles is a Jehovah-elected mouthpiece calling priestly kings to ascend into the Order of Melchizedek with an enlightened understanding of not only who Melchizedek is; but also, who they are within the order.

While some may drowsily hit the snooze control and portions of the Church seem content to roll back over to sleep, others are sounding an end-time alarm to awaken the Bride of Christ to prepare themselves to be equally yoked with their Groom Jesus. Imperative to this initiative is the rallying shout we hear clearly and emphatically between the lines from Dr. Myles, "Awake! Awake! Awake!"

Just as the rabbis teach, there is a requirement of two for a witness, and three witnesses are a perfect witness.* In this manner, Dr. Myles brings scriptural truth to spiritual life in highlighting the importance of the three witnesses from holy writ — Abraham, David, and the Apostle Paul — who establish the three-fold witness of Melchizedek. The two eye-opening testimonies from our Patriarch Abraham and King David from the Old Covenant would have been sufficient to convince us to "Awake! Awake!" However, Dr. Myles profoundly relays the importance in the reconciling account of the Apostle Paul in the New Covenant Book of Hebrews as the third Biblical unction to "Awake!"

You will be stirred to rise up as you read *"The Order of Melchizedek Chronicles: Volume I."* Not only will you come to know Christ Jesus as Our Royal High Priest, you will have your eyes opened more fully to your kingdom assignment. Francis will challenge you to raise your understanding, and thereby take your stand to a higher plane of righteousness in this day and hour.

What Dr. Myles covered initially in his book on *"The Order of Melchizedek,"* was powerfully conveyed. It has truly resulted in a multitude of lives and ministries positively changing their awareness of their King/Priest mandate. In this Chronicle, any remaining speculative considerations regarding the Order of Melchizedek, its importance, and necessary implementation are addressed head on to bring a conclusion that this ancient pattern has present-day relevance.

B'Shalom,

— Dr. Pamala Denise Smith, *Gate-View Bible Institute and Ministry Arts Training Center, Mesa, Arizona*

A masterpiece - deliberate and intricate. In this transforming guide to understanding the inner workings of Christ Jesus' Melchizedek Priesthood, as taught in the Book of Hebrews, Dr. Francis Myles offers indisputable truths that the Melchizedek Priesthood is indeed the Eternal Royal Priesthood of Christ, prior to His incarnation.

This anointed work is a must-read for all who aspire to kingdom leadership status. It forces a decision relative to spiritual maturity and its role in equipping the believer to discern and understand the mystery of the Melchizedek Priesthood. The author has set forth a step by step notation and discussion of the Epistle to the Hebrews, releasing preponderant proof of New Testament Grace along with evidence that superbly insists that Christ is The Pattern Son, The Eternal God, The Creator, Who has a passion for righteousness and Whose name is greater than the angels. This is The Order of Melchizedek - the integral dynamics of the ministry of our Eternal High Priest and King, Christ Jesus.

— Apostle James Brewton, *Author of "Back Porch Meditations, Holy Spirit Revelations" (2012)*

www.community-empowerment-ministries.org

WWW.GEMSNETWORK.ORG

www.scopevision.org

Dear reader, it is no coincidence that this book is in your hands and now, at the most perfect time, it has found you, and I am so glad that is has! Now, I beseech you by the mercies of God, to take one moment and think about everything that is going on around you; and then ask yourself this question, is the Body of Christ truly effective in the war on culture, and is she really influencing this earth like she could? If the answer is no, then get ready to find out why. This amazing expose' that Dr. Francis Myles has written of the book of Hebrews, will simply but very powerfully reveal to you the Scriptures that have been here all along, just waiting on us to see them the way our Great King intended for us to see them. We have become masters at quoting Scriptures, but if we do not understand by the Spirit of revelation what is really being said, then we will continue to be servants of only the types and shadows which continue to perpetuate the same cycles of bondage; when all along, since the Holy Spirit has been sent back to us, He has been trying to reveal to us what Priesthood we are of. If we do not understand what Priesthood we are of, then without realizing it, we are left living in the one we are most familiar with, that is only an earthly one, and Aaron was the high priest of this one. Jesus the Christ was, is and always will be the High Priest of the Heavenly Temple in Heavenly Jerusalem, which is the mother of us all, and is the only place you are supposed to be living from since you were born again. So let Dr. Francis Myles guide you through some of the most misunderstood Scriptures in church history, and I am convinced that you will finally ascend to the Place That Jesus our Christ prepared for you, and you will finally quit just quoting 1 Peter 2:9, and instead, You Will Be The Royal Priesthood after the Order of Melchizedek.

— Pastor Jamie Bokelmann,
College Station, TX

Thank you Dr. Myles for not only asking the tough questions that are raised in the book of Hebrews, but for bringing such depth of eye-opening understanding and clarity for the Body of Christ. As with all of your previous books, you have opened a new window into heaven's great reservoir of revelation and Kingdom knowledge that has been hidden in the pages of Scripture for centuries! Every serious Christian and student of the Word will be deeply rewarded as they discover the enormous wealth of knowledge offered up in, "CHRIST JESUS: Our Royal High Priest". I could not recommend any work or study of the book of Hebrews more highly!

— Pastor Michael Sims,
The Bridge, Tolleson, AZ

FOREWORD

"Come unto me, all ye that labour and are heavy laden, and I will give you rest. Take my yoke upon you and learn of me; for I am meek and lowly in heart: and ye shall find rest for your souls. For my yoke is easy, and my burden is light."

Matthew 11:29

THESE words contain a powerful and profound truth about how to find the one thing that seems to be the common goal of mankind, no matter what race, religion, creed or color is involved. It is the idea of finding rest from struggles and peace with life itself. The Lord Jesus Christ gave a very simple answer to a seemingly complex problem of life. People search everywhere to find rest and in turn often complicate matters and incur more work and frustration than when they began, simply because they've been searching in all of the wrong places and for the wrong solution. Jesus Himself is the answer to the problem of restlessness in life. The lack of knowledge of the one true source of peace is enough to set any and everyone on a collision course with discontent, disaster and dismay. When we truly learn about Jesus and take His yoke upon us, we enter into a "rest for our souls" and a sense of peace that is real and enduring.

The word "yoke" has an amazing meaning in the Greek text. It is taken from the term *"Zeugnumi,"* meaning: *To join, as in a coupling or connection, or a beam of balance as when connecting scales that are used to weigh something.* This implies that our connection to Jesus is not only a connection to the Father and the Holy Spirit but also a connection to how to "weigh in" on the governmental grace and power of God that comes through the knowledge of Christ. Scales are used as a symbol of governance, judgment and justice and represent the activation of supernatural authority and government that gives us leverage in every situation in life on earth. Isaiah 9:7 says of Christ... *"Of the increase of his government and peace there shall be no end."* This proves that governance and authority lead to a state of prolonged peace because the justice of God is in effect in our lives. It testifies to the fact that knowing how to carry that authority and knowing how to wield its power are essential to ruling and reigning in the natural life. Learning about Jesus is essential to the full display of that power and peace.

The average believer today is unaware of the power of the ancient order called the Order of Melchizedek and may even shy away from study or research on this profound subject. But it is completely Biblical and legitimate and we cannot afford to ignore the potency and potential of this message. Enter Dr. Francis Myles and his book entitled The Oder of Melchizedek - Rediscovering the Eternal Priesthood of Jesus Christ and How it Affects Us Today! (2009) What an eye-opener it was and how it paved the way for us to walk in a truly supernatural understanding of all that Jesus Christ accomplished for us!

Now, this latest writing by Dr. Francis Myles on Christ Jesus Our Royal High Priest - Understanding the Book of Hebrews and the Inner Workings of Yeshua Ha Mashiach's Melchizedek Priesthood builds upon everything that was given to us before and perfects the message to an even greater level. It is a true masterpiece in exegesis, explanation and expression about how we benefit from truly "learning" about our Lord beyond His sacrifice on the cross and His resurrection from the dead. So much more was accomplished through the establishment of that great royal priesthood...the Order of Melchizedek! I don't know a person alive with a greater revelation of the "technology" of the Order of Melchizedek and how it applies to believers today! Although it is an ancient order, God has given us fresh manna and fresh and up to date material to thrive on in today's world through the revelation and writings of Dr. Myles. This is a feast!

>   – Dr. Gordon E. Bradshaw
> President - *Global Effect Movers & Shakers Network (GEMS) TM*
>
> President - *The SCOPEVision Group TM*
>
> Senior Scholar of Spiritual Formation and Leadership - *Hope Schools of Ministry Consortium*
>
> Author - *The Technology of Apostolic Succession*
>
> Author - *Authority for Assignment - Releasing the Mantle of God's Government in the Marketplace*

TABLE OF CONTENTS

PREFACE

WHEN I published my book on the Order of Melchizedek in October of 2008, the revelation on Christ's Melchizedek priesthood contained in the book quickly touched a nerve of an untapped spiritual hunger in many members of the Body of Christ. They had long-desired to understand the mystery of the Melchizedek Priesthood and how it impacts the Church today. For many marketplace leaders and ministers, their revelation on the Melchizedek Priesthood, inspired by my book, has brought tremendous healing and a narrowing of the proverbial theological divide (which has existed for centuries) between the institutional Church and the Marketplace. The Bible alludes to the Melchizedek Priesthood in the books of Genesis, Psalms and Hebrews. A vortex of spiritual hunger to better understand this ancient priesthood has quickly created a sales funnel from all over the world for my book. Thousands of copies have been sold as a consequence.

This tornado of spiritual hunger precipitated the birthing of the Order of Melchizedek Leadership University (www.ancientorderofmelchizedek.com). This one-of-a-kind School of Ministry is being used by God to train Kingdom Citizens on how to operate as Kings and Priests, under the spiritual covering of Christ's Melchizedek Priesthood. This Leadership Institute is now at the forefront of teaching believers how to advance the Kingdom of God, from the Temple to the Marketplace.

While thousands around the world were celebrating the breaking of the veil over this important biblical truth and New Testament reality; I quickly realized that the vast majority of Christians are not aware of the present day relevance of the Melchizedek priesthood. Most of them did not know how to apply this ancient priesthood to their spiritual walk. I discovered that many Christians viewed my teaching on the Order of Melchizedek as an introduction of a new and strange doctrine to the Body of Christ. But nothing could be further from the Truth.

The Order of Melchizedek Priesthood predates both Judaism and Christianity. This divine priesthood is referenced by four key biblical figures: Abraham, David, Moses and the Apostle Paul. Moses wrote the Torah that contains the book of Genesis so by revelation; God also introduced Moses to the Order of Melchizedek. It is the undisputed testimony of Scripture, that the importance and validity of a biblical truth is established permanently on the testimony of two or three witnesses. What is of note is that the above aforementioned biblical figures have contributed greatly to the unfolding and progressive revelation of the Kingdom of God through the ancient Hebrew Scriptures.

Additional affirmation of this ancient Priesthood is invoked indirectly by the Apostle Peter in 1 Peter 2:9 when he declares that..."we are a chosen generation and royal priesthood." This passage is particularly powerful because Peter was an apostle to Orthodox Jews who were very familiar with the Law of Moses and the inner workings of the Levitical Priesthood. Any bona fide orthodox Jew would have quickly realized that Peter was not inferring that they were priests after the Order of Levi, because they all knew that the Levitical Priesthood was based upon both gender and natural birthright. The Levitical Priesthood excluded all females and any man who was not born from the Tribe of Levi. Most importantly, Orthodox Jews would have also picked up on the fact that Peter was inferring a higher priesthood than the priesthood of Levi because there was no royal bloodline that flowed through the Priesthood of Levi. The only God-sanctioned priesthood that the nation of Israel had ever been exposed to in its prophetic history that carried a royal lineage was the Melchizedek priesthood.

Nevertheless, many Christians have never heard a sermon in their Church about the Order of Melchizedek. This unfortunate omission by most Church leaders is the main reason why most Christians do not fully appreciate Christ as our Royal High Priest. Consequently, many Christians do not know how Christ's Melchizedek priesthood affects the priesthood of the believer today, within the economy of the Kingdom of God.

Although my book, "The Order of Melchizedek", does an amazing job of reintroducing this royal priesthood to the greater Body of Christ, it proved to be too "deep" for many Christians who attend churches where much of what is taught from the pulpit is extremely watered down as not to offend the many. Nevertheless, knowing the importance of the priesthood of the believer, I asked the Holy Spirit to show me another way to present the Priesthood of Yeshua Ha-Mashiach (Jesus Christ) to many Christians who have never heard a message on the Order of Melchizedek. The Holy Spirit immediately told me to write an apostolic exposé on the Book of Hebrews.

It suddenly dawned on me that aside from the book of Hebrews, there is no other book of the Bible that is more dedicated to explaining the New Covenant, the Deity and Priesthood of Christ Jesus. Without the New Testament emphasis on the Melchizedek Priesthood that is found in the book of Hebrews, the importance of Christ's Melchizedek Priesthood and its inner workings would have been lost in translation. The supernatural encounter between Abram and Melchizedek's Priesthood in Genesis 14:17-20, would have been relegated to the annals of history and at the expense of embracing the present day relevance of this powerful eternal royal priesthood. It is this same priesthood that brought our father Abram into a living covenant with God. This encounter with Melchizedek's Priesthood changed the spiritual matrix of Abram's name, from "Abram" to "Abraham." Ignoring the power and present-day relevance of such a powerful priesthood has greatly hindered the Church from entering into its full inheritance in Christ.

With God given forensic aptitude, I will endeavor to bring you into an accurate understanding of the most apologetic book ever written by the Apostle Paul. Most Bible scholars agree that the style and pattern of writing in the book of Hebrews overwhelmingly suggests that the Apostle Paul authored this priceless epistle. Besides the style and pattern of writing, the writer of Hebrews demonstrates an uncanny understanding of the inner workings of the Mosaic Law and Priesthood. Both of these factors suggest that Paul was the author as he was a prolific student of Gamaliel, the best rabbinical teacher of the times. The emphasis on Christology that is littered throughout the book of Hebrews, further suggests that the Apostle Paul is the book's author because his epistles are filled with more references to Christ than any of the other epistles written by the other apostles. Without a shadow of doubt, "Christology" is Saint Paul's primary doctrinal contribution to the New Testament.

What makes the book of Hebrews particularly interesting is that it is the only epistle of Paul that was written for a primarily Jewish audience. All of his other epistles were written for Gentile believers who had turned to the Lord under his apostolic ministry. The letter to the Hebrews was written to orthodox Jewish believers who had accepted Yeshua as the promised Jewish Messiah. But these Messianic Jewish believers were having a difficult time letting go of some of the Levitical ceremonial aspects of the Law given by God to Moses, which was so deeply ingrained in them from childhood. Most of these Hebrew believers were constantly mixing the New and Old Covenant. They kept vacillating between the Old and New Covenant. Unfortunately the problem that these Hebrew believers were experiencing concerning mixing the Law with Grace still plagues us today for both Catholic and Protestant believers.

It is my prayer and desire that once you finish reading this book that you will come out with greater clarity on the following:

1. Christ as the Image of God and Pattern Son

2. The High Priest Ministry of Christ Jesus

3. The Differences between the Old and New Covenants

4. The Differences between the Levitical Priesthood and the Melchizedek Priesthood

5. Christ as a High Priest after the Order of Melchizedek

6. The Two Tithing Systems

7. The Superiority of Christ over Moses

8. The Elementary Principles of the Doctrine of Christ

9. The Role of Faith in the Kingdom Economy

10. The Unchanging Nature of Jesus Christ

11. Christ Jesus as the Perfect Sacrifice

12. The Atoning Power of the Blood of Christ

It is also my prayer that once your appetite for the nature and inner workings of the Melchizedek Priesthood has been rekindled, that you would also get yourself a copy of my book, "The Order of Melchizedek" which has since been revised and renamed: "A Kingdom of Kings and Priests: Rediscovering the Order of Melchizedek." The book title was revised and updated to include deeper revelations on the Melchizedek Priesthood that I did not fully grasp when I first wrote, "The Order of Melchizedek."

May God bless your reading with the spirit of revelation and understanding in the knowledge of Him!

God's Servant
Dr. Francis Myles, *Chancellor*
The Order of Melchizedek Leadership University
www.francismyles.com or www.royalpriesthoodchurch.com

CHRIST:
THE ETERNAL GOD AND PATTERN SON

A Higher Technology of Communication

1God, who at sundry times and in divers manners spake in time past unto the fathers by the prophets, 2Hath in these last days spoken unto us by his Son, whom he hath appointed heir of all things, by whom also he made the worlds;

Hebrews 1:1-2

THE book of Hebrews opens its sacred pages with a verse that contrasts the method of divine communication between the Old Testament forefathers and God's method for communicating to His people under the New Covenant. In the Old Testament God spoke to the forefathers through the prophets, but under the New Covenant, God's voice has been highly amplified by the fact that Christ, God's pattern Son, is <u>NOW</u> God's primary means of communicating His divine agenda to the people of our planet. Under the Old Covenant, God employed several spiritual technologies for communicating His Will to His people through His anointed servants, the prophets. God spoke to the people under the Old Covenant (The Jewish people) through the prophets by means of prophetic signs, prophetic acts, audible sounds, visions, dreams and Urims. While the integrity of the Word of the LORD through the prophets whom God used to pen the Old Testament is indisputable, having God speak to us through His Son (Yeshua) is much more powerful! Paul the apostle declares that in the last days God is speaking to US (mankind) through His dear Son (Christ) whom He has made heir of all things. Why would God do such a thing? The answer is staggeringly simple. God has a deep-seated passion to be understood by men, who are the primary recipients of His ferocious love for His creation. In Christ, God could communicate His perfect Will and unwavering love for mankind without any interference whatsoever. *In Christ, the invisible God became visible, reachable and touchable.*

The Empowerment Question: *Who Is Christ?*

Who being the brightness of his glory, and the express image of his person, and upholding all things by the word of his power, when he had by himself purged our sins, sat down on the right hand of the Majesty on high:

Hebrews 1:3

The first being to pose a question in Scripture was the Serpent (the devil) in Genesis 3, when the serpent asked Eve a question that was designed to lure her into doubting the integrity of God's Word. The Serpent placed a question mark in the place were God had placed a period in Eve's relationship with God. Since then the Devil has used questions as a means of luring men from operating within our God given spiritual inheritance. But God in His redemptive nature quickly turned the tables on the devil when He introduced Adam and Eve to empowerment questions. God entered the Garden of Eden after the Fall and started asking them empowerment questions that were designed to show them why and how they had fallen from grace. Every question God has ever asked us since then is designed to help us break free from the enemy's deception as well as be restored back to our rightful inheritance in Christ.

In *Christ*, THE INVISIBLE *God* BECAME VISIBLE, REACHABLE AND TOUCHABLE.

One of the most profound questions Jesus ever asked his disciples while he was on earth was asked while He was walking along the coasts of Caesarea Philippi. He asked his disciples, *"Whom do men say that I the Son of man am? (Matthew 16:13)* The disciples threw several answers at Him that were all wrong. But in the midst of it all Peter was raptured into the throne room and got a life changing revelation from the heavenly Father concerning the true identity of the Rabbi from the tribe of Judah, whom they knew simply as Yeshua, son of Joseph and Mary. Peter proclaimed, *""Thou art the Christ, the Son of the living God"*. The writer of the book of Hebrews goes deeper into answering the question that Jesus asked His disciples concerning His true identity. The apostle Paul lists the following concerning Christ's true identity:

1. Christ is the brightness or apex of God's glory

2. Christ is the express or exact image of the Invisible God

3. Christ is the power and eternal Word of God that holds all of creation together

Unfortunately, many Christians fail to appreciate the far-reaching implications of Christ's true identity because most fail to go past Christ's humanity. Christ's flawless humanity is only surpassed by His divinity. The Church's obsession with Christ's humanity, while failing to comprehend His divinity, is also the reason most Christians fail to fully appreciate and appropriate Christ's royal Priesthood. If we truly knew who Christ is and who He is in us - many of us would live very differently. We would gain the courage and grace to go past the limitation of our own humanity by drawing on the limitless resources of the Christ in us.

An Excellent Name

Being made so much better than the angels, as he hath by inheritance obtained a more excellent name than they.

Hebrews 1:4

One of the most powerful spiritual technologies for manifesting dominion is *"The Technology of Names"* that God introduced to Adam in Genesis 2:19. When the angel Gabriel appeared to Joseph in a dream, he told him to call the child who was going to be born out of Mary's womb, Jesus! Jesus means "Savior." These incidences clearly showcase the importance of names in the spirit realm. An incorrect name can give birth to an inaccurate expression of a person or an entity's intended purpose.

*And out of the ground the Lord God formed every beast of the field, and every fowl of the air; and brought them unto Adam to see what he would call them: and whatsoever Adam called every living creature, that was the **name** thereof.*

Genesis 2:19 KJV

It is my concern that many members of the Body of Christ do not really respect the "technology of names" as much as God does. But the truth is that this ancient spiritual technology is the method that God uses to *determine the capacity, function, and nature of a thing.* God imparted this technology of names to Adam. The Bible says that God brought all the animals on earth to Adam to see what he would call or name them. The Bible tells us that whatever name Adam gave to any animal the name would enshrine that particular animal's purpose, potential, and nature. The technology of names also shows us that whoever names a person, a product, or an organization has inherent power over what they name. The writer of Hebrews informs that the name of Jesus carries more tremendous weight in the spirit than any other names of angels we could ever name; and it is so because of the finished work of Christ. This powerful name is now ours by Inheritance.

The Pattern Son

For unto which of the angels said he at any time, Thou art my Son, this day have I begotten thee? And again, I will be to him a Father, and he shall be to me a Son?

Hebrews 1:5

The writer of Hebrews shows us that Christ is the "Pattern Son." Since Jesus Christ is God's pattern Son, His life and ministry style are the true blueprints for real Kingdom living here on earth. Christ as the pattern Son is the very essence of Sonship in the economy of the Kingdom. Under the New Testament, God has purged us from sin and recreated our spirits in order to transform us into sons. Just as Jesus Christ, the Pattern Son is the desire of all nations. We have also become the desire of all of creation through our union with Him as sons of the living God. This is the testimony of the Apostle Paul in Romans 8:19-23. All of creation is groaning for the manifestation of the sons of God. I have news for you! All of creation is not groaning or travailing for the manifestation of Christians, but for the manifestation of true sons who relate to the Heavenly Father in the same way that Christ did while He was on earth. The world is full of people who profess to be Christians on almost every corner and yet nature continues to groan in a holy travail for the manifestation of Sons who will put fear in the heart of the devil, just like Jesus Christ did. Failure to understand that our highest calling is to become like the Pattern Son will limit our ability to manifest Christ's royal priesthood here on this earth.

Greater Than the Angels

And again, when he bringeth in the firstbegotten into the world, he saith, And let all the angels of God worship him. 7And of the angels he saith, Who maketh his angels spirits, and his ministers a flame of fire.

Hebrews 1:6-7

The writer of the book of Hebrews drops another bombshell. Christ is greater than all of the angels combined. This is why Saint Paul warns against the worship of angels in the epistle to the Colossians. There is a lot of talk about angelic appearances and visitations among certain sections of the Christian church. While I applaud the ministry of angels, some Christian's undue emphasis and obsession with the manifestation of angelic beings concerns me deeply. For some of them their obsession with generating angelic experiences borders on the worship of angels. Any time we talk more about angels than about Christ, who is the express image of the invisible God, we are sliding down a slippery slope. When the healing revivals swept through America in the early fifties, many anointed healing evangelists lost their way as they attributed their crusade miracles to the special healing angels, who patronized their ministries, more than they referred to the finished work of Christ on the cross. But the truth of the matter is that our obsession must always center on Christ Jesus, with angels as a distant after thought.

The Eternal God

But unto the Son he saith, Thy throne, O God, is forever and ever: a sceptre of righteousness is the sceptre of thy kingdom.

Hebrews 1:8

While it is powerful that Christ Jesus is greater than the angels, what the Apostle Paul declares next is even more mind blowing. Christ, the Pattern Son, is also the eternal "God" who sits on an ancient throne that exists beyond the peripherals of time. This statement blows a hole in the doctrine of the Jehovah's Witnesses who say that Jesus Christ is not equal to God the Father as an equal and distinct member of the eternal Godhead. But the staggering truth is that the "Pattern Son" is also God Most High! Wow! How can we fail to live in victory in this world, with such a Savior living inside us? The fact that Christ Jesus is also the eternal God has deep and far reaching spiritual implications on the present day priesthood of the believer.

A Passion for Righteousness

Thou hast loved righteousness, and hated iniquity; therefore God, even thy God, hath anointed thee with the oil of gladness above thy fellows.

Hebrews 1:9

There is nothing that defines any relationship more than passion. A passionless relationship is either dead or on the verge of dying. Passion also reveals what is most important to a person and the driving motivation behind all that they say and do. The writer of Hebrews opens the veil into the very heart and nature of Christ Jesus. The divine nature of Jesus Christ is a blazing holy inferno of righteousness. Righteousness is and was the primary passion of Jesus Christ while He walked the earth. This means that the Church will fail to fully unlock the Priesthood of the believer if it fails to embrace the same passion for righteousness that burns in the Pattern Son. In fact, righteousness is the essential ingredient of the Melchizedek Priesthood (Hebrews 7). We will dig into this fact in a later chapter. But it suffices to say that Christ is so passionate about righteousness that He has made it the scepter of his glorious and eternal Kingdom.

The Creator

And, Thou, Lord, in the beginning hast laid the foundation of the earth; and the heavens are the works of thine hands: 11They shall perish; but thou remainest; and they all shall wax old as doth a garment; 12And as a vesture shalt thou fold them up, and they shall be changed: but thou art the same, and thy years shall not fail.

Hebrews 1:10-12

Most Christians are so focused on Jesus Christ as Savior from sin that we fail to appreciate the fact that He is first and foremost, the creator of the Universe. Before the world existed, Christ was. According to the above passage, Christ (the Living Word) formed and fashioned the heavens and the earth. The heavens mentioned here encompasses all that is found in the third, second and first heavens. If the Christ, who came to live inside us after we heard and responded to the preaching of the Gospel, is also the creator, then Christians ought to be the most creative thinkers or people on planet earth! My dear friend there is an abundance of creative genius flowing through our veins. We need only believe and act upon it. It is so sad that most Churches lack imagination and are instead stuck in long-held man made traditions.

SINCE *Jesus Christ* IS *God's* PATTER SON, HIS LIFE AND MINISTRY STYLE ARE THE TRUE BLUEPRINTS FOR REAL KINGDOM LIVING HERE ON EARTH.

Destined for Dominion

But to which of the angels said he at any time, Sit on my right hand, until I make thine enemies thy footstool?

Hebrews 1:13

The above passage of Scripture is a reference to Psalm 110:1-4, where David is given a supernatural and staggering revelation concerning Christ's Melchizedek Priesthood. David is shown that Christ is destined for complete dominion over His enemies through a functional body of priests; who operate after the Order of Melchizedek. Since Christ is the head of the Church, the feet in the proverbial prophecy refers to the work and ministry of the priesthood of New Testament believers. We will fully discuss the nature and inner workings of the Melchizedek Priesthood in later chapters; and how Christians can operate under this powerful and eternal royal priesthood.

Our Angelic Servants

Are they not all ministering spirits, sent forth to minister for them who shall be heirs of salvation?

Hebrews 1:14

MANY *Christians* ARE NOT MAKING FULL USE OF THEIR GUARDIAN *Angels* BECAUSE OF FALSE HUMILITY TOWARDS THESE GLORIOUS BEINGS

The final verse in the first chapter of Hebrews staggers the mind and causes believers to stumble who are bound by a religious and inferior sense of self. This Scripture is also sacrilegious to people who are caught up in the unhealthy veneration of angels. This Scripture was both offensive and difficult to accept for orthodox Hebrew believers who came out of a covenant of performance and condemnation. How could angels be servants of New Testament heirs of salvation? The very thought is intimidating. How can these holy angels who have never sinned a day in their lives be servants of men and women who are still struggling with sin in their humanity? A baffling question indeed, unless we truly understand the far-reaching power of Christ's finished work. Jesus Christ's atonement and redemption is so far reaching that it has caused holy angels to bow in attendance to the needs of mere mortals who have been washed by the blood of Christ.

Many Christians are not making full use of their guardian angels because of false religious teachings coupled with false humility towards these glorious beings. The last time I checked, servants are employed and deployed to serve. According to the Apostle Paul, angels are no different. They are servants or ministering spirits sent to "minister for them" who shall be heirs of salvation. The expression "minister for them" implies that guardian angels have a God given assignment to cater to the needs of the redeemed.

How many Christians are struggling to make ends meet who never even think of invoking angelic help in bringing much needed financial resources in their lives? Most of the ministering spirits (angels) assigned to many Christians are sitting around doing nothing - because they have not been commanded to serve.

A MERCIFUL AND FAITHFUL HIGH PRIEST

The Sin of Omission

Therefore we ought to give the more earnest heed to the things, which we have heard, lest at any time we should let them slip. 2For if the word spoken by angels was stedfast, and every transgression and disobedience received a just recompence of reward; 3How shall we escape, if we neglect so great salvation; which at the first began to be spoken by the Lord, and was confirmed unto us by them that heard him;

Hebrews 2:1-3

THE second chapter of the book of Hebrews opens with a warning about a common human misnomer. One of the weaknesses of all humans is our inherent ability to easily forget the things we have learned. This inherent flaw opens us up to what theologians call sins of omission. Sins of omission are sins that we make by simply neglecting what we know we ought to do. The apostle Paul warns us against the danger of neglecting the benefits of so great a salvation that the Lord has offered us under His New Covenant. The great apostle admonishes us that if disobedience to the Word that was spoken by angels under the Old Covenant warranted quick punishment; how can we escape if we reject the Gospel of the Kingdom that was preached by the Lord himself? This warning about the sin of omission causes the entire book of Hebrews to take on a new level of seriousness. God intended for the New Testament church to both understand and walk-out the book of Hebrews. It is my humble opinion that the book of Romans and the book of Hebrews are two of the most important epistles in the entire Bible for believers who want to understand New Testament kingdom living under the New Covenant.

The Witness of Signs and Wonders

God also bearing them witness, both with signs and wonders, and with divers miracles, and gifts of the Holy Ghost, according to his own will?

Hebrews 2:4

The writer of the book of Hebrews calls the finished work of Christ on the cross, the "so great salvation". It is the "so great salvation," because it is so much easier for a human being to be saved under the New Covenant than under the Old Covenant of works. The Bible actually calls our own works of righteousness filthy rags. This is why our sincere effort to make ourselves righteous before God ends in total frustration. I once saw a toddler fall into a puddle of dirty, muddy water, and the more the toddler tried to clean himself up the dirtier he became. It was not long before his mom came to the rescue. She scooped him up from the dirty water and cleaned him up in no time. This is exactly what Jesus Christ did for human kind on the cross. He picked us up from the dirty pond of sin that we were swimming in and then cleaned us up in righteousness by His precious blood. Salvation through the sacrificial death of our Lord Jesus Christ is so important to God that in His eternal wisdom He has chosen to accompany the preaching of the gospel of the Kingdom with signs and wonders and various gifts of the Holy Spirit. This means that signs and wonders, and the various gifts of the Holy Spirit are God's way of catching the attention of a lost and dying world.

Man: God's Crown Jewel

For unto the angels hath he not put in subjection the world to come, whereof we speak. 6But one in a certain place testified, saying, What is man, that thou art mindful of him? or the son of man that thou visitest him? 7Thou madest him a little lower than the angels; thou crownedst him with glory and honour, and didst set him over the works of thy hands: 8Thou hast put all things in subjection under his feet. For in that he put all in subjection under him, he left nothing that is not put under him. But now we see not yet all things put under him

Hebrews 2:5-8

We are living in a scientifically and technologically advanced age. Science and technology are changing very rapidly and changing the way the masses engage the marketplace. But while the world is desperately looking for new methods of doing things, God's method has not changed. Man is and has always been God's method. When God decided to extend His invisible kingdom to planet Earth, He created a man and gave him an ambassadorial assignment to advance the kingdom of God here on earth. When that man committed high treason and was excommunicated from the governor's mansion in the Garden of Eden, God moved through the pages of history to find a man he could use.

When God wanted to give birth to a nation of the just who live by faith, he found a man He could work through called Abram. When God wanted to atone for the sins of the whole world, he found a perfect and willing sacrifice in the face of Jesus Christ. Time and time again, we see that man is God's crown jewel. This is why the psalmist David was so captivated by the passionate, obsessive, loving-affection that God lavishes on man. King David was so moved by the divine obsession for the species called mankind that he was compelled to ask the question that is echoed throughout the ages, "What is man that thou art mindful of him?" Many people who committed suicide in ages past would never have done so had they been able to find the answer to King David's question. They would have discovered, to their dismay, that people are God's most treasured inheritance.

The great King David also echoes God's original design for the species called mankind. Man was created for God's pleasure and to exercise dominion over all of God's creation in the visible planet called Earth. Even though modern translations of Scripture state that man was created a little lower than the angels; the ancient Hebrew Scriptures disagree. In the original Hebrew version of the Bible, the Scriptures actually declare that man was created a little a lower than "Eloim" not Angels. "Eloim" is the name of God. This means that before the fall of man in the Garden of Eden, man was actually created just a little lower than God himself. This would explain why the Devil coveted man's position in the Garden of Eden.

God's METHOD HAS NOT CHANGED; MAN IS AND HAS ALWAYS BEEN *God's* METHOD.

We See Jesus

But we see Jesus, who was made a little lower than the angels for the suffering of death, crowned with glory and honour; that he by the grace of God should taste death for every man. ¹⁰*For it became him, for whom are all things, and by whom are all things, in bringing many sons unto glory, to make the captain of their salvation perfect through sufferings.*

Hebrews 2:9-10

Even though man, "God's Crown Jewel", lost his exalted position of authority to the Devil in the Garden of Eden, God has never given up on His big idea of having spirit children housed in tents of flesh living on earth to extend His invisible Kingdom. Unfortunately, Adam and Eve's sin temporary interrupted the execution of God's divine agenda. From the excommunication of the first Adam to the incarnation of the last Adam, demonic powers have terrorized and subjugated mankind. But the demonic reign of terror came to an abrupt end when the eyes of all mankind feasted on the birth of Jesus Christ, who was wrapped in swaddling clothes in a manger in Bethlehem.

The writer of the book of Hebrews tells us that Jesus was made a little lower than the angels for the suffering of death. The expression, a little lower than the angels for the suffering of death, has far and deep reaching implications. The expression means that that the only reason why the humanity of Christ was made a little lower than the angels, was to make it possible for the body of Jesus to die on the cross. Had the body of Jesus been celestial like the Angels, death would have never been able to contact his body; because angels do not die physically. Since the redemption of all mankind from the penalty of sin required death, the body of Jesus was made a little lower than the angels. However, ever since his glorious resurrection from the dead, the Lord Jesus Christ's body is no longer lower than the angels. The resurrected body that the Lord Jesus Christ now has, is the same type of spiritual body that born again believers will inherit in the resurrection.

Jesus: Our Brother

For both he that sanctifieth and they who are sanctified are all of one: for which cause he is not ashamed to call them brethren, 12 Saying, I will declare thy name unto my brethren, in the midst of the church will I sing praise unto thee. 13 And again, I will put my trust in him. And again, Behold I and the children, which God hath given me.

Hebrews 2:11-13

For the deeply religious, what I am about to say next will sound sacrilegious. According to the writer of the book of Hebrews, Jesus Christ is not only our Lord and Savior He is also our brother. We share a deep brotherly bond with the Lord Jesus Christ after we are born again. Sharing this deep bond with the Lord Jesus Christ is one of the primary purposes of the sanctification that we experience through the blood of the cross. The apostle Paul tells us that He that sanctifies (Jesus Christ) and those who are being sanctified (the Body of Christ) are children of the same Heavenly Father.

THE BLESSING OF ABRAHAM IS THE SUPERNATURAL PRIVILEGE OF BEING IDENTIFIED WITH THE MOST HIGH *God*.

Coming to terms with the fact that the Lord Jesus Christ is both our Savior and brother would radically change our entire outlook on life itself. How many of us would walk differently if we discovered that our brother was the most powerful and richest person on earth. I believe that we would walk differently. Unfortunately, this powerful truth has not yet dawned on many members of the Body of Christ. Many members of the body of Christ are walking through life as though they were orphans or mere pawns on a chessboard. But I challenge you to begin to see the Lord Jesus Christ as your closest and most trusted brother. This does not in any way diminish the Lordship of Jesus Christ over the life of the believer. It just breaks the stronghold of fear and man-made traditions that have stifled a relationship of intimacy with the Lord Jesus Christ in the lives of many believers.

The Destruction of the Technology of Death

Forasmuch then as the children are partakers of flesh and blood, he also himself likewise took part of the same; that through death he might destroy him that had the power of death, that is, the devil; ¹⁵And deliver them who through fear of death were all their lifetime subject to bondage.

Hebrews 2:14-15

The fall from Grace of the first Kingdom ambassadors (Adam and Eve) opened the portals of sin and death onto our planet. The entity called "Sin", and the technology of death that accompanies it, entered the world. Since then, streets stained with the blood of those killed by war, crime and pestilence, continue to display the devastating impact of death agencies on our troubled planet. No matter how long mankind has been in existence we still cannot bring ourselves to accept death as a fact of life. We are all afraid of it; even those who desire to go to heaven do not want to die. This is because death was never intended for mankind. All you have to do to acknowledge this fact is visit a funeral and the frantic emotions of those who have lost a loved one is enough to demonstrate man's disdain for the one inevitable event in his existence.

Before the incarnation of the Lord Jesus Christ, everyman who had ever dared to challenge the Angel of death lost the bout. Death agencies, fueled by the entrance of sin in the spirit, soul and body of man, eventually proved to be too strong, even for the most righteous of Old Testament saints. But in the body of Jesus Christ, death met a challenger who proved to be too powerful! Ganged up on by both Sin and Death on the cross, Jesus triumphed glorious over Sin, Hell and the Grave. According to the writer of Hebrews by conquering death in His body, the Lord Jesus Christ set us all free from "the fear of death."

We are the Seed of Abraham

For verily he took not on him the nature of angels; but he took on him the seed of Abraham.

Hebrews 2:16

One of the most powerful prophetic statements that the writer of Hebrews makes is that we are the "seed of Abraham." This expression connects our present day to the past prophetic history of the dealings of God with Abraham, who is the father of Israel and Gentiles who walk by faith and not by sight. This powerful expression "seed of Abraham" gives us an abiding inheritance in what God bequeathed on Abraham. In Abraham, God set a prophetic pattern for accessing an unlimited multigenerational blessing.

Several generations after the death of Abraham, God appeared in human form in the face of the baby Jesus, in a manger in Bethlehem. God supernaturally became one of us. The writer of Hebrews tells us that the Messiah's incarnation did not result in Him being born in a celestial body like the angels; instead, He was born in a terrestrial body like the sons of men. This is because He came to this planet to redeem the children of Abraham; first the Jews then the Gentiles. In the third chapter of the book of Galatians, the Apostle Paul tells us that Christ Jesus suffered the shameful death of the cross, becoming a curse for us in the process so that the blessing of Abraham might come upon the Gentiles through faith. What is the blessing of Abraham? The blessing of Abraham is the supernatural privilege of being identified with the Most High God here on Earth, while demonstrating the supernatural ability to possess both Heaven and Earth (Genesis 14:18-20).

A Merciful and Faithful High Priest

Wherefore in all things it behoved him to be made like unto his brethren, that he might be a merciful and faithful high priest in things pertaining to God, to make reconciliation for the sins of the people. 18For in that he himself hath suffered being tempted, he is able to succour them that are tempted.

Hebrews 2:17-18

The Apostle Paul tells us that even though Christ's priesthood is based upon His divinity, His humanity gave Him the proper perspective on the fragilities of the human condition. Before Christ became the "Word made flesh", He had no concept of what it feels like to wrestle with sin and temptation in the human body. But the apostle Paul tells us that Christ became a human being and wrapped human flesh around His divinity and appeared to us in the face of Yeshua.

Once Christ became a man, that is to say both human and divine, He could be tempted by the Devil. Christ's human condition made Him susceptible to the fragilities of the human condition in much the same way as the first Adam. If this were not the case, Jesus Christ's 40 days of temptation in the wilderness by the devil would have been meaningless and unhelpful in Christ's ability to be a merciful and faithful High Priest. If the masses in our world really knew just how merciful and faithful Christ is as

High Priest, they would run for refuge under His eternal Royal Priesthood. Yeshua Ha-Mashiach is truly a faithful and merciful High Priest; meaning that He delights more in exercising mercy than dishing out punishment. Glory to God!

THE APOSTLE AND HIGH PRIEST OF OUR PROFESSION

The Apostle and High Priest of our Profession

Wherefore, holy brethren, partakers of the heavenly calling, consider the Apostle and High Priest of our profession, Christ Jesus;
Hebrews 3:1

THE writer of the book of Hebrews goes on to tell us that Christ Jesus is the apostle and high Priest of our profession. The word apostle comes from the Greek word "Proton." The word "proton" means *that which is "first" in rank, time and order of importance.* As the apostle of our profession, Jesus Christ is "first" in rank, time and order of importance. Any teaching that does not place Jesus Christ in a position where He is the "Proton" of all that we say and do is a demonic and erroneous doctrine. Such a doctrine would only serve to take us out of our ambassadorial profession of representing Christ and His kingdom here on earth.

The writer of the book of Hebrews also goes on to tell us that Jesus Christ is also the High Priest of our profession. What I love about the book of Hebrews is that it is the only epistle in the New Testament that boldly calls the Lord Jesus Christ a High Priest. I truly believe that without the book of Hebrews many Christians would not have been aware of Christ's eternal position as High Priest. What is also interesting about the above passage of Scripture is that the apostle Paul makes it very clear that born again believers have a profession here on earth given to them by God. So we will quickly get into a deeper understanding of the word "Profession."

The online thesaurus defines "Profession" as:

1. *A vocation requiring knowledge of some department of learning or science.* This means that our profession as Ambassadors of Christ here on earth requires a working knowledge of the Kingdom of God. We need to know our King, His Kingdom, the principles of His Kingdom, the laws of His Kingdom and the culture of His Kingdom.

2. Any vocation or business. As citizens of the Kingdom of God, our vocation is to be ambassadors of Christ and our primary business here on earth is the business of advancing the Kingdom of God into all spheres of human enterprise. Advancing the Kingdom is what the Lord Jesus Christ meant when He told Joseph and Mary, "I must be about my Father's business!" <u>Luke 2:49</u> *"And he said unto them, how is it that ye sought me? wist ye not that I must be about my Father's business?"*

3. *The body of persons engaged in an occupation or calling.* As a body of persons, the Body of Christ is engaged in an occupation or calling to teach, reach and demonstrate the Gospel of the Kingdom until the kingdoms of this world have become the kingdoms of God and of His Christ. This is why I detest the spirit of division, which divides the Body of Christ along denominational lines. The reality is that whether our church affiliation is Baptist, Pentecostal, Charismatic or Fundamentalist, if we are blood-washed and acknowledge Christ as our Lord, then we are all members of the body of Christ. This means that we have one Lord, one faith and one baptism, and that baptism is the baptism into the body of Christ.

AS THE APOSTLE OF OUR PROFESSION, *Jesus Christ* IS "FIRST" IN RANK, TIME AND ORDER OF IMPORTANCE.

THE APOSTLE AND HIGH PRIEST OF OUR PROFESSION

4. *The act of <u>professing</u>; avowal; a declaration, whether true or false.* The writer of the book of Hebrews tells us that the Lord Jesus Christ is the Apostle and High Priest of our profession. The word profession also means the act of professing or declaring something that is true or false. This means that the blessings of the New Covenant are activated by words of faith spoken by the believer. This is why the words we speak can either release the inheritance secured for us in Christ Jesus, or they can delay the inheritance, impacting the quality of our life. This also means that the Lord Jesus Christ is not going to be an apostle and high priest over doubt filled words. He is the apostle and high priest of our faith, not our unbelief. Unbelief can only diminish our ability to function as the Royal priesthood of Jesus Christ.

Jesus Christ: The King Priest

Wherefore, holy brethren, partakers of the heavenly calling, consider the Apostle and High Priest of our profession, Christ Jesus;
                                                          Hebrews 3:1

The apostle Paul in his epistle to the Hebrews tells us that Jesus Christ has become the High Priest of everyone who is a partaker of the divine nature. Since it has been proven that Jesus Christ is a true King, it follows then that Christ's new order of priesthood has to be a royal priesthood. Since Jesus Christ is a King, His priestly ministry is greatly influenced by His kingship. It is impossible to separate His kingship from His priesthood.

Kings, by nature, own and control everything that is within the sphere of their kingdom. All the praying, preaching, and marketplace activities within a kingdom must reflect the personal will of the king. The priesthood of a king is designated to reflect and carry out the will of the king to all the citizens of the kingdom and to all aspects of His kingdom.

This means that Christ's priesthood has jurisdiction over the affairs of Kingdom citizens in the arenas of finance, business, law, media, sports, family, and church. Therefore, what Kingdom citizens do in the House of God (local church) and what they do in the marketplace, are both holy and spiritual when they are done in accordance with the King's will.

Under Christ's New Testament Order of Melchizedek priesthood, we can be most assured that our Kingdom assignment is important and spiritual, whether it is carried out in the temple or in the marketplace. Under this Order of Melchizedek priesthood, we are all in full-time ministry even though for some (pastors), that ministry is primarily carried out in the House of God. On the other hand, full-time ministry for many others (marketplace ministers) may involve spending a majority of their time representing the Kingdom of God in the marketplace.

Partakers of the Heavenly Calling

Wherefore, holy brethren, partakers of the heavenly calling, consider the Apostle and High Priest of our profession, Christ Jesus;
Hebrews 3:1

The writer of the book of Hebrews makes another powerful statement. He tells us that members of the body of Christ are partakers of the heavenly calling. The expression "heavenly calling" implies that there is an internal pull on the life of the believer to be more heavenly-minded than to be earthly-minded while we are stationed here on earth. This means that our citizenship is heavenly. We are part of the universal family of God the father that is in heaven and on earth. This is why born-again believers should have no fear when it is time to die. At the moment of death, those who die in the Lord, appear immediately in the presence of God in the heavenly realm. This is because the Lord Jesus Christ paid the price for our complete redemption and made us partakers of the heavenly calling.

The Power of Faithfulness

Who was faithful to him that appointed him, as also Moses was faithful in all his house.
Hebrews 3:2

In the world that we live in, it is so easy to bump into men and women who are driven to succeed at all costs. They have such massive egos and conflicting selfish agendas that it's becoming increasingly difficult, both in the church and in the marketplace, to find men and women who are truly faithful. Faithfulness has become as rare as dinosaurs in our high tech, fast paced societies, especially faithfulness to that which belongs to another man. We live in a world where we have exalted natural talent, anointing and personal charisma above faithfulness. But in the economy of the Kingdom of God, "faithfulness" is indescribably more valuable than natural talent and charisma combined.

SINCE *Jesus Christ* IS A KING, HIS PRIESTLY MINISTRY IS GREATLY INFLUENCED BY HIS KINGSHIP.

The writer of the book of Hebrews tells us that the Lord Jesus Christ and Moses both excelled in this rare spiritual virtue. Moses was completely faithful to God as a servant in God's house, while the Lord Jesus demonstrated unparalleled faithfulness to the will and work of God. I shudder to think of what would've happened to our eternal redemption had the Lord Jesus Christ faltered in His faithfulness towards God and what He required in order to redeem the souls of men from the power of Sin, death and the devil. But thank God that the Lord Jesus Christ was faithful to the end. When He cried, "it is finished" from the cross, the work the Father had sent Him to do was truly finished in every sense of the word. God wants to raise a prophetic company of believers who are truly faithful to God in all that they say and do. When our time here on earth is done, it is not our talent that will be celebrated at the pearly gates; it will be our faithfulness to God. When we stand in His presence when our time here on earth expires, will He say to us well done, my good and faithful servant? I truly wonder.

More Glorious and Honorable than Moses

For this man was counted worthy of more glory than Moses, inasmuch as he who hath builded the house hath more honour than the house.

Hebrews 3:3

The writer of the book of Hebrews tells us that the Lord Jesus Christ was counted to be worthy of more glory and honor than Moses. This is a very important prophetic statement for us to understand. Without a doubt, the Bible tells us that Moses was one of the highest spiritual delegated authorities of the Old Testament era. Under Moses' leadership, the Lord supernaturally delivered the people of Israel out of captivity from the hands of the Egyptians. Some of the most notable miracles in human history happened under the leadership of Moses. Under his anointed leadership, the people of Israel received the Covenant of LAW on tablets of stone that governed the affairs of their lives for the next four thousand years.

But the writer of the book of Hebrews tells us that even though the man Moses was a great man, his life and ministry pales, in comparison to the life and ministry of the Lord Jesus Christ. Moses introduced the Covenant of Law, but the Lord Jesus Christ introduced the Covenant of Grace and Truth. This is not to say that the concept of grace was not available in the Old Covenant; it was. But in Yeshua grace and truth found their complete and highest expression. The Lord Jesus Christ carries a higher level of glory and honor than Moses. This also means that the New Covenant is much more glorious than the Old Covenant.

God the Master Builder

For every house is builded by some man; but he that built all things is God.

Hebrews 3:4

The writer of the book of Hebrews tells us that God is the builder of all things. This means that in order for us to build anything that will be of any eternal consequence and value, we have to make sure that we are building what God has already built. It is the testimony of the writer of the Psalms who tells us that they that build without the Lord build in vain. This is because God is a God of foreknowledge. Everything He does, He does it from a position of foreknowledge. Foreknowledge means that the Lord knows the end from the beginning. Then He (God) turns around and commissions us (mankind) to "build in time" what is already "finished" in heaven. This is why building into the spirit requires that we command a place of intimacy with the Lord so that we know how to build into the spirit and into people's lives, for the advancement of the kingdom.

Servants versus Sons

And Moses verily was faithful in all his house, as a servant, for a testimony of those things which were to be spoken after; 6But Christ as a son over his own house; whose house are we, if we hold fast the confidence and the rejoicing of the hope firm unto the end.

Hebrews 3:5-6

From the closure of the Garden of Eden to the opening of the gates of the New Jerusalem, God has never given up on the idea of having a family of "sons" stationed here on earth as kings and priests. One of the most famous parables of Jesus Christ addresses this critical subject: the subject of "divine sonship." In the parable of the "Prodigal Son" (Luke 15), the Lord Jesus told a parable about two sons and their perception of their relationship with their Father. Even though the younger son who asked his Father for his inheritance has been much maligned in many sermons from the pulpit, there is yet much to be learned about the difference between the mindset of a "son" to that of a "servant."

THE NEW COVENANT IS MUCH MORE GLORIOUS THAN THE OLD COVENANT.

One of the main points that the Lord Jesus was trying to get across is that we can either choose to live like a "son" in the father's house or we can live like a servant in the father's house. The younger brother in the parable had such a strong sense of "sonship" that he was not afraid to ask for his inheritance and his father gave it to him generously. His only mistake was that he broke off his relationship with his father after he got his inheritance. But after he squandered his inheritance in a foreign land and found himself in dire distress, the devil attacked his mind and made him feel like his mistake had cancelled his sonship. So when he came to his senses, he told himself that he would return to his father's house; but he would return not as a son but as servant. He was convinced he was no longer worthy to be a son. Nothing could have been further from the truth. In the parable Jesus tells us that his father never stopped anticipating the return of his dear son. As soon as he saw him from a far distance, the Father ran towards him and embraced him vigorously as a son.

The Father restored the prodigal son to his rightful inheritance in the Father's house. The Father arranged for a lavish party to celebrate the return of his son. When the elder brother returned from the field after finishing the day's chores, he was welcomed by sounds of jubilation at the Father's house. When he inquired about the lavish festivities, one of the servants told him that his father had thrown a party to welcome the return of his younger brother. The elder brother was so upset that he refused to come to the celebration. When the Father found out, he went after his eldest son and asked him why he was pouting. The older son pointed to all the "good works" that he had done for his Father and that his father had never thrown him such a lavish party. The father's response in this parable represents the staggering difference between the Old and the New Covenant. The father told his eldest son that he was the one in error, because he thought he could earn the Father's favor through his "works." His father already loved and favored him, because he his son. But he had been living under his Father's covering as a "servant" instead of a "son." You see, servants do not get paid until they work for it, but sons do not have to perform to have access to the Father's wealth.

The writer of Hebrews tells us that, Moses, as powerful as he was, operated like a "servant" in the Father's house. But the Lord Jesus Christ operates as a "Son" in the Father's house. Moses in this analogy represents the Old Covenant, while the Lord Jesus Christ represents the New Covenant. The two covenants build upon each other but are also radically different in how they each positioned man before God. Under the Old Covenant, the people of Israel lived under a "covenant of written on tablets of stone," instead of having the Law of God inscribed on their hearts by the Spirit. Consequently the people of Israel struggled trying to live up to the righteous demands of the law without the circumcision of the heart. This would explain why many people under the Old Covenant fell into the trap of wanting to please "God through their works." *This is not to say that "works" are not important to faith but it is to say that "works alone" can never justify a man or woman before a holy God.* Under the New Covenant we do not have to perform for God; He is already pleased with us through our Lord Jesus Christ. He loves and approves of us as much as he loves and approves of the Lord Jesus Christ. Unfortunately, many Christians operate like the elder brother in the parable of the prodigal son. This is why most Christians struggle with an ongoing "sin consciousness" because they do not believe they are good enough to be recipients of God's favor. They are constantly looking to their good works to supplement whatever they feel is lacking in the "finished work of Christ."

SONS DO NOT HAVE TO PERFORM TO HAVE ACCESS TO THE FATHER'S WEALTH.

Harden Not your Heart

Wherefore (as the Holy Ghost saith, To day if ye will hear his voice, 8Harden not your hearts, as in the provocation, in the day of temptation in the wilderness:

Hebrews 3:7-8

Even though the New Testament is a powerful covenant of grace, one of the most dangerous things we can do is harden our hearts when the Holy Spirit is speaking. The writer of Hebrews tells us that some of the people of Israel who came out of Egypt provoked God in the wilderness when they refused to listen to His voice. By hardening their heart when God was speaking to them, they provoked the judgment of God. Many of them died in the wilderness and never got a chance to enter the Promised Land, because they allowed sin to harden their hearts. We must be careful not to allow sin to harden our hearts. We need to confront sin immediately and ask for God's empowerment to overcome it. We must cultivate a heart that is both pliable and soft towards the Lord. This is why I personally love to cultivate an ongoing atmosphere of worship, prayer and communion with the Lord just to make sure that my heart is always tender towards the Lord.

Knowing the Ways of the Spirit

When your fathers tempted me, proved me, and saw my works forty years. 10Wherefore I was grieved with that generation, and said, They do alway err in their heart; and they have not known my ways.

Hebrews 3:9-10

The writer of the book of Psalms tells us that Moses knew His ways, but the people of Israel only knew His acts. God's "acts" deal with the result of what He does, while His "ways" deal with the how and why behind the acts of God. In short, the children of Israel were only interested in seeking God's hand, while Moses was interested in seeking his face. Christendom is full of Christians who are just like the children of Israel who came out of Egypt. They are only interested in what God can do for them. But to truly know God we need to look past His acts and begin to understand the ways of His Spirit.

When God wanted to destroy the walls of Jericho, he told Joshua to tell the people of Israel to walk around the city walls seven times. Can you imagine how ridiculous their march around the city walls of

Jericho must have looked like to the people of Jericho? They probably thought the children of Israel were insane. But after marching around the city walls for seven days, the children of Israel stopped and under Joshua's leadership gave a resounding shout of praise to the Lord. As soon as their shouts of praise and the trumpets of their musicians rose into the atmosphere, the walls of Jericho began to tremble and tumbled to the ground. What had seemed like a stupid war strategy to the naked eye suddenly became the most lethal war strategy that had ever been employed in the history of mankind. This story illustrates the big difference between knowing his ways and knowing His acts.

Entering His Rest

*So I sware in my wrath, They shall not enter into my rest.)
15While it is said, To day if ye will hear his voice, harden not
your hearts, as in the provocation. 16For some, when they had
heard, did provoke: howbeit not all that came out of Egypt
by Moses. 19So we see that they could not enter in because of
unbelief.*

Hebrews 3:11,15-16,19

We live in a world terrorized by the spirit of unrest. Restlessness is everywhere and in everything. But the Kingdom of God does NOT operate in an atmosphere of unrest. To the contrary, the Kingdom of God will arrest every chaotic frequency in the creation that exalts itself above the Knowledge of God. I have never seen so many Christians as I see now; whose lives are governed by the spirit of restlessness. But REST is an inheritance that God has reserved for the sons of God. The Lord longs for us to know the power of rest by entering into His rest.

There is too much striving in the body of Christ, the engines of greed and fear are driving much of this striving. Unfortunately, the Christianity of today is more about "personal survival" than manifesting the "Triumph" of Christ over the principalities and powers in the heavenly realms. But the Lord wants to demonstrate His manifold wisdom to the "fallen angels" through His universal body (the Church). This will not happen if Christians do not understand the power of entering His rest. Restlessness leads to bad choices and bad choices can place undue pressure on our future destiny.

THE KINGDOM OF *God* DOES NOT OPERATE IN AN ATMOSPHERE OF UNREST.

An Evil Heart of Unbelief

Take heed, brethren, lest there be in any of you an evil heart of unbelief, in departing from the living God. 13But exhort one another daily, while it is called To day; lest any of you be hardened through the deceitfulness of sin. 17But with whom was he grieved forty years? was it not with them that had sinned, whose carcases fell in the wilderness? 18And to whom sware he that they should not enter into his rest, but to them that believed not?

Hebrews 3:12-13, 17-18

The writer of the book of Hebrews tells us that one of the greatest dangers to entering into His rest is having an evil heart of unbelief. God so hates unbelief that he calls the heart of unbelief "evil." Wow, this is a serious matter never to be taken lightly. The Apostle tells us that an "evil heart of unbelief" can:

Cause us to depart from following the Living God

- Harden our hearts from responding to the soft and gentle prompting of the Holy Spirit by enticing us with the deceitfulness of sin.

- Stop us from entering His REST

But the writer of the book of Hebrews also shows us how we can stop ourselves from generating an "evil heart" of "unbelief." We must stay in close fellowship with other like-minded believers who are on fire for God, who can exhort us unto good works. It is my testimony that whenever I have felt like I was slipping in my passion for the Lord, fellowship with brothers and sisters in Christ who are fired up about God, tends to rekindle my own passion quite rapidly.

Partakers of Christ

For we are made partakers of Christ, if we hold the beginning of our confidence stedfast unto the end;

Hebrews 3:14

The Apostle makes another startling statement when he declares, "we have been made partakers of Christ!" Being partakers of the mystery that is Christ is in my opinion the highest calling in the life of the believer. There is nothing more worthy of our participation than partaking of the Christ nature. Christ is the visible expression of the invisible God. It does not get better than living and feeding on the nature of Christ.

This is why true apostolic ministry is not just about planting churches, it is about having the supernatural ability to "form the Christ nature" in the saints of the Most High.

ENTERING HIS REST

Mixing the Word with Faith

Let us therefore fear, lest, a promise being left us of entering into his rest, any of you should seem to come short of it. ²For unto us was the gospel preached, as well as unto them: but the word preached did not profit them, not being mixed with faith in them that heard it.

Hebrews 4:1-2

THE fourth chapter of the book of Hebrews starts with the expression, "let us therefore," implying that the apostle is not finished with the body of thought on the "issue of rest", that he started in the previous chapter. The Apostle Paul admonishes the Hebrew believers not to disqualify themselves from "entering into His rest" because of unbelief. It is clear from the passage that there is a promise that has been left for us to enter into His rest!

I must at this time point out that "the place of rest" that the Apostle is referring to here has nothing to do with where believers will spend eternity. The death, burial and resurrection of Jesus Christ has already paid the price for our complete redemption. Once we profess our faith in Christ, all our sins, past, present and future are dealt with. But this does NOT in any way suggest that we have a license to sin. I am merely stating the scope and completeness of our redemption. Nevertheless, the rest the Apostle Paul is referring to in the above passage is our entrance into our God given spiritual inheritance here on earth. For the Children of Israel their place of "rest" was entering the Promised Land; a land that flowed with milk and honey. When we enter into our God given spiritual inheritance, we "cease" from our own works as God did from His.

We cannot fulfill our spiritual destiny by employing fleshly technologies and methodologies. Spiritual destiny requires spiritual technology for its seamless fulfillment. But many Christians are striving through "flesh generated effort" to accomplish the spiritual destiny upon their lives. God never intended for spiritual destiny to be so laborious to reach. When I look on the faces of many Christians; I see a sickening weariness and contortions of defeat plastered on their faces. Our goal is to enter His rest, but we cannot do so until we "MIX" the Word (the prophecy) we have received from heaven with "faith."

Entering His Rest

For we which have believed do enter into rest, as he said, As I have sworn in my wrath, if they shall enter into my rest: although the works were finished from the foundation of the world. 4For he spake in a certain place of the seventh day on this wise, And God did rest the seventh day from all his works. 5And in this place again, If they shall enter into my rest. 6Seeing therefore it remaineth that some must enter therein, and they to whom it was first preached entered not in because of unbelief:

Hebrews 4:3-6

The Apostle Paul continues to hammer the point that believers need to enter into a place of rest: His rest- to be specific. He describes this rest as the place "where we cease from our works as God did from His." When God rested on the seventh day after He created the heavens and the earth, He introduced the principle of rest into the very fabric of creation. This is why everything that is feeding into the mainframe of God's created order, seeks to find a place of rest. If rest doesn't come, the person, animal or organization crashes and burns. Rest is an important part of the rhythm of creation. The Stock Market goes through seasons of rest, where it is neither a bull or bear market.

The night season was God's way of forcing mankind to find the place of rest from the day's chores! Nutritionists say that most of the body's activity of burning fat and digestion is done while a person is sleeping.

WHEN WE ENTER INTO OUR *God* GIVEN SPIRITUAL INHERITANCE, WE "CEASE" FROM OUR OWN WORKS AS *God* DID FROM HIS.

I have seen businessmen and pastors who are so driven by their desire to succeed that they literally have run their health into the ground. For many of them the price of unrest resulted in the demise of their marriages or wayward children who feel abandoned by their workaholic parents. Beloved let us release our faith to enter this powerful place of rest. It is time to stop all fleshly striving and enter into the "finished work of Christ."

Obedience Leads to Rest

Again, he limiteth a certain day, saying in David, To day, after so long a time; as it is said, Today if ye will hear his voice, harden not your hearts. 8For if Jesus had given them rest, then would he not afterward have spoken of another day. 9There remaineth therefore a rest to the people of God.

Hebrews 4:7-9

The writer of the book of Hebrews unveils the secret to entering His rest - obedience! The apostle tells us that if we do not harden our hearts when we hear His voice we will enter into His rest. Obeying His voice in the "NOW" is the master key to entering the place of supernatural rest in the Spirit. Said simply, obedience leads to rest. When the prophet Elisha told Namaan, the Syrian army general, to go and dip himself seven times in the dirty Jordan river to be healed of his leprosy; Namaan was infuriated (2 Kings 5). He felt that dipping himself in a dirty river like the Jordan River, when there were beautiful rivers in Damascus was beneath him. He would have returned to Syria with his leprosy had his pride not been intercepted by the wisdom of one of his servants.

When Namaan finally gave in and begrudgingly dipped himself seven times in the Jordan River, he came up from the water a healed man after the seventh dip. God gave him brand new skin. He was so delighted at the obvious change in his body. To think that he almost missed his miracle because of pride and unbelief is quite telling. But when he obeyed the voice of God through the man of God, he found a place of rest from his affliction.

Rest: The Place of the Inheritance

For he that is entered into his rest, he also hath ceased from his own works, as God did from his. 11Let us labour therefore to enter into that rest, lest any man fall after the same example of unbelief.

Hebrews 4:10-11

God never created mankind to struggle for anything. Struggle for provision in human life is an insult to the original plan and purpose of God. God never created man until He had finished preparing the Garden of Eden. When Adam opened his eyes after God breathed life into him, he was welcomed by a glistening world of abundance. There was nothing missing or out of place in the Garden of God.

Since God had already provided the resources for man's purposeful existence, He gave Adam the "Work" of "Managing or Stewarding" the "Finished Work!" Managing the "Finished Work of Christ" is mankind's true spiritual inheritance. There is a huge difference between "striving for the provision" and "managing the provision." The writer of Hebrews shows us that the place of REST is the place of Inheritance. If we work for something, it is called "wages", but if something is just given to us because of a relationship we have with the "testator" it is called "Inheritance." Let us enter His rest so we can live in our rightful spiritual inheritance. Nevertheless, we will not enter our full inheritance in Christ until after the return of Yeshua;

when He comes again to redeem the earth. In the meantime the Holy Spirit is the down payment of our total redemption.

The Power of the Quickened Word

For the word of God is quick, and powerful, and sharper than any twoedged sword, piercing even to the dividing asunder of soul and spirit, and of the joints and marrow, and is a discerner of the thoughts and intents of the heart. Hebrews 4:12

The writer of Hebrews tells us about the inherent dynamics of the proceeding Word of God. It will serve us well to understand these spiritual dynamics that come into play when we expose ourselves to the Word of God. Below are the distinct dynamics of the Word of God that the apostle gives us.

- The Word of God is "Quick." This means that the Word of God has the inherent ability to act upon us very rapidly. When we apply the word to our lives, we should expect quick and immediate changes in our lives.

- The Word of God is "Powerful." This means that the Word of God is more powerful than a nuclear bomb. It has inherent authority over all of God's creation. This is why miracles happen when we stand on the Word!

- The Word of God is "Sharper than a two edged sword." The only thing that is sharper than a two edged sword is a "laser beam." The world of technology and science has introduced us to the amazing power of the laser beam that is able to cut into any object with a 360 degree laser sharp edge. The writer of Hebrews compares the sharpness and precision of the laser beam to the Word of God. This is why I trust the Word of God to change any person or situation.

- The Word of God divides between the "Soul and the Spirit" of a man, separating the spiritual from that which is "soulish or fleshly." This is truly a powerful dynamic of the Word of God. Without the Word of God, we would never be able to know the difference between, spirit, soul and fleshly operations.

OBEYING HIS VOICE IN THE "NOW" IS THE MASKER KEY TO ENTERING THE PLACE OF SUPERNATURAL REST IN THE SPIRIT.

You Can Run but You Can't Hide

Neither is there any creature that is not manifest in his sight: but all things are naked and opened unto the eyes of him with whom we have to do.

Hebrews 4:13

The proverbial saying, "you can run but you can't hide", is certainly true when we relate it to God. The writer of the book of Hebrews tells us that there is no creature in the universe that is not on God's eternal radar. Everything is naked in the sight of God, even the secret things that people do. The world we live in is full of secret societies; but the reality is that there is no secret before God. This is why it's important for us not to live our faith trying to please people, when pleasing God is the only thing that matters.

Don't Let Go of Your Confession

Seeing then that we have a great high priest, that is passed into the heavens, Jesus the Son of God, let us hold fast our profession. 15For we have not an high priest which cannot be touched with the feeling of our infirmities; but was in all points tempted like as we are, yet without sin.

Hebrews 4:14-15

The writer of the book of Hebrews makes a startling conclusion. He concludes, that since we have a great high priest that is passed into the heavens, Jesus the Son of God, we cannot afford to let go of our confession. In other words, it is foolish for us to abandon our confession of the word of God over our lives when the Lord Jesus Christ is seated on the right hand of God to mediate our profession of faith. The above passage of Scripture, tells us that we have a high priest in Yeshua who is touched by the feelings and inherent weaknesses of our fleshly existence. Yeshua is not sitting at the right hand of the Father to condemn us but to give us grace and forgiveness in time of need.

Enter Boldly

Let us therefore come boldly unto the throne of grace, that we may obtain mercy, and find grace to help in time of need.

Hebrews 4:16

In conclusion, the fourth chapter of the book of Hebrews ends on a very powerful note. Based upon the fact that we have a high priest in the heavens in the face of the Lord Jesus Christ, we can come boldly to the throne of grace. What is interesting about this final verse in the fourth chapter of the book of Hebrews is the manner of approach that we are commanded to take. *We are commanded to come to the throne of grace boldly.* This one word demonstrates the vast difference in approaching God between the Old and the New Covenant.

Under the Old Covenant, the high priest from the tribe of Levi would enter the holy of holies once a year. But it was never with boldness, but it was with great fear and dread. Approaching the Ark of the Covenant was a frightening experience for the people under the Old Covenant, because you could live or die through the experience. But under the New Covenant, we are commanded to approach the throne of grace with boldness. The word boldness is defined as unwavering confidence. This means that the apostle Paul is encouraging us to approach the throne of grace with unwavering confidence that God wants us there. He wants us to obtain mercy and the grace that we need in our time of need. This is very powerful my dear friends. This is why understanding the book of Hebrews is a key to enjoying the New Covenant.

CHRIST THE HIGH PRIEST AFTER THE ORDER OF MELCHIZEDEK

The Ministry of a High Priest

For every high priest taken from among men is ordained for men in things pertaining to God, that he may offer both gifts and sacrifices for sins:

Hebrews 5:1

ONE of the most powerful ministries in Scripture is the ministry of the High Priest. The writer of the book of Hebrews tells us that candidates for the ministry of the high priest were taken from among men. These candidates were given a supernatural ordination to represent the spiritual needs of the people of Israel before God. The ministry of these earthly high priests involved offering gifts and sacrifices for sins on behalf of the people of Israel.

Under the Levitical priestly order, the high priest had the tremendous burden of cleansing and preparing himself for his one appointment with the glory of God in the holy of holies to atone for the sins of the people of Israel. He would go beyond the veil bearing the blood of an innocent scapegoat that he sprinkled on the mercy seat. This is also what the Lord Jesus Christ did for us when he rose from the dead. He went before the mercy seat in heaven, bearing his blood and sprinkled the heavenly mercy seat with his precious blood. The sprinkling of his precious blood onto the heavenly mercy seat transformed it into the throne of grace.

Compassion and the Ministry of a High Priest

Who can have compassion on the ignorant, and on them that are out of the way; for that he himself also is compassed with infirmity. 3And by reason hereof he ought, as for the people, so also for himself, to offer for sins.

Hebrews 5:2-3

The writer of the book of Hebrews delves deeper into the ministry of the high priest; by demonstrating that one of the primary reasons why the high priest was chosen from among men was to ensure that he had compassion for the people he was representing because he was one of them. The apostle Paul tells us that since the high priest was taken from among men, he was affected by the same inherent weaknesses of human nature that his people were also dealing with. It is interesting to me how critical we can be of people who have gone through moral failures that we can never see ourselves committing. But we are very compassionate and understanding of the weakness or failures of those who are going through what we have also gone through.

This is why Christ, the High Priest of the eternal Melchizedek priesthood, became a man through the mystery of the incarnation. From this point onwards, we will delve deeper into the nature and inner workings of the Melchizedek priesthood and the role that Christ plays in it. The Order of Melchizedek is the eternal priestly ministry of Christ before He wrapped himself with flesh in Mary's womb (Psalm 110). However, His priesthood had not yet been tempered by the humanity factor. But once the Messiah became a man in the face of Yeshua, what He could not understand in His divinity he came to comprehend through his sanctified humanity. For instance, in His divinity as the "Christ", He could never get tired or hungry. But in His humanity as "Jesus", He could experience these cravings that are common to the human experience.

The Honor of the Ministry of a High Priest

And no man taketh this honour unto himself, but he that is called of God, as was Aaron. 5So also Christ glorified not himself to be made an high priest; but he that said unto him, Thou art my Son, today have I begotten thee.

Hebrews 5:4-5

The writer of the book of Hebrews delves deeper into the integral dynamics of the ministry of the High Priest. The apostle Paul now tells us that God has placed "great honor" on the ministry of the High Priest. The "honor" of the high priest is that He is by divine election placed in a spiritual position where he is responsible for representing the spiritual needs of the people before God. Imagine the sense of honor that comes with knowing that you have been given the ability to negotiate with God for the destiny of many.

THE ORDER OF MELCHIZEDEK IS THE ETERNAL PRIESTLY MINISTRY OF *Christ* BEFORE HE WRAPPED HIMSELF WITH FLESH IN MARY'S WOMB (PSALM 110).

Saint Paul is adamantly clear that "no man", even if he or she tried, can take this honor upon him or herself. The ministry of the high priest is not a ministry one can just unilaterally decide to operate in through mere human volition. God is the initiator of this supernatural ordination. No man can take this honor upon himself without a bona fide call from God. Just like Aaron, Christ did not glorify himself to be a high priest, but he was consecrated to this lofty spiritual office by a call of God from within the realms of eternity (Psalm 110). This call was again reaffirmed on earth when Christ put on flesh to become the son of man in the face of Jesus.

A Priest Forever After the Order of Melchizedek

As he saith also in another place, Thou art a priest forever after the order of Melchisedec.

Hebrews 5:6

The above passage of Scripture is probably one of the most powerful proclamations of the eternal royal priesthood of Christ. What is of note here is that Hebrews 5:6 is a direct quote from Psalm 110. This Psalm of David was written at least 2000 years before the incarnation of the Christ through the virgin birth. This passage of Scripture demonstrates that the Melchizedek Priesthood is the eternal royal priesthood of Christ before He came to our planet. In this writing, we will endeavor to bring you into a deeper and accurate understanding of the Order of Melchizedek.

King David, the man after the heart of God was given a powerful prophetic encounter in which he found himself in the throne room of God. In this prophetic experience, King David overheard God the Father tell the Son that he was a priest forever after the Order of Melchizedek. What is of note is that in this powerful prophetic experience, David is actually given a breath-taking preview of future events that took place immediately after the resurrection and ascension of Jesus Christ. What is interesting is that King David had this open vision two thousand years before the death, resurrection and ascension of Jesus Christ. He supernaturally stepped into New Testament realities while he was living under the Old Covenant.

Prayer and the Ministry of a High Priest

Who in the days of his flesh, when he had offered up prayers and supplications with strong crying and tears unto him that was able to save him from death, and was heard in that he feared;

Hebrews 5:7

The Apostle Paul now shows us that prayer is a critical aspect of the ministry of the High Priest. It is clear from the progressive revelation of Scripture that prayer has a very important and enduring purpose in the manifestation of the eternal purposes of God here on earth. The one common defining factor between the great men and women of God of the Bible is a prevailing life of prayer. It is clear that he who is weak as a factor in prayer is weak as factor in the work of God.

The writer of the book of Hebrews draws our attention to this aspect of the life of Christ, while He was on earth. He gives us a glimpse into the intensity of the prevailing prayers of intercession that Christ was engaged in while He was on earth. This passage ought to be a rallying cry to a life of prevailing prayer in the life of each follower of Christ. The passage also seems to suggest that walking in the fear of the Lord enhances our prayer lives.

Learning Obedience

Though he were a Son, yet learned he obedience by the things which he suffered; 9And being made perfect, he became the author of eternal salvation unto all them that obey him;

Hebrews 5:8-9

The writer of the book of Hebrews tells us something that we do not normally associate with the Lord Jesus Christ. He tells us that even though the Lord Jesus Christ was the Son of God, He had to learn obedience through the things that he suffered. Now we know that Christ in His divinity does not need to learn obedience, but in his humanity as Jesus of Nazareth, He needed to learn how to obey God in the human body. This passage of Scripture also uncovers a very powerful principle about the whole subject of obeying God. One of the ways that we learn obedience is through suffering. Now the suffering that is implied in this passage is not synonymous with poverty. It is not a suffering that is derived from having a poor economic standing in life; it is the suffering that is created in our minds, emotions and will when we have to choose the will of God above the dictates of our own humanity. Every born-again believer has to learn obedience through denying his or her own will. If the Lord

Jesus Christ had to learn obedience, then born-again believers also have to learn obedience by carrying their cross daily.

THE ONE COMMON DEFINING FACTOR BETWEEN THE GREAT MEN AND WOMEN OF *God* OF THE BIBLE IS A PREVAILING LIFE OF PRAYER.

Called of God

Called of God an high priest after the order of Melchisedec.

Hebrews 5:10

The apostle Paul now informs us that the Lord Jesus Christ is a high priest, called of God, after the Order of Melchizedek. What is so unfortunate is that many members of the body of Christ do not have an accurate understanding of the Order of Melchizedek. But if the Lord Jesus Christ is a high priest after the Order of Melchizedek, it follows that all New Testament believers are called to a priestly ministry that is patterned after the Order of Melchizedek. If the Lord Jesus Christ, who is our head and High Priest is called of God after the Order of Melchizedek, it is safe to assume that New Testament believers have a calling to be kings and priests after the Order of Melchizedek. There is much to be said about the Melchizedek Priesthood that can greatly benefit the Body of Christ and change how churches function in the Community at large.

The Curse of Itching Ears

Of whom we have many things to say, and hard to be uttered, seeing ye are dull of hearing.

Hebrews 5:11

At this juncture, the apostle Paul taps into a nerve of his personal frustration. He is consumed by a deep desire to take the Hebrew believers into a deeper understanding of the Melchizedek priesthood of Jesus Christ and yet he is forced to stop teaching on the subject because the people had become dull of hearing. They had become desensitized by their own carnal desires from desiring the deep things of God. This passage of Scripture demonstrates that the stream of divine revelation does not flow in the direction of people who are not hungry for more of God. The Bible calls this spiritual condition itching ears. It is a curse for us to have itching ears when it comes to the knowledge of the truth.

Unfortunately, the rise of the user-friendly gospel and churches that promote this tooth-less gospel has given birth to spiritual wimps. They have created a man-centered gospel which has given birth to a mass proliferation of believers who are more interested in what God can do for them, rather than what they can do for God. This new company of believers has little taste for the deep things of God, especially if the truths that govern access to the "deep things of God" require sacrifice of personal agenda, so they can embrace God's agenda. Consequently, Christendom is full of believers who have "Itching ears". They have become what the Apostle calls, "dull of hearing." The Apostle Paul also makes it clear that those who are dull of hearing can never understand the Order of Melchizedek. This would explain why many Christians have very little understanding of the Melchizedek Priesthood of Jesus Christ, even though the book of Hebrews dedicates a large portion of its dissertation to this important priestly order.

The Folly of Spiritual Immaturity

For when the time ye ought to be teachers, ye have need that one teach you again which be the first principles of the oracles of God; and are become such as have need of milk, and not of strong meat. 13For every one that useth milk is unskilful in the word of righteousness: for he is a babe.

Hebrews 5:12-13

Spiritual immaturity is not wickedness but it can delay the manifestation of God's best in the life of the believer, as is the case with the Hebrew believers whom the apostle Paul was referring to. The apostle had a strong desire to take the Hebrew believers into a deep understanding of the Melchizedek priesthood of Jesus Christ and its benefits for them. However, the apostle was forced to stop his dissertation.

IT IS A CURSE FOR US TO HAVE ITCHING EARS WHEN IT COMES TO THE KNOWLEDGE OF THE TRUTH.

In the above passage of Scripture, the apostle Paul makes it very clear that believers who are still babies in Christ can never come into a functional understanding of the Order of Melchizedek. Operating as a king and priest under the Order of Melchizedek requires an appreciation for the meaty portion of the Word of God. The meaty portion of the Word of God is not found by skimping around the edges of the ocean of Revelation. We have to take a dive into the deepest parts of the ocean of Revelation.

Spiritual Discernment and the Order of Melchizedek

But strong meat belongeth to them that are of full age, even those who by reason of use have their senses exercised to discern both good and evil.

Hebrews 5:14

The apostle Paul finally concludes the fifth chapter by establishing the connection between spiritual maturity and the spirit of discernment. He first establishes the fact that strong meat belongs to them that are of full age. The expression "of full age" in the passage above denotes a level of spiritual maturity where the believer is able to discern the difference between good and evil. The spirit of discernment is developed over time when the believers allow the Lord to exercise their five senses, to discern the difference between right and wrong in relation to His kingdom.

What is of note here is that the apostle Paul is implying that without the spirit of discernment that comes from operating from a place of spiritual maturity, many believers will never be able to discern and understand the Order of Melchizedek. If there was ever a time when the church needed to understand the Order of Melchizedek it is NOW! We need to win the cultural war and take on a leadership role in the transformation of nations. It is my deepest prayer that the Lord will give you a taste for the "deeper things of God" as you read this book. If you desire to acquire a deeper understanding of the nature, scope and inner workings of the Order of Melchizedek, I strongly suggest that you get a copy of my book, *"The Order of Melchizedek."*

ELEMENTARY PRINCIPLES OF THE DOCTRINE OF CHRIST

THE writer of the Psalms poses a very probing question, *"If the foundations are destroyed, what shall the righteous do?"* The greater body of Christ around the world needs to ask itself this question. When I came to the Lord in 1989 there was a very serious discipleship movement in the local church that I attended. I will be forever grateful to the Lord for this. But as I travel around the United States and some Western nations, I am deeply saddened by the trend that I see. I am coming across a generation of Christians who are being raised on "spiritual sound bites" in the place of foundational principles of the doctrines of Christ. Consequently, when the pressure to conform to the shifting sands of new cultural norms, these "sound bite" Christians have nothing to stand on.

The Elementary Principles of the Doctrine of Christ

Therefore leaving the principles of the doctrine of Christ, let us go on unto perfection; not laying again the foundation of repentance from dead works, and of faith toward God, 2 Of the doctrine of baptisms, and of laying on of hands, and of the resurrection of the dead, and of eternal judgment.

Hebrews 6:1-2

The writer of the book of Hebrews has an ancient solution to the aforementioned spiritual ills of the church. This ageless solution to the lack of a solid rock foundation in the lives of so many citizens of the Kingdom of God comes in the form of six elementary principles of the doctrine of Christ.

1. Repentance from dead works

Dead works are "things" (activity) not done out of faith or obedience to God. These things are not necessarily sinful. For instance, giving is good but when we do it begrudgingly we forfeit any eternal rewards associated with the act of giving. This is because our giving in such a case was coerced instead of being driven by faith in God who multiplies the seed sown. This also includes all religious acts based upon our own righteousness and not the finished work of Christ on the cross. This is why the Bible calls every human being under the sun to repent. Repentance is the doorway into the Kingdom of God.

The word "Repentance" comes from a Greek word that actually means, "To change your mind." This means that true repentance is not based on emotion or mere intellectual acknowledgement. True repentance is a decision to change one's mind after being confronted by the immutable truths of God's Word. Repentance is a complete change in the direction of a person's life driven by a supernatural change of heart. It is an inner acknowledgement by a person in which he or she becomes convinced of their sinful condition before God. True repentance does not treat sin as though it is a mere error in judgment, but as a cancer of the soul that only God can heal through the shed blood of Christ.

"IF THE FOUNDATIONS ARE DESTROYED, WHAT SHALL THE RIGHTEOUS DO?"

On the other hand, "remorse" is a false kind of repentance, because it never involves a true change of heart. For the most part a person who is remorseful may regret their actions or may be just embarrassed that they got caught. But such a person has not made paradigm shift in their spiritual disposition. A perfect biblical example of true repentance is the story of the prodigal son (Luke 15:17-20). He came to his senses in a moment of truth. He quickly made a decision to change his life and return to his father's house. He immediately acted out his decision to demonstrate his inward heart change. On the other hand, Judas Iscariot became remorseful over his betrayal of Jesus but he never really repented (Matthew 27:3-5).

2   Faith toward God

> The second elementary principle of the doctrine of Christ is "Faith towards God." Faith comes from and relates to God's Word according to Romans 10:17. This means that true biblical faith comes only through the Word of God. This is why faith can be easily galvanized in a climate saturated with the Word of God.
>
> According to Hebrews 11:1, faith is a spiritual substance; hope is built on the substance of faith. First and foremost, faith is a "present" substance in the heart of all of mankind. This means that every human being has a measure of faith residing in his or her heart (Romans 10:10). This is why no one can accuse God of not giving him or her access to faith. When people, saved or unsaved, board a plane flown by a pilot they do not know, while hoping that he or she will fly them to their destination safely, are actually exercising faith.

On the other hand "Hope"....is a *future* expectation in the mind (1 Thessalonians 5:8). But in order to substantiate this future expectation the optimist has to engage "faith." This is because true biblical faith relates to the unseen. But this "unseen" element is not mere wishful thinking or daydreaming. This unseen element that faith is designed to reach for is the "unseen reality of the Word of God (Hebrews 11:3).

On the other hand, faith's number one nemesis is "sight." Sight unlike faith deals not with the "unseen reality of the Word of God" but with only what can be perceived by the carnal eye. According to Scripture, "Faith and sight" are completely exclusive of each other (2 Corinthians 5:7). The Bible teaches that we have to believe before we can see (John 11:39-40).

Dr. Derek Prince in his foundational series says that, "Faith is primarily character." Faithfulness or loyalty expresses the character aspect of faith better than any other attribute. This especially means that "Faith" is essentially an abiding commitment to a person (2 Timothy 1:12) and that person is none other than the Lord Jesus Christ (Luke 22:28). In this sense, true biblical faith is an abiding commitment or loyalty to the Lord Jesus Christ. If we fail at this first embassy of faith, we will make shipwreck of our faith.

Dr. Derek Prince in his foundational series also says, "Faith is secondarily doctrine." In this second embassy, "Faith" becomes something that can be taught. It also becomes something that can be "confessed." The Bible tells us that when we confess our faith in the Lord Jesus Christ and His finished work on the cross, the way is made unto salvation. Faith as confession relates us to Christ Jesus as our eternal High Priest (Hebrews 3:1). The Lord Jesus Christ is the Apostle over our confession of faith.

3. Doctrine of baptisms

The third elementary principle of the doctrine of Christ is the "doctrine of baptisms." There are three different baptisms in the New Testament.

i. John's baptism

ii. The New Creation baptism

iii. Holy Spirit baptism

The word, "baptize" means to immerse or fully cover with water. It also means to put something down into water or pour water from above. Baptism in Scripture is always "in" and "into." "In" refers to an element in which you are baptized, while "into" refers to the result that is produced by the baptism.

"Remorse" is a false kind of repentance, because it never involves a true change of heart.

John's Baptism: A baptism performed to prepare the nation of Israel for the coming Messiah. The baptism of John awoke the consciousness of Israel to the advent of the promised Jewish Messiah (Mark 1:2-5). The Messiah could not come until they were prepared for His arrival. In the same way, the second coming of Jesus Christ will not happen until the Church is prepared to receive Him as the spotless bride. The Baptism of John also serves as the dispensational link between the Old and New covenant, between the end of Law and the beginning of Grace.

New Creation Baptism: A baptism that born again believers are required to go through in order to identify with the death, burial and resurrection of the Lord Jesus Christ. It is an outward sign of what happened inwardly. It is a pattern of how to fulfill all righteousness: Jesus (Matthew 3:13–17). New creation baptism, or the baptism into the body of Christ, has the approval of all three members of the Godhead. Jesus charged the apostles to go and disciple nations baptizing them in the name of the Father, Son and Holy Ghost (Matthew 28). This baptism also infers that we have been "acquitted, reckoned righteous and made righteous: justified (Romans 5:1)." The primary message of this baptism is that our lives do not belong to us after baptism. The requirements for New Creation baptism are that we first hear the gospel (Matthew 28:19-20). Then we also have to believe that Jesus died, was buried, and then rose from the dead so we can enter into the newness of life. We must first go through repentance (Acts 2:38) before this baptism can even be meaningful. New Creation baptism helps us with obtaining a good conscience toward

God (1 Peter 3:21). The spiritual significance of this baptism is that it empowers us in our identification with Jesus in death (Romans 6:3–11).

The Baptism of the Holy Spirit: Perhaps there is no other baptism that has been the source of deep and far reaching theological disputes among Christians like the baptism in the Holy Ghost. But since the advent of the Holy Spirit on the day of Pentecost (Acts 2), the clear evidence of the recipient speaking in other tongues as the Spirit gives utterance has accompanied this baptism. What is of note is that this baptism seems to be the tipping point to the release of the supernatural ministry of the Holy Spirit through the Body of Christ. It is not within the scope of this writing to discuss this vast subject. There are many books on this specific baptism in most Christian bookstores.

4. **Laying on of hands**

> The fourth elementary principle of the doctrine of Christ is the "doctrine of the laying on of hands." This doctrine ensures continuity of life and the leadership of God's people. This doctrine is the cornerstone of apostolic succession. It contains the spiritual technology for transferring the purposes of God to the next generation of Kingdom citizens.

In Scripture, the doctrine of "laying on of hands" has been used to connect spiritual purposes, mantles and mandates to common human practices. This principle has been used in Scripture to transmit blessings, authority, wisdom, impart the Holy Spirit, and spiritual gifts or ministry. This elementary principle has also been used to commission, to set apart, as well as to give authority to those so chosen.

Examples from the Old Testament: Jacob laid his hands on the sons of Joseph (Genesis 48:8–19), imparted a blessing and determined their destiny. Moses also laid hands on Joshua (Numbers 27:18–23; Deut. 34:9), his faithful apprentice, to set him apart, to endorse as well as equip him for the service that lay ahead.

Purposes for the Laying on of hands Indicated in New Testament:

A. To impart healing to the sick

1. To the unsaved (Mark 16:17–18; Luke 4:40–41)

2. For church members, accompanied by anointing with oil (James 5:14–15)

B. *To impart (the gift of) the Holy Spirit*

1. The Samaritans (Acts 8:14–20)

2. Saul of Tarsus (Acts 9:17–18)

3. Disciples of Ephesus (Acts 19:1–6)

C. *To commission church servants/deacons (Acts 6:1–7)*

1. Transmit authority

2. Set apart, endorse, equip

D. *To send out apostles (Acts 13:1–4, 14:26–27)*

1. Transmit authority

2. Set apart, endorse, equip

E. *To appoint elders (Acts 14:23; 1 Timothy 5:17–22; Titus 1:5)*

1. Transmit authority

2. Set apart, endorse, equip

F. *To impart a spiritual gift (charisma)*

1. Romans 1:11–12

2. 2 Timothy 1:6

Dangers and Safeguards: While the laying on of hands is one of the fundamental principles of the doctrine of Christ, there are inherent dangers to the task of laying on of hands. We are warned in the book of Timothy against the danger of endorsing someone who is unfit or unworthy (1 Timothy 5:22) to hold an office in the church. Laying hands on people too quickly can also expose us to spiritual contamination. This is because we become associated with the person that we lay hands on. It is also possible to transfer the wrong spirit on the lives of those who are having hands laid on them, if the person doing so is living in some secret sin.

The safeguards to the laying on of hands come in the form of:

1. Prayer accompanied by a spirit of humility

2. Being directed by the Holy Spirit before we lay hands on anybody (Romans 8:14).

3. Being protected by the blood of Jesus, while we lay hands on anybody (Hebrews 13:12)

4. Being empowered against evil forces by the Holy Spirit (Luke 10:19)

5. Resurrection of the dead

   The fifth elementary principle of the doctrine of Christ is the "Resurrection from the dead." The word resurrection means: "To stand up again." Man's personality consists of the spirit, soul and body (1 Thessalonians 5:23). The body dies and will be resurrected, while the spirit and soul continue to exist after physical death.

"REMORSE" IS A FALSE KIND OF REPENTANCE, BECAUSE IT NEVER INVOLVES A TRUE CHANGE OF HEART.

From the closure of the Garden of Eden to the opening of the gates of the New Jerusalem, the ageless question that has haunted the mind of every human being is "Is there life after death?" But the story of the rich man and Lazarus demonstrates that the departed soul/spirit in Sheol/Hades (Luke 16:22–26) has the following:

1. Persistence of personality—no loss of identity

2. Recognition of persons

3. Recollection of life on earth

4. Consciousness of present conditions

5. A complete separation between righteous and unrighteous

The Bible shows that before Jesus' death on the cross:

1. All souls passed into Hades (Greek)—Sheol (Hebrew)

2. Hades or Sheol was the place of departed souls. There were two separate areas in Sheol for the righteous and unrighteous person. The righteous dead went to Abraham's bosom, while the wicked dead went straight into the burning flames of hell.

At Jesus' death, His spirit was committed to the Heavenly Father (Luke 23:46), while His soul descended into Sheol/Hades (Acts 2:31; 1 Peter 3:18–19). Jesus' body on one hand was laid in the tomb (John 19:40–42). At Jesus' resurrection — His spirit and soul reunited with His body in a glorious resurrection that changed the spiritual projectile of the people of our planet. After the death and resurrection of Jesus, the destiny of righteous believers changed drastically. At death, the spirits of born-again believers can now ascend directly to God (Acts 7:59, Philippians 1:23-24). Jesus' death and resurrection affected the whole universe. When He rose from the dead, He released the righteous from Hades. Many of the righteous dead actually went into the City of Jerusalem before they were caught up in the clouds with Jesus as He took His precious blood to the Father's throne.

THE DOCTRINE OF "LAYING ON OF HANDS"
HAS BEEN USED TO CONNECT SPIRITUAL
PURPOSES, MANTLES AND MANDATES TO

COMMON HUMAN PRACTICES.

Importance of Resurrection: The resurrection is God's vindication of Jesus Christ (Romans 1:3–4). It is also the basis for our justification (Romans 4:25). The resurrection is the eternal guarantee of Christ's power to save (Hebrews 7:25). The resurrection is also the completion of our redemption. Our resurrected body is the completion of our salvation (Philippians 3:10–12). The resurrection is also the consummation of union with Christ (1 Thessalonians 4:17). I sincerely believe that if many born again Christians (Kingdom citizens to be more accurate) truly understood the doctrine of the resurrection of the dead, they would live their lives in the fear of the Lord. The resurrection is in three phases namely:

1. Christ the first fruits (Leviticus 23:10–11; Matthew 27:51–53)

2. Those who are Christ's at His coming (1 Thessalonians 4:16–17)

3. Final general resurrection (Revelation 20:12–13)

6. **Eternal judgment**

   The sixth elementary principle of the doctrine of Christ is the "doctrine of Eternal Judgment." There are two kinds of judgment mentioned in Scripture:

   1. In history: God's punishment or blessing on succeeding

      Generations for:

      a. Idolatry (Exodus 20:4–6)

      b. Iniquity (Jeremiah 32:18)

      c. Righteousness (Psalm 103:17–18)

   2. In eternity: Each individual will answer for his or her own life (Ezekiel 18:1–4, 20)

They are five principles or criteria of God's judgment based upon (Romans 2:1–16).

1. It is according to *truth* (Romans 2. 1–2)

2. It is according to *deeds* (Romans 2:6). These deeds are faithfully recorded in the "books" of heaven (Revelation 20:2).

3. There is no respect of persons—(v. 11)

4. It is according to our measure of light (Romans 2:12, Matthew 11:20–24)

5. Includes *secret thoughts* and *motives of men's hearts and minds.* (Romans 2:16)

Christians (born-again believers) will appear before the judgment seat of Christ. The judgment seat of Christ is for born-again *Christians only!* (2 Corinthians 5:10, 1 Peter 1:17, 4:17) There are five main features of the judgment of the saints after death:

1. Individual—each one will answer for himself.

2. The judgment will be about things done in the body, after the salvation experience.

3. The judgment will be about only two categories: *good* or *bad—no neutrality will be accepted.*

4. The judgment will not be for condemnation (Romans 8:1).

5. The judgment will be about assessment of our service to the Lord while we are living here on earth (1 Corinthians 3:11–15). Our service to the Lord will be tested by fire, so God can prove the quality of our work. If our work fails to pass the test of fire, it will be burnt to ashes and we will forfeit our reward.

At the Judgment Seat of Christ there will be three requirements for our "work" to stand the test of fire, namely:

1. The primary motive for our service must be: *For God's glory* (1 Corinthians 10:31).

2. Our Obedience to God's Word (Matthew 7:21–27).

3. Proof that the Holy Spirit powered our service to the Lord and not the arm of the flesh (Romans 15:18–19).

The final and most dreaded judgment is before the Great White Throne. This is the judgment seat for all the remaining dead (Revelation 20:11–15). Every life is recorded in a book of records. (Revelation 20:12). God will grant mercy to those enrolled in Book of Life (Revelation 20:12, 15). It's not within the scope of this writing to do a full expose' on this very important doctrine. I highly recommend you get a copy of Derek Prince's foundational series, among many others, for detailed explanation of these important principles of the doctrine of Christ.

If God Permits

And this will we do, if God permit.

Hebrews 6:3

The writer of the book of Hebrews makes a very interesting statement that demands further investigation. He uses the expression, "If God permits" to insinuate the possibility of God resisting us from coming into our full inheritance in Christ if we fail to grapple with the elementary principles of the doctrine of Christ. What I am about to say may shock or annoy many in Christendom who are living under the impression that much of their struggle to come into their full inheritance in Christ has a lot to do with the Devil's ability to resist them. In most cases, this is not the case. Much of their struggle actually originates from the fact that God is resisting their soulish efforts to possess their spiritual inheritance because they have NOT given God a proper foundation of truth to build on within the circumference of their lives. God is a builder and like all builders, the LORD respects foundations. The Lord knows that anything of worth that is built on a false or inadequate foundation is already doomed for destruction in its future destiny. This is why I wrote this book. I want to help you to come into a deeper and accurate understanding of the elementary principles of the doctrine of Christ. The Holy Spirit wants to bestow the blessing of Abraham upon your life; once you become serious about building on the foundation that is Christ. If you take to heart the aforementioned doctrines of Christ, the Lord will permit you to move on to perfection (spiritual maturity).

The Unpardonable Sin

For it is impossible for those who were once enlightened, and have tasted of the heavenly gift, and were made partakers of the Holy Ghost, 5And have tasted the good word of God, and the powers of the world to come, 6If they shall fall away, to renew them again unto repentance; seeing they crucify to themselves the Son of God afresh, and put him to an open shame.

Hebrews 6:4-6

Perhaps there is no passage of Scripture, in the book of Hebrews, that has suffered more than its share of misinterpretation, like that of Hebrews 6:4-6. This passage is one of the favorite passages of Christian legalists who place undue burden on a believer's ability to live a righteous life rather than on God's faithfulness to keep us blameless until the day of Jesus Christ. Unfortunately, this passage has been used by well meaning pastors and teachers of the Word to heap condemnation on many brothers and sisters who have fallen into sin. I have actually counseled born again believers who were living under heavy condemnation because they had been convinced by very bad theology that they had actually lost their salvation because of past sinful indiscretions. Bad teaching had convinced them they had already committed the "unpardonable sin."

I got saved in an Assemblies of God church in Africa, under an evangelist-pastor who preached fire and brimstone messages every

Sunday. He was a great preacher but a bad theologian. The unintended consequence of his teaching style was such that the church was full of "Sin Conscious" believers. We were all afraid of committing the unpardonable sin and going to hell. We did penance every day; every chance we got. Even a passing evil thought sent shivers of the fear of divine retribution down our spine. There were times I was even afraid to read the sixth chapter of Hebrews for fear that I would discover that I had already committed the unpardonable sin.

Years later I discovered to my utter dismay that Hebrews 6:4-6 has little to do with a believer losing his or her salvation because of sin. If you read the passage carefully, you will quickly notice that the Apostle Paul is not at all concerned about any born-again believer losing their salvation because of sin. The context for the loss of salvation in this particular passage is "Choice and not Sin." The reason the Apostle Paul does not insinuate that Sin can cause a born again believer to lose his or her salvation is because Christ paid for our sins, past, present and future on the Cross. This statement is NOT a license for any believer to live in sin. If we do so we are using the grace of God as a cloak of unrighteousness. This kind of lifestyle can only attract the judgment of God. Sin is to have no dominion over us. We have died to Sin and its passions through out blessed Messiah. Sin was effectively vanquished on the cross when the Lord laid on Him (Yeshua) the iniquity of us all. This may come as a huge shock to many Christian legalists, but after Jesus Christ died on the Cross- no one is necessarily going to hell because of sin. Any human being, who ends up in hell post Calvary, is there not because they sinned, but because they failed to "choose" Christ as the appropriation for their sins. On the other hand, born again believers who forfeit their salvation are those who knowingly choose to deny Christ as the appropriation for their sin after...

1. They were once enlightened (Came to the saving knowledge of Jesus Christ).

2. They have tasted of the heavenly gift (They experienced the baptism in the Holy Ghost with the evidence of speaking in tongues).

3. They were made partakers of the Holy Ghost (They experienced all the above, plus began to function in the nine gifts of the Spirit).

4. They have tasted the good word of God (They experienced all the above, plus began to function in deep Kingdom and Christ centered revelation).

5. They have experienced the powers of the world to come (They experienced all the above, plus were used by God to operate in signs, wonders and mighty deeds).

As you can clearly see from the above qualifications, those who qualify to be judged by God under the tenets of Hebrews 6:4-6 are a major minority. I have been saved for many years and I have spent many of those years at the frontlines of cutting edge ministry. I have been blessed to know powerful and famous preachers in the body of Christ. Yet I can count on one hand, how many of them satisfy all the qualifications listed above. Many of our beloved Baptist brothers who do not believe in the baptism of the Holy Ghost will never be in danger of falling under the judgment tenets of Hebrews 6:4-6, because they have not even arrived on second base. Most Christians who attended churches controlled by the user-friendly gospel, can never fall under the tenets above either. Many believers who patronize most seeker sensitive churches have never really tasted the "good Word of God."

THE *Holy Spirit* WANTS TO BESTOW THE BLESSING OF ABRAHAM UPON YOUR LIFE, ONCE YOU BECOME SERIOUS ABOUT BUILDING ON THE FOUNDATION.

The more the Holy Spirit revealed to me the proper context of Hebrews 6:4-6, the more I realized just how deep the grace of God is towards all mankind, especially those of the household of faith. The passage is actually showing us how far God is willing to go before he can let our foolish choices determine our eternal position. The writer of the book of Hebrews makes it staggeringly clear that if a believer who has experienced the aforementioned blessings of the Kingdom of God chooses to walk away from God, they can never ever be renewed to repentance again. Their choice of denouncing Christ at this stage of spiritual maturity and experience is tantamount to crucifying Christ all over again. Hebrews 6:4-6 was not written to Christ loving believers who sin from time to time. This does not mean that I am encouraging any born-again believer to live in sin.

The Blessing of God

For the earth which drinketh in the rain that cometh oft upon it, and bringeth forth herbs meet for them by whom it is dressed, receiveth blessing from God: 8But that which beareth thorns and briers is rejected, and is nigh unto cursing; whose end is to be burned. 9But, beloved, we are persuaded better things of you, and things that accompany salvation, though we thus speak.

Hebrews 6:7-9

There is a lot of talk about the blessing of God within the circumference of the Body of Christ. Everyone is striving to live under the blessing of God. Unfortunately, many believers do not know that there are two kinds of blessings. Namely:

1. The Blessing of God

2. The Blessing of the Father (Ephesians 1)

Many believers are striving to experience the blessing of God upon their lives, when in reality they should be striving to live under the blessing of the Father. There is a big difference between the blessing of the Father and the blessing of God. The blessing of God is the general goodness of God to all of His creation without discrimination. The blessing of God can be accessed by both the just and the unjust. For example, when God sends the seasonal rains, they rain on the fields of both the wicked and the righteous. If a wicked farmer has worked and planted seed in his fields, when the rain comes, it will cause his crop to grow too, regardless of his inability to acknowledge divine providence.

I truly believe that as the Body of Christ comes into a deeper understanding of Christ's Melchizedek priesthood, many believers will experience the joy of living under the blessing of the Father. The blessing of Abraham is of this order. Unbelievers can never experience the blessing of Abraham. This powerful generational blessing is reserved for the children of God. It is not within the reach of the unbeliever no matter how hard he works for it.

God is Not Unrighteous

For God is not unrighteous to forget your work and labour of love, which ye have shewed toward his name, in that ye have ministered to the saints, and do minister. [11]And we desire that every one of you do shew the same diligence to the full assurance of hope unto the end:
Hebrews 6:10-11

The above passage of Scripture is probably one of my favorite passages in the book of Hebrews. It has given me much comfort over the years, especially during my season of obscurity. We were all born for significance; it is the way God created us. The cry for significance is the eternal echo of the seed of dominion that God deposited in man. But during times of obscurity while the Lord is forming and fashioning us into His chosen instruments, it would seem like our labor in the Lord is lost on those closest to us. I used to feel that way until I stumbled upon this powerful passage, then I saw it. God is NOT unrighteous to forget our labor of love and the fact that we have faithfully ministered to His children. When I saw this, a sense of relief swept over me and I was instantly delivered from the feelings of insignificance that I used to wrestle with. Suddenly it did not matter whether people recognized my service in the Lord or not. I realized that the Lord would never forget my labor of love.

Faith and Patience

That ye be not slothful, but followers of them who through faith and patience inherit the promises. 13For when God made promise to Abraham, because he could swear by no greater, he sware by himself, 14Saying, Surely blessing I will bless thee, and multiplying I will multiply thee. 15And so, after he had patiently endured, he obtained the promise.

Hebrews 6:12-15

Much has been said about faith and the merits of it within Christendom. Unfortunately, faith has a twin that makes it even more efficacious if this second element is properly applied. This second spiritual element that must be added to our faith is "Patience." This is a word that makes many "Word of Faith" believers nervous. In the fast paced microwave world that we live in, the pressure for things to happen fast has caused many believers to make shipwreck their faith. It would seem to most that faith and patience are like an odd couple. At a distance, it would seem so, but closer inspection will quickly convince us otherwise.

Think of "Faith" as the hand that reaches into the spirit world and lays hold of the promises of God. Now I want you to think of "Patience" as the muscle that supplies the strength (energy) to the hand to hold onto until the promise is pulled into your material world. If you can think of faith and patience from this perspective, you will quickly come to appreciate the above scriptural passage. The writer of the book of Hebrews shows us that all the patriarchs who came into their inheritance did so by deploying both "faith and patience." As you are reading this book, it is my prayer that you will add patience to your faith.

The Immutability of His Counsel

For men verily swear by the greater: and an oath for confirmation is to them an end of all strife. 17Wherein God, willing more abundantly to shew unto the heirs of promise the immutability of his counsel, confirmed it by an oath: 18That by two immutable things, in which it was impossible for God to lie, we might have a strong consolation, who have fled for refuge to lay hold upon the hope set before us:

Hebrews 6:16-18

God does everything from a position of purpose and foreknowledge. The marriage of God's eternal purpose to His foreknowledge forms His eternal counsel. The writer of the book of Hebrews tells us that even though God's Counsel is already immutable, the Lord went out of His way to reassure the heirs of the promise He gave to Abraham. Even though it's impossible for God to lie, the Lord swore to bless Abraham and his descendants, both Jews and Gentiles. Why would a God who cannot lie bind Himself to an Oath? This is a question that begs an answer. The answer to the question will explode both your hope and faith. God swore to demonstrate how deeply He desires to bless us with everything contained inside the blessing of Abraham. If many Christians (Kingdom citizens is a better definition) understood this, their level of hope in life would be higher than that of most humans.

Hope an Anchor of the Soul

Which hope we have as an anchor of the soul, both sure and stedfast, and which entereth into that within the veil;

Hebrews 6:19

When a ship docks into the harbor, sailors throw down an anchor into the water below to hold the ship in place and stop it from drifting away. The writer of the book of Hebrews tells us that the "hope" that we derive from the knowledge of the immutability of His counsel has now become the anchor for the soul. Why the soul? The soul is the seat of our will, mind and emotions. It is truly the seat of our self-consciousness. Ever since the fall of man in the Garden of Eden, nothing can get us into trouble faster than the soul that is not anchored in God.

The unsanctified soul is a magnet for worry; fear, stress and envy, just to name a few. But the Apostle Paul tells us that this overpowering surge of hope that comes from knowing that God is not a liar and that He is fully committed to backing up His word is a "sure and steadfast" anchor of hope for our soul. This means that instead of our soul wallowing in self-pity or drowned in sorrow, it can rest in the calming knowledge of the immutability of His counsel. This river of hope actually goes beyond the veil into the very presence of God.

THINK OF "FAITH" AS THE HAND THAT REACHES INTO THE SPIRIT WORLD AND LAYS HOLD OF THE PROMISES OF *God*

A Forerunner after the Order of Melchizedek

Whither the forerunner is for us entered, even Jesus, made an high priest for ever after the order of Melchizedek.

Hebrews 6:20

Without the book of Hebrews, understanding the royal priesthood of Jesus Christ and its inner workings, would have been lost on the consciousness of the Body of Christ. Without the book of Hebrews, the New Testament significance of the Order of Melchizedek would have also been lost on many generations of Christians. The writer of the book of Hebrews tells us that our Lord Jesus Christ is our forerunner. A forerunner is a person who goes ahead of those who are yet to come and prepares the way. According to Hebrews 6:20, Jesus, our forerunner, has gone beyond the veil; beyond the veil He has been made a High Priest forever after the Order of Melchizedek. Since Jesus is a forerunner high priest after the Order of Melchizedek, it follows that those of us (born again believers) who are following in His footsteps are also called to operate beyond the veil as kings and priests under the Order of Melchizedek.

ABRAHAM MEETS MELCHIZEDEK

Deciphering the Identity of Melchizedek

For this Melchisedec, king of Salem, priest of the most high God, who met Abraham returning from the slaughter of the kings, and blessed him; 2To whom also Abraham gave a tenth part of all; first being by interpretation King of righteousness, and after that also King of Salem, which is, King of peace; 3Without father, without mother, without descent, having neither beginning of days, nor end of life; but made like unto the Son of God; abideth a priest continually.

Hebrews 7:1-3

Who Was this Heavenly Man?

THERE are several schools of thought regarding the identity of this mysterious high priest who appeared to Abram in the valley of Shaveh. We will quickly examine some of these schools of thought and then I will tell you what I believe is the most logical answer as to the identity of this mysterious man. But in the last chapter of this book, I will fully answer the question, *"Is Jesus Melchizedek?"* Some think Melchizedek was:

- The first Adam

- Shem, the son of Noah

- The priest-king of ancient Salem

- The pre-incarnation appearance of Christ

There are those who believe that *Melchizedek was the first Adam* returning in his glory because Adam was the only man in Scripture who had no earthly genealogy. But this belief stands on slippery ice because:

- **First,** Adam had no earthly genealogy. Nevertheless, he had a spiritual genesis. The Bible clearly tells us when he was created, which means that Adam had a clear and traceable "beginning." This is in direct contrast to what the apostle Paul tells us in Hebrews chapter 7 about the Melchizedek, who met Abram in Genesis chapter 14. Paul says that this particular Melchizedek was "without beginning of days or end of life." Adam's life on the other hand had a beginning and a sure ending.

- **Second,** Adam became a slave to sin and its insidious powers after he fell from grace in the Garden of Eden. This means that in his fallen sinful condition there is simply no way Adam could be referred to as the king of righteousness. The name Melchizedek literally means "king of righteousness." Adam was anything but the king of righteousness. Even before they fell short of God's glory, Adam and Eve were both innocent, but not righteous. They were as innocent as a newborn baby is innocent, but not righteous; so there is no way Adam could be the Melchizedek that appeared to Abraham.

- **Third,** the first Adam died without ever having broken the sentence of death over his own life. This in itself disqualifies him from being the prophetic representation of an eternal priesthood that is driven by the power of an endless life. The Order of Melchizedek exists beyond the perimeters of death in the realms of eternity.

THE NAME MELCHIZEDEK LITERALLY MEANS "KING OF RIGHTEOUSNESS."

There are also those who believe that *Melchizedek was Shem*, the son of Noah. They say that Shem was both a king and a priest, and that he received this priesthood from his father Noah. This belief stands on thinner ice than those who believe that Melchizedek was the first Adam returning in his glory. Here is why:

- The Bible clearly sets out the genealogy of Noah's family in the book of Genesis, which includes Shem. This in itself clearly disqualifies Shem from being the Melchizedek who met Abram in the valley of Shaveh. Once again, the apostle Paul is quite clear that this Melchizedek who met Abram in the Valley of the Kings "had no earthly genealogy or beginning of days." There is no way God would use someone whose natural genealogy could be so easily proven to represent an eternal priesthood that is not of this world.

- Finally, if Melchizedek were Shem the son of Noah, it would mean that he would have had to have lived a very long time. If this were the case, it is highly probable that his appearance in the book of Genesis would have been duly noted, before and after Genesis 14. The fact that Melchizedek is not mentioned in the historical accounts of the book of Genesis except for this one meeting with Abram suggests that he was not Shem. Furthermore, the Bible does tell us when Shem died. Again, the apostle Paul is clear in letting us know that this Melchizedek had "no beginning of days or end of life."

Then there are those who believe that the Melchizedek who met Abram when he was returning from the slaughter of the kings was *the king-priest of the ancient City of Salem.* I admit that this school of thought is much more plausible than the previous two concerning the identity of this mysterious priest.

I personally believe that the king-priest over the ancient City of Salem was not the one who commissioned Abram in Genesis 14; even though he was certainly a priest of Jehovah. The Melchizedek priesthood which was stationed in the ancient City of Salem was merely a "shadow and forerunner" of the true heavenly Order of Melchizedek priesthood of our Lord Jesus Christ.

There are three more reasons why I believe that the Melchizedek who met Abram in the Valley of Shaveh was not the same Melchizedek who ruled the earthly City of Salem (Jerusalem). In the prophetic vision of King David in Psalm 110, David makes it very clear that the Order of Melchizedek is an eternal priestly ministry of Christ that has always existed in the realms of eternity before God created the world.

- After the fall of Adam, every human being born of a woman has been born a slave to sin, in terrible need of a Savior. I just do not see how God can pattern the eternal priestly ministry of Christ after a sin-compromised earthly priesthood. The supernatural never bows to the natural. The natural can be patterned after the supernatural, but never the other way around. The Melchizedek priesthood in ancient Salem was patterned after the heavenly.

- The Bible teaches that all have sinned and come short of the glory of God. (See Romans 3:23.) If the Melchizedek who met Abram in the Valley of Shaveh was a mere mortal, I fail to see how he could possibly assume such a lofty title as the king of righteousness and prince of peace.

- While I agree that there was a king-priest over the ancient City of Salem who represented the eternal priesthood of Christ, I do not believe that he is the one who brought Abram into a living covenant with God. This is because the writer of Hebrews makes it quite clear that the Melchizedek who met Abram in Genesis 14 was greater than Abram. If the Melchizedek who met Abram was a mere mortal, then it would mean that there was a man on earth who was greater and of a superior spiritual pedigree than Abram. If this were the case, then Abram is not qualified to be the father of many nations and the spiritual father of the New Creation. The "greater" is always more honorable and more blessed than the "lesser." Melchizedek, the king-priest of the ancient City of Salem, was therefore more suited to be

ABRAHAM MEETS MELCHIZEDEK

the father of many nations and the spiritual father of the New Creation than was Abraham. If we insist that the Melchizedek who met Abram was a mere mortal who was stationed here on earth, then we also have to conclude that Abram was not the best candidate to be "the father of many nations."

Which leads us to what I believe is the most probable identity of the Melchizedek who intercepted Abram in the kings' valley. My extensive study on this subject has convinced me that the Melchizedek who met Abram in the Valley of Shaveh was different in both glory and stature from the earthly Melchizedek. I believe that this heavenly man was actually Christ manifesting Himself in bodily form to Abram before the virgin birth.

Perhaps this is what Jesus meant when He told the astounded Jews of His era that, "Abraham saw my day!" (See John 8:56.) What the Bible tells us in Genesis 14 is that this man was the "King of Salem," which corresponds to the heavenly City of Jerusalem. The Bible also tells us that this man was also the "King of righteousness," a term that is only befitting of Christ. The very name Melchizedek means, "King over the whole domain of righteousness." Who else is fully qualified to properly assume the lofty title of "King of righteousness" other than the Lord Jesus Christ?

REGRETTABLY, BOTH THE REVELATION AND ATTITUDE BEHIND ABRAM'S TITHING ARE UNMISTAKABLY MISSING IN MANY OF THE POPULAR METHODS OF TITHING.

The Bible also tells us in Genesis chapter 14 that this man whom Abram met when he was returning from the slaughter of the kings was also the "Priest of God Most High." The man carried "bread and wine" which he offered to the stunned Abram. Abram was so impressed with this awesome man that he gave Him a tenth of all the spoils. This priestly man seemed to know everything about Abram. He even told

Abram why he triumphed over such a mighty foreign army with only 318 men who were trained in his own house. Melchizedek informed Abram that the God of heaven and earth had sent his warring angels ahead of him into the battlefield. By the time Abram got to the camp of his enemies, their fate had already been delivered into his hands.

Tithes of Honor

Now consider how great this man was, unto whom even the patriarch Abraham gave the tenth of the spoils.

Hebrews 7:4

One of the defining moments in the encounter that Abram had with Melchizedek, the High Priest of God Most High, had to do with the covenant exchange that took place between Melchizedek and Abram. The Bible tells us that Melchizedek, who was representing the Godhead in this supernatural transaction, gave Abram sacred bread and wine. Abram, on the other hand, who was representing humanity in this heavenly transaction, responded by sowing tithes of honor into this divine priesthood. Melchizedek blessed Abram with this blessing:

"Blessed be Abram by God Most High, Creator of heaven and earth. And blessed be God Most High, who has defeated your enemies for you." Then Abram gave Melchizedek a tenth of all the goods he had recovered.

Genesis 14:19-20

We will not discuss the deep and profound spiritual implications of this divine exchange between the Order of Melchizedek and Abram in this chapter. At this point I will simply say that tithing under the Order of Melchizedek is very different and much more honorable than the way tithing is taught today by many of the proponents of Malachi 3:8-12. Regrettably, both the revelation and attitude behind Abram's tithing are unmistakably missing in many of the popular methods of tithing. Understanding the Order of Melchizedek will both restore and upgrade the technology of tithing in the global Church.

Abram was so moved by this man's spiritual stature and divine-royalty that Abram did something that was customary to the people of the ancient world. His response to Melchizedek was inspired by his personal sense of awe and by the prevailing culture and protocol of hosting a king. The men of the ancient world did not go to a king without presenting a gift or royal endowment. As far as Abram was concerned, Melchizedek was the greatest and most glorious King he had ever met.

Out of his deep sense of honor and personal awe, Abram, the father of the faithful, gave his first tithe into the priestly Order of Melchizedek thereby establishing a prophetic pattern of tithing for all of his spiritual descendants. Abram did not tithe into Melchizedek because he thought Melchizedek could use the money. Abram knew that there was nothing that he owned that could pay for the services of such a great King. Abram's motivation and reason for tithing are sadly missing in much of today's tithing patterns. This is why it's imperative that we rediscover the spiritual ramifications of belonging to the priestly Order of Melchizedek.

Abram had visited and entertained many other kings before he met Melchizedek the king-priest in the valley of Shaveh, but Abram knew during his encounter that this Melchizedek was the loftiest king he had ever met. *I truly believe that Abram sensed that he was standing in the presence of God when he had a face-to-face encounter with Melchizedek.* Out of a heart filled with worship, honor, and inspiration, Abram gave his endowment of tithes to the Order of Melchizedek. He gave Melchizedek the king-priest tithes of honor. The Church must rediscover this prophetic pattern of tithing that was set by our father Abraham.

The Levitical Priesthood

And verily they that are of the sons of Levi, who receive the office of the priesthood, have a commandment to take tithes of the people according to the law, that is, of their brethren, though they come out of the loins of Abraham:

Hebrews 7:5

Call for your brother, Aaron, and his sons, Nadab, Abihu, Eleazar, and Ithamar. Set them apart from the rest of the people of Israel so they may minister to me and be my priests.

Exodus 28:1

There are only two priestly Orders that God ever gave to His people—the priestly Order of Aaron (commonly known as the Levitical priesthood) and the priestly Order of Melchizedek. For this reason both of these priesthoods are very important to God's revealed will for His people. The priestly Order of Aaron came out of the Mountain of Law, which is Mount Sinai where God gave Moses the Covenant of Law. The following is a summarized overview of the spiritual characteristics of the Order of Aaron.

1   ***The priestly Order of Aaron was based on the Mountain of Law.***

So if the priesthood of Levi, on which the law was based, could have achieved the perfection God intended, why did God need to establish a different priesthood, with a priest in the Order of Melchizedek instead of the order of Levi and Aaron?

Hebrews 7:11

2. ***The priestly Order of Aaron derived all its high priests from the sons of Aaron.***

"Now take Aaron your brother, and his sons with him, from among the children of Israel, that he may minister to Me as priest, Aaron and Aaron's sons: Nadab, Abihu, Elemazar, and Ithamar"

Exodus 28:1 NKJV

3. ***The priestly Order of Aaron was commanded to receive a tithe of their brethren according to the Law.***

Now the law of Moses required that the priests, who are descendants of Levi, must collect a tithe from the rest of the people of Israel, who are also descendants of Abraham.

Hebrews 7:5

4. **The tithe under the priestly Order of Aaron was simply payment for priestly services rendered to the people.**

As for the tribe of Levi, your relatives, I will compensate them for their service in the Tabernacle. Instead of an allotment of land, I will give them the tithes from the entire land of Israel.

Numbers 18:21

Tithing under the Levitical priesthood was intricately connected to service. It was a payment to the priesthood for services rendered. On the other hand, tithing under the Order of Melchizedek is based upon the *principle of honor*. Whenever I hear spiritual leaders tell their people to *"pay their tithes,"* I know instantly that they are trapped in a Levitical priestly mindset because under the Levitical priesthood *"tithes were paid out"* in the same way one would pay an electric bill that is due. Under the Order of Melchizedek, tithes are never paid out; they are always "given" in honor.

5. **Under the priestly Order of Aaron, the priesthood was only chosen from the tribe of Levi.**

So if the priesthood of Levi, on which the law was based, could have achieved the perfection God intended, why did God need to establish a different priesthood, with a priest in the Order of Melchizedek instead of the order of Levi and Aaron?

Hebrews 7:11

Under the Levitical priesthood, members of the other eleven tribes of Israel could never be admitted to the priesthood. The priesthood was passed on as a right of birth to the sons of Levi. Women who were also born into the tribe of Levi were not included in the staffing of the priesthood. The Levitical priesthood created a growing divide between those who were in full-time ministry (the Levites) and those who were in the marketplace (the remainder of Israel).

THE MEN OF THE ANCIENT WORLD DID NOT GO TO A KING WITHOUT PRESENTING A GIFT OR ROYAL ENDOWMENT.

A quick look at how many Christian denominations there are quickly exposes the fact that many of today's church leaders are not operating after the Order of Melchizedek. They function more like Old Testament Levites. How many of these church leaders use the phrase full-time ministry to refer to their vocation, while simultaneously separating themselves from those in the church who are serving God in the marketplace? What's more, how many Christian denominations have problems admitting God's daughters (women) into the priesthood?

The Power to Bless

But he whose descent is not counted from them received tithes of Abraham, and blessed him that had the promises. 7And without all contradiction the less is blessed of the better.

Hebrews 7:6-7

Before Melchizedek, the priest of God Most High, left the scene, he blessed Abram, who was the custodian of the covenant of promise. The fact that this king-priest blessed Abram proves that he was far more powerful and loftier than Abram. Even though Abram was the custodian of the faith promise to become the father of many nations, he never truly entered into the blessing until after the supernatural encounter with Melchizedek's priesthood. Abram had the "promises" but the "power to bless" or activate those faith promises lay in the hands of Melchizedek.

Most Christians think that Abram was blessed in Genesis 12, but that is not the case. In Genesis 12, Abram was "called of God" and was given futuristic "faith promises." God told him, "I will bless you" and not "I have blessed you", when He called him out of Chaldea. But when Melchizedek met him in the Valley of the Kings, "I will bless you" was transformed into "I have blessed you!" Melchizedek also gave Abram the supernatural bread and wine that he had brought for him from His eternal priestly Order. Bread and wine are the eternal emblems of the priestly Order of Melchizedek. What is interesting is that these spiritual elements are the same ones that the Lord Jesus Christ used to induct his apostles into the New Covenant secured by his blood and the death of his body.

Tithing Under the Order of Melchizedek

And here men that die receive tithes; but there he receiveth them, of whom it is witnessed that he liveth.

Hebrews 7:8

When Abraham met Melchizedek, the priest of God Most High, he was aware that he was giving tithes to a King and not just to a priest. Since every king has a kingdom, it is safe to assume that **Abraham's tithes were used to support a "Kingdom."** Everything that is given to a king becomes part of his royal estate. This means then that the Abrahamic tithing model" is a Kingdom driven and Kingdom minded tithing model. This is why it is the highest form and level of tithing mentioned in the Scriptures. Under the Levitical priesthood, tithes were given to support the priesthood (the clergy) whereas under the Order of Melchizedek, tithes are given to support and sustain the advancement of God's Kingdom on earth. Since Abraham's tithes were employed to advance a "Kingdom" it is quite redundant for us to say that there is no requirement for tithing in the New Testament. Consider this: New Testament living has a greater emphasis on advancing God's Kingdom on earth than under the Old

Testament. Since New Testament living revolves around advancing the Kingdom, the giving of "tithes of honor" will continue until the Kingdom is established. Dr Myles Munroe describes tithes as a form of "Kingdom tax" that Kingdom citizens give into the Kingdom treasury to show their allegiance to the Kingdom.

BREAD AND WINE ARE THE ETERNAL EMBLEMS OF THE PRIESTLY ORDER OF MELCHIZEDEK.

Seven Reasons to Give to a King

Dr. Myles Munroe, in his best-selling book *Kingdom Principles,* lists seven reasons why citizens of a kingdom give to a reigning king. I have taken the liberty to quote him verbatim so we can gain a greater understanding as to why and how Abraham tithed into Melchizedek. Please remember that Melchizedek was both the King of Jerusalem, as well as the Priest of God Most High.

1. *Royal protocol requires that a gift must be presented when visiting a king.* This is why the queen of Sheba brought such lavish gifts to King Solomon even though he was richer than she was. It was royal protocol. He would have done the same had he visited her.

2. *The gift must be fitting for the king.* Worse than approaching a king with no gift is to bring a gift unworthy of him. An inappropriate or inadequate gift amounts to an insult to the king. It shows that the giver does not properly respect the king or his authority.

3. *The gift reveals our value or "worth-ship" of the king.* The quality of what we offer the king and the attitude with which we offer it, reveals much more than the value or worthiness that we attach to our words.

4. ***Worship demands a gift and giving is worship.*** "Worthship" is where we get "worship." To worship the king means to ascribe worth or worthiness to Him. And as we have already seen, that always involves bringing him a gift. There is no genuine worship without gift-giving. But giving is itself an act of worship and worship is always fitting for the king. The Magi who saw His star in the east understood this, which is why they brought gifts as they journeyed to find Him.

5. ***Giving to a king attracts his favor.*** Kings are attracted to people who give with a willing and grateful spirit. Like anyone else, a king likes to know he is loved and appreciated. The King of Heaven is the same way. The Giver is attracted to the giver and extends His favor. Gifts open doors to blessings, opportunities and prosperity.

6. ***Giving to a king acknowledges his ownership of everything.*** Remember, kings are lords; they own everything in their domain. So giving to a king is simply returning to him what is already his. That's why in the Kingdom of Heaven we are always stewards and never owners.

7. ***Giving to a king is thanksgiving.*** One of the best ways to express gratitude is with a gift. Gratitude expressed is in itself a gift.1

Before Melchizedek left the scene, he blessed Abram, who was the custodian of the covenant of promise. The fact that this king-priest blessed Abram proves that he was far more powerful and loftier than Abram. Melchizedek also gave Abram the supernatural bread and wine that he had brought for him from His eternal priestly Order. Bread and wine are the eternal emblems of the priestly Order of Melchizedek. Tithing under the Order of Melchizedek is the highest form of tithing mentioned in Scripture; it is tremendously more powerful than the popular Malachi 3 tithing model. The church will change how it exacts the "Tithe" once it rediscovers the Order of Melchizedek. For an in-depth teaching on tithing please get my book, "Tithes of Honor" (Formerly: Tithing Under the Order of Melchizedek.)

Melchizedek's Priesthood is Superior

And as I may so say, Levi also, who receiveth tithes, payed tithes in Abraham. 10For he was yet in the loins of his father, when Melchisedec met him.

Hebrews 7:9

One of the most powerful Kingdom principles is the principle of apostolic succession. The apostle Paul uses this principle to demonstrate the superiority of the Melchizedek priesthood over the Old Testament Levitical priesthood. The apostle Paul declares that Levi who receives tithes from his brethren, the people of Israel, also paid tithes in Abraham. This is because the tribe of Levi was still in the loins of Abraham when Melchizedek met him in the Valley of the Kings. Through this powerful principle of apostolic succession, Levi tithed-up to Melchizedek. This implies that the priesthood of Melchizedek was much more loftier than that of Levi, who came 400 years after Abraham's encounter with Melchizedek. This is why the entire ministry of the Church to the world will change once it rediscovers the scope, nature and inner workings of the Melchizedek Priesthood of Jesus Christ.

EVERYTHING THAT IS GIVEN TO A KING BECOMES PART OF HIS ROYAL ESTATE. THIS MEANS THEN THAT THE ABRAHAMIC TITHING MODEL IS A KINGDOM DRIVEN AND KINGDOM MINDED TITHING MODEL.

Consider that Paul's epistle to the Hebrews was written to the Jews who lived in Asia Minor and that it is the strongest and most intelligent apologetic epistle ever written by an apostle. This epistle was written to convince men and women of Jewish descent who were having a tough time walking away from some of the ceremonial and sacrificial laws within the Torah; even though the Messiah had already fulfilled those aspects of Torah. These Jewish believers kept mixing the Old Covenant with the New Covenant in their spiritual practices. We must remember that these Messianic Jews who were converting to a life of faith in Christ Jesus had spent over 4,000 years of their national history under the Levitical priesthood, and changing gears to a new priestly Order was no simple task.

This is why it was necessary for the apostle Paul to intelligently walk them through the writings of the Old and New Testaments and show them the utter superiority of the priestly Order of Melchizedek over the Levitical priesthood. Saint Paul had to show them that they were not abandoning their ancient Jewish faith in the God of Abraham, Isaac, and Jacob when they brought themselves under the priestly Order of Melchizedek.

The most important argument Paul presented to establish the surpassing superiority of the priestly Order of Melchizedek over the priestly Order of Aaron, is that Abraham, the father of the Jewish nation, had himself tithed into this eternal priesthood of the Order of Melchizedek. This is significant because Abraham never tithed into the priestly Order of Aaron, a priesthood established on Mount Sinai over 400 years after Abraham's death.

The apostle Paul seals his argument when he states:, That if Abraham who is the father of the Jewish nation tithed into Melchizedek, it also follows that Levi who was in the spiritual loins of Abraham when Abraham met Melchizedek, also tithed into this powerful priestly Order. Paul's argument affected these Hebrew believers in a very profound way. They were beginning to realize that the tribe of Levi, whose priesthood they had previously followed, had also tithed into Melchizedek, when Levi was yet in the loins of their forefather Abraham. This is why I flinch when I hear preachers teach on tithing using Malachi 3:8-12 because I know that they are training New Testament believers to access the wrong priesthood concerning their tithes and offerings.

Perfection is Tied to the Melchizedek Priesthood

Therefore, if perfection were through the Levitical priesthood (for under it the people received the law), what further need was there that another priest should rise according to the Order of Melchizedek, and not be called according to the order of Aaron? Therefore He is also able to save to the uttermost those who come to God through Him, since He always lives to make intercession for them.

Hebrews 7:11,25 NKJV

Ever since Adam and Eve opened the portals of time to the entrance of sin, death, and demons, men and women in every era have been in search of a utopian society where they would not have to deal with the idiosyncrasies of this broken down planet. *The search for a perfect society is the motivating factor behind most world religions and political ideologies.*

The rise of Marxism—the philosophy of Karl Marx that gave birth to the ideology of communism—is the result of the global pursuit for a perfect or utopian society. Currently the United States is rocking from the shock waves of mass legal and illegal immigration because men and women worldwide want to live in a society where they can prosper and live in peace. They are invading the United States by the millions hoping to get their share of the great American dream.

For on the one hand there is an annulling of the former commandment because of its weakness and unprofitableness, for the law made nothing perfect; on the other hand, there is the bringing in of a better hope, through which we draw near to God.

Hebrews 7:18-19 NKJV

This frantic search for a utopian society is not a foreign experience in the human pursuit for perfection. The formation of human civilizations and the ensuing industrial and technological revolutions are all by-products of this global search for a perfect society. Every little girl dreams of growing into a beautiful woman and marrying the most amazing man on earth and living happily ever after. I can imagine the feeling of emotional devastation and spiritual disillusionment some of these women go through once they are married and discover that their husband is the devil's first cousin.

How many times have politicians promised the masses a land of milk and honey while campaigning for office only to deliver stale bread and bitter drink after they are elected? Why is this so? The answer is simple. Once sin and death entered the world, the machinery of death has been working endlessly, and as such, whatever man touches or promises becomes subject to this machinery of death.

The question that comes to mind is simply: Is there a sure way of creating a perfect society? The answer is a resounding "YES"! There is a spiritual technology for creating the perfect marriage and the perfect society and it is locked up in the priestly Order of Melchizedek. The apostle Paul concludes by telling the Hebrew believers that the Order of Aaron had no power to bring about the fulfillment of man's greatest search, the search for utopia. The Levitical priesthood had too many inherent flaws that made it impossible for the proper outworking of this spiritual technology. But under the priestly Order of Melchizedek, perfection in its purest form is a surety because this priestly Order already exists in a perfect state in the realms of eternity.

THIS FRANTIC SEARCH FOR A UTOPIAN SOCIETY IS NOT A FOREIGN EXPERIENCE IN THE HUMAN PURSUIT FOR PERFECTION.

The Priesthood has been Changed

For the priesthood being changed, there is made of necessity a change also of the law. 13For he of whom these things are spoken pertaineth to another tribe, of which no man gave attendance at the altar. 14For it is evident that our Lord sprang out of Juda; of which tribe Moses spake nothing concerning the priesthood.

Hebrews 7:12-14

God has laws that govern whatever He wants to do in the earth. When God established the Levitical priesthood, He gave Moses specific laws from the Mountain of Law (Mount Sinai), which regulated the priestly Order of Aaron. These specific laws were to govern the inflow and outflow of this priesthood and the way people tithed into it. These laws were then sealed and ratified by the blood of bulls and goats. But once God changed the law governing the priesthood, He immediately created a vacancy for another priesthood, loftier than the former, governed by different Law(s).

The apostle Paul shows us that the priestly Order of Melchizedek also has its own law that governs the outflow and inflow of this eternal priesthood. The law that the apostle Paul is referring to is the Law of the Spirit of Life in Christ Jesus. This is the primary law that governs the priestly Order of Melchizedek.

There is therefore now no condemnation to them which are in Christ Jesus, who walk not after the flesh, but after the Spirit. For the law of the Spirit of life in Christ Jesus hath made me free from the law of sin and death.

Romans 8:1-2 KJV

Unfortunately, many Christians do not know or appreciate the ramifications of being under the New Covenant. As a result, most churches tend to be very legalistic in their theology and inner dynamics. Even though many Christians would give you a mental assent that God has not called us to a "Covenant of works," the reality is that most Christians can't get over working in order to earn God's favor.

A Priesthood Backed by the Power of an Endless Life

And it is yet far more evident: for that after the similitude of Melchisedec there ariseth another priest, 16Who is made, not after the law of a carnal commandment, but after the power of an endless life.

Hebrews 7:15-16

Another very powerful spiritual ingredient of the Melchizedek Priesthood of Jesus Christ, that sets it apart from the Old Testament Levitical priesthood, is the fact that the engines of an endless life propels the Order of Melchizedek. Everything that happens under the Melchizedek Priesthood is backed by the "Power of an Endless Life!" The Law of carnal commandments produced men who became high priests after the flesh. The phrase "the Law of carnal commandments" is not an insinuation that the "Law" was carnal because it was spiritual. The word "carnal" in the phrase means "external." Rephrasing it, it should read "the Law of external commandments." This expression shows us that the "Law" was not written on people's hearts but on external tablets of stone is the reason the Old Covenant failed.

Flawed people (sinful men) could never keep a perfect Law unless it was written on their hearts and minds, supernaturally. Consequently under the Levitical priesthood they could only minister to the shadow of heavenly things, but they could never substantiate their practices with heavenly things. These high priests, no matter how devoted they were to the service of God, were forced to retire from the priesthood through the technology of death. Death always managed to get the best of them. But when Jesus Christ rose from the dead, He broke the technology of death over the priesthood of God. As a result, New Testament believers do not have to live under the cloud of the fear of death. God has called us to life in abundance.

The Melchizedek Priesthood is Eternal

For he testifieth, Thou art a priest for ever after the order of Melchisedec.

Hebrews 7:17

113

The Lord has sworn and will not relent, "You are a priest forever according to the order of Melchizedek".

Psalm 110:4 NKJV

The first thing that the apostle Paul and King David tell us about the priestly Order of Melchizedek is that unlike the priestly Order of Aaron, this priesthood is an eternal or everlasting priesthood. This powerful priestly Order exists in an infinite eternal state, which cannot be improved upon because everything in this realm is completely perfect—there is nothing missing or broken in this spiritual Order. The fact that the priestly Order of Melchizedek is eternal has far-reaching spiritual implications. It means that there is simply no end to the level and quality of representation we can expect from this glorious Order when we yield ourselves to it.

UNFORTUNATELY, MANY CHRISTIANS DO NOT KNOW OR APPRECIATE THE RAMIFICATIONS OF BEING UNDER THE NEW COVENANT.

The Power of Disannulment

For there is verily a disannulling of the commandment going before for the weakness and unprofitableness thereof.

Hebrews 7:18

I find no New Testament Scripture that demonstrates the abolishment of the Old Covenant like the above passage from the book of Hebrews. The Apostle Paul uses a very powerful legal word to demonstrate what God has done with the Old Covenant of Works! This word is the word, "Disannulment." There is perhaps no weightier word in LAW than the word "Disannulment." This word means to ***"cancel or utterly make void as though the said contract never even existed."***

When a Judge "Disannuls" a legal contract, the judge's ruling actually wipes off the said contract from judicial history. When the judge's gavel hits his table, it becomes as though the contract in question never existed. When a marriage goes through a divorce, the original marriage contract is still seen as valid during its pre-divorce tenure. But this not the case with a disannulment; in such cases any transactions that occurred during the time affected by the disannulment are considered totally void. This is why it is quite unfortunate to see the Body of Christ vacillate between "Law and Grace!" It is no wonder the writer of Hebrews calls works done by born again believers to earn God's favor "dead works."

The Apostle Paul gives us two main reasons for the disannulment of the Old Testament Covenant of Law.

1. The Law of external commandments was "weak because the people charged to keep it were flawed." It was weak not inherently but externally. It was weak because the Old Covenant required men, flooded with inherent character weaknesses, to keep the vigorous righteous demands of the Law. We know how that ended up. No one ever managed to satisfy the righteous demands of the Law in its fullness. The Scriptures declare (Galatians 3) that is you break the Law in one part you were guilty of breaking the whole Law.

2. The Law of external commandments was "Unprofitable." The Old Covenant was unprofitable not because it was not spiritual or perfect but because it only excited the engines of sin in those who dared to keep it. It was not profitable as a means of producing "sustainable righteousness." This is what the Apostle Paul was alluding to in the passage below.

> *If God's promise is only for those who obey the law, then faith is not necessary and the promise is pointless. 15For the law always brings punishment on those who try to obey it. (The only way to avoid breaking the law is to have no law to break!) 16So the promise is received by faith. It is given as a free gift. And we are all certain to receive it, whether or not we live according to the law of*

Moses, if we have faith like Abraham's. For Abraham is
the father of all who believe.

Romans 4:14-16 (NLT)

The Law Made Nothing Perfect

For the law made nothing perfect, but the bringing in of a better
hope did; by the which we draw nigh unto God.

Hebrews 7:19

The writer of the book of Hebrews goes on to say, "The Law made nothing perfect!" This very startling statement t probably shook the foundation of Hebrew believers who were mixing the Law with Grace. The expression "the Law made nothing perfect," implies that the Law could never bring anyone who kept it, into the "full righteousness of God." This is because there is no human being who can work hard enough to earn a batch of the eternal and lofty righteousness of God. Our best efforts at being good are as "filthy rags."

The only way to bring about perfection in the spirit of man is by the bringing of a "better hope." This bringing of a better hope is the "imputation of the righteousness of God that comes by expressing faith in the finished Work of Christ!" Righteousness imputed by faith will instantly make us partakers of the divine nature. This supernatural partaking of the righteousness by faith will cause us to easily "draw near unto God."

An Oath Backs the Melchizedek Priesthood

And inasmuch as not without an oath he was made priest:
21(For those priests were made without an oath; but this with
an oath by him that said unto him, The Lord sware and will not
repent, Thou art a priest for ever after the order of Melchisedec:)

Hebrews 7:20-21

We live in a world that is constantly changing and changing the people around us as the earth rotates on its axis. In the rapid changes that are taking place, we sometimes lose sight of vital principles that drive the engines of life. One of those vital principles, which sometimes gets lost in translation, is our ability to trust delegated authority. Many of us have seen leadership change hands so many times that we have become weary of trusting the engines of human leadership because we do not know who will be in power from one day to the next. This is especially true in democratic societies. In the United States, for instance, there is a change of leadership every four or eight years.

> *The law appointed high priests who were limited by human weakness. But after the law was given, God appointed his Son with an oath, and his Son has been made the perfect High Priest forever.*
>
> Hebrews 7:28

People may like and trust the present structures of leadership, but they are never sure whether the leaders that they trust in one day, will be available to lead them in the next. This has caused many people to have very loose connections with authority figures, choosing rather to be laws unto themselves. In many cases the people's loose connections with their secular leaders usually translates into loose connections with their spiritual fathers and mothers in the Kingdom of God.

The frustrations of a constantly changing leadership structure and climate, was one of the horrifying things that plagued the people who lived under the priestly Order of Aaron. The high priests kept changing every few years as each previous high priest died away. Even more frightening was the fact that a corrupt high priest, lacking in spiritual power, sometimes replaced some very good and honorable high priests. It's like being in a marriage where your wife or husband is constantly changing from one day to the next. How terrifying is that?

With great excitement, the apostle Paul tells us that under the priestly Order of Melchizedek, we never have to live in fear of a sudden change in the structure and climate of leadership. The structure of leadership and the eternal position of our presiding High Priest, Jesus Christ, has already been sealed by an unchangeable oath from the mouth of God.

Jesus Christ is the same yesterday, today, and forever.
Hebrews 13:8

Hebrews 13:8 means that under the priestly Order of Melchizedek we can fully surrender ourselves to our Leader, Jesus Christ, while He outworks His eternal purposes through our lives. The priestly Order of Melchizedek creates a spiritual climate in which people can establish very strong spiritual connections with their spiritual fathers and mothers in the Lord.

The Order of Melchizedek destroys the loose connections between the people and their shepherds. It unleashes strong spiritual connections between those who lead and those who follow. These supernatural dimensions of strong spirit connections and loyalty will help us establish strong father-son type of churches, which have the favor to possess, faith to prevail, and power to finish. Under the Order of Melchizedek we can truly build churches and businesses that can take cities and impact nations.

The Surety of a Better Covenant

By so much was Jesus made a surety of a better testament.
Hebrews 7:22

The writer of the book of Hebrews tells us, "Jesus has been made a surety of a better Covenant." The usage of the word "Surety" is designed to invoke a feeling of total confidence in us and in the finished work of Christ. The word "Surety" is not a religious term, it's always a legal term. The word "Surety" in Law carries tremendous weight.

The online thesaurus dictionary defines the word, "Surety" as follows:

1. Security against loss or damage or for the fulfillment of an obligation, the payment of a debt, etc.; a pledge, guaranty, or bond.

2. A person who has made himself or herself responsible for another, as a sponsor, godparent, or bondsman.

3. The state or quality of being sure.

4. Certainty.

5. Something that makes sure; ground of confidence or safety.

Looking at the above definitions of this powerful legal word, "Surety", gets me very excited. It drives away the fear of losing my salvation over minor shortcomings. The Heavenly Father truly desires to bless and confer the benefits of redemption on the Children of God by making Yeshua the "Surety" for everything that He has promised us. The fact that the Lord Jesus has been made a surety of the New Covenant is the reason the "Covenant of Grace" is more important than the "Covenant of Works," which was the Old Covenant.

Looking at the above definitions of this powerful legal word, "Surety", gets me very excited. It drives away the fear of losing my salvation or failing to enjoy the blessings of redemption. The Heavenly Father truly desires to bless and confer the benefits of redemption on the Children of God by making Jesus a "Surety" for everything that He has promised us. The fact that the Lord Jesus has been made a surety of the New Covenant is the reason the "Covenant of Grace" is more important than the "Covenant of Works," which was the Old Covenant.

A Priesthood Harassed by Death

And they truly were many priests, because they were not suffered to continue by reason of death:

Hebrews 7:23

God told Adam and Eve that if they chose to disobey Him and eat from the Tree of the Knowledge of Good and Evil, they would surely die. At the time when God told them this, Adam and Eve could not comprehend the horrors of death because they had never seen anything die. You can imagine the sense of horror and dismay that they must have experienced when they discovered the lifeless body of their son, Abel, who had been murdered by his own brother. Death agencies had struck close to home, and the emotional pain was almost unbearable. There is nothing more painful to a parent than the death of his or her child. Countless generations have wrestled with the angels of death while trying to make sense of the loss of loved ones.

Because God's children are human beings—made of flesh and blood—the Son also became flesh and blood. For only as a human being could he die, and only by dying could he break the power of the devil, who had the power of death. Only in this way could he set free all who have lived their lives as slaves to the fear of dying.

Hebrews 2:14-15

Since the first funeral in the Garden of Eden, the fear of death has terrorized men and women for centuries. What is death? Death in its most basic form is the cessation of life or the absence of animation—the primary assignment of death agencies is to shut down the flow of life. If a marriage is filled with life and laughter, death agencies will look for ways to bring death into the marriage. The high rate of divorce in our modern societies is evidence that death agencies are working overtime to quarantine the flow of life. Death is more than a corpse lying in a casket; it's a demonic technology, which stops the flow of life!

Jesus died to break the power that the devil had over the human race by manipulating us through our fear of death. Before the resurrection of Jesus Christ, death agencies terrorized the world using man's inherent fear of death. According to the apostle Paul, the priestly Order of Melchizedek has complete authority over the spirit of death. The Order of Melchizedek is the custodian for the divine technology called—the Law of the Spirit of Life in Christ Jesus, which is infinitely superior to the demonic technology called the Law of Sin and Death. Under the priestly Order of Aaron, the high priests kept changing because they could not serve forever by reason of death. Their ministerial assignments to the Jewish nation were always cut short by death.

When we bring ourselves under the priestly Order of Melchizedek, God will give us the power to conquer death and its auxiliary agencies. The priestly Order of Melchizedek will cancel and quarantine the sentence of death over our lives—spiritually, emotionally, and physically. Under this Order, death itself receives a sentence of death. Death is told to die!

There is no doubt that many people would pay astronomical amounts of money if a scientist could invent a pill that contained the secret to the fountain of youth. A magic pill that, once swallowed; would arrest the machinery of death inside their bodies and reverse the aging process. I know that if such a pill were ever introduced, its originator would be a multibillionaire within hours of its release on the global market. There would be mass hysteria as the rich and famous fought their way to the front of the queue to buy the pill that would allow them to live longer. Such is the universal fear of death that exists in the inner sanctum of the human soul.

> *Then, when our dying bodies have been transformed into bodies that will never die, this Scripture will be fulfilled: "Death is swallowed up in victory. O death, where is your victory? O death, where is your sting?"*
>
> 1 Corinthians 15:54-55

What multiplied millions of people on our planet do not know, is that there is now a Priestly Order where the sentence and machinery of death at work in the human body can be restrained and even reversed. The miracle pill with the secret to the fountain of youth has already been invented under this Priestly Order of Melchizedek. It comes in the form of the divine bread and wine offered to people who submit themselves to this powerful Priestly Order.

DEATH IN ITS MOST BASIC FORM IS THE CESSATION OF LIFE OR THE ABSENCE OF ANIMATION — THE PRIMARY ASSIGNMENT OF DEATH AGENCIES IS TO SHUT DOWN THE FLOW OF LIFE.

Unchangeable Priesthood

But this man, because he continueth ever, hath an unchangeable priesthood.

Hebrews 7:24

What makes the Melchizedek Priesthood of Jesus Christ so powerful is that it is an unchangeable priesthood because the Lord Jesus Christ will never die. He will never die or abdicate His eternal position as our faithful and merciful High Priest. This means that when believers rediscover the Order of Melchizedek and begin to function under it, they start their earthly internship in an eternal and heavenly priesthood. Jesus has an unchangeable priesthood because He is the same yesterday, today and forever. As a result, His priesthood resonates at the same spiritual frequency. Christ is the life behind His own priesthood.

The Great Intercessor

Wherefore he is able also to save them to the uttermost that come unto God by him, seeing he ever liveth to make intercession for them.

Hebrews 7:25

Without any contradiction, the Lord Jesus Christ is the greatest intercessor of our faith and profession. We all know that an intercessor is one who prays to God on behalf of another. This is truly a ministry of "selflessness!" The ministry of the Intercessor is one ministry we can never participate in if "self" is on the throne. Christ Jesus crucified Himself on the cross in order to stand in the gap for our betterment. While intercession is mostly associated with praying, the ministry of Intercession that the Lord Jesus Christ is now engaged in as described above is of a different order.

When the writer of the book of Hebrews says that "He ever liveth to make intercession," this expression conveys the idea of an attorney arguing the merits of his case in front of a judge on behalf of his client. The intercessor in this passage is an "Advocate." This is why 1 John 2 warns us not to sin, but if we do sin, we need to know that we have an advocate with the Father, Christ Jesus the righteous one. Under the banner of His everlasting Melchizedek Priesthood, the Lord Jesus Christ is constantly arguing the merits of His finished work against the charges brought against the saints, by the accuser of the Brethren.

The Condition of Our High Priest

For such an high priest became us, who is holy, harmless, undefiled, separate from sinners, and made higher than the heavens 26; Who needeth not daily, as those high priests, to offer up sacrifice, first for his own sins, and then for the people's: for this he did once, when he offered up himself 27.

Hebrews 7:26-27

Another aspect of Yeshua's Melchizedek priesthood that makes it quite different and superior to the Old Testament Levitical priesthood is the spiritual condition of our High Priest. We are told the following things about the spiritual condition of our High Priest:

- He became one of us, through the blessed incarnation at the virgin birth. In Mary's womb, God put on flesh and became one of us.

- He is holy. Holiness is His permanent and unbroken condition. This is why He calls all His children (royal priesthood) to a life of holiness.

- He is harmless. This reference to "harmless" must not be construed to mean that he is "powerless or naïve." This quality of "harmlessness" is a divine invitation for mankind to place their trust in Him fully, knowing that He would never use that trust to destroy us. This also means that the Lord will never use our weaknesses and sins to manipulate us into submission or embarrass us in front of the public.

- He is "Undefiled." This statement means that our High Priest (Jesus Christ) lives beyond the parameters of any kind of spiritual, mental or physical defilement. He longs to impart this grace to all of His people on earth.

- He is "Separate from sinners." This statement is not intended to imply that the Lord has an elitist attitude against sinners. By no means. The Lord loves sinners; but in order to save them, he cannot share in their sin nature. This statement implies that when Christ appeared to us in human flesh, there was no stain of sin in him. He was truly the Son of man with the incorruptible body.

- He is the "Perfect Sacrifice" who sacrificed Himself once and for all time. The writer of Hebrews tells us that the reason the Old Covenant system of worship was full of daily and yearly sacrifices is because the blood of bulls and goats was not potent enough to wipe out sin and the sin nature. But when Jesus Christ died on the cross, He was truly the perfect sacrifice. As soon as He sacrificed himself on the cross, sin was completely vanquished. The sins of all mankind throughout all the ages was paid for, past, present and future.

Our High Priest is also the Pattern Son

For the law maketh men high priests which have infirmity; but the word of the oath, which was since the law, maketh the Son, who is consecrated for evermore.

Hebrews 7:28

The writer of the book of Hebrews tells us that the Covenant of Law made men high priests, with their inherent weaknesses. However, the "Word of Oath," which was before the Law, has designated only one eternal high priest and that high priest is the Lord Jesus Christ, the begotten Son of God who is "consecrated forever!"

There is no well-versed, post-Calvary preacher of the Gospel or theologian who can deny the fact that the Lord Jesus Christ preached on the message of the Kingdom more than any other spiritual leader in recorded human history. Jesus Christ talked about the Kingdom of God and Kingdom living much more often than the prophets Moses, David, and Daniel combined.

In Christ's eternal perspective, everything that He came to do on earth was centered on uncovering and restoring the Kingdom of God to our troubled planet. As the Creator incarnate, Jesus Christ knew that Adam and Eve did not lose a religion in the Garden of Eden— they lost their place in the Kingdom that God had given them here on earth. Jesus knew that only the restoration of the Kingdom of God in the hearts of sinful men could turn the tide of humankind's self-engineered spiritual suicide. Since Jesus Christ is God's pattern Son, His life and ministry style are the blueprints for real Kingdom living here on earth. Understanding the Order of Melchizedek will help us advance and spread the message of the Gospel of the Kingdom to every sphere of human endeavor.

DONE AWAY WITH

A Powerful Summation

Now of the things which we have spoken this is the sum: We have such an high priest, who is set on the right hand of the throne of the Majesty in the heavens;

Hebrews 8:1

MOST career attorneys will tell you that in adjudicating a legal case, securing a favorable verdict more often than not comes down to the power of the final legal summations. In the eighth chapter of the book of Hebrews, the writer brings us into his final summations about the key issues of his letter to the Hebrews. The Apostle Paul begins his final summations by giving us three Cornerstones of the revelation contained in the book of Hebrews concerning the Melchizedek priesthood of Jesus Christ, namely:

1. We have a lofty High Priest, the Lord Jesus Christ

2. Our High Priest, the Lord Jesus Christ has a seat of great honor next to the throne of God

3. His Priesthood is a heavenly priesthood and is 'set' in Majestic splendor

These three Cornerstone revelations sum up the vast difference between the Levitical priesthood and the Melchizedek priesthood. A lower, earthly, Levitical priesthood serviced the Old Covenant, with earthly high priests who were limited by both space and time. But under the New Covenant, Kingdom citizens (both Jews and

Gentiles) are being serviced by a loftier, heavenly priestly order (the Melchizedek priesthood), which is not limited by both time and space.

A True Tabernacle

A minister of the sanctuary, and of the true tabernacle, which the Lord pitched, and not man.

Hebrews 8:2

As he continues with his final summations, the Apostle Paul now tells us that the Lord Jesus Christ is a minister in the heavenly sanctuary. This heavenly sanctuary is also the "True Tabernacle" of God, formed by the hands of God. The Tabernacle of Moses was a foreshadowing of this heavenly tabernacle. The expression "True Tabernacle" in the second verse implies that Christ Jesus serves as High Priest in a heavenly Sanctuary, which is the "True Habitation of God" in the Spirit. This means that the priesthood of Jesus is the only priesthood that can transform worshippers into becoming a true habitation of God in the Spirit. The expression "not made with human hands," in the verse introduces us to the order and nature of worship under the Melchizedek Priesthood of Jesus Christ. This powerful expression implies that God does not want "fleshly effort" in how we worship Him. True worship happens in the spirit, because God is a "Spirit" and those who worship Him must do so in spirit and truth (John 4:24).

The Work of a High Priest

For every high priest is ordained to offer gifts and sacrifices: wherefore it is of necessity that this man have somewhat also to offer.

Hebrews 8:3

Every high priest is required by divine law to offer both gifts and sacrifices. This was also true of pagan priesthoods. Pagan high priests would sometimes sacrifice women and infants to demon-gods in order to appeal to them for national prosperity. Under the

Levitical priesthood there were numerous gifts and sacrifices that the high priest offered daily to appease the God of Israel.

UNDER THE NEW COVENANT, KINGDOM CITIZENS ARE BEING SERVICED BY A LOFTIER, HEAVENLY PRIESTLY ORDER, WHICH IS NOT LIMITED BY BOTH TIME AND SPACE.

For us to be effective members of the New Testament royal priesthood of Jesus Christ, we must understand what the gifts and sacrifices are, that we need to present to God. When we present the appropriate gifts and sacrifices, Yeshua our High Priest will take them and offer them to God as a sweet smelling savor. The New Testament shows us the following gifts and sacrifices that we can give God:

1. **Our Bodies**

   *I beseech you therefore, brethren, by the mercies of God, that ye present your bodies a living **sacrifice,** holy, acceptable unto God, which is your reasonable service* (Romans 12:1 KJV).

2. **Walking in the Love of God**

   *And walk in love, as Christ also hath loved us, and hath given himself for us an offering and a **sacrifice** to God for a sweet smelling savor* (Ephesians 5:2 KJV).

3. **Service of Faith**

   *Yea, and if I be offered upon the **sacrifice** and service of your faith, I joy, and rejoice with you all* (Philippians 2:17 KJV).

4. **Sacrificial Offerings**

*But I have all, and abound: I am full, having received of Epaphroditus the things which were sent from you, an odor of a sweet smell, a **sacrifice** acceptable, well pleasing to God* (Philippians 4:18 KJV).

5. Tithes

...but he whose genealogy is not derived from them received tithes from Abraham and blessed him who had the promises. Now beyond all contradiction the lesser is blessed by the better. Here mortal men receive tithes, but there he receives them, of whom it is witnessed that he lives (Hebrews 7:6-8 NKJV).

6. Praise and Worship

But you are a chosen generation, a royal priesthood, a holy nation, His own special people, that you may proclaim the praises of Him who called you out of darkness into His marvelous light (1 Peter 2:9 NKJV).

7. Talents and Skills

*If any man speak, let him speak as the oracles of God; if any man minister, let him do it as of the **ability** which God giveth: that God in all things may be glorified through Jesus Christ, to whom be praise and dominion for ever and ever. Amen* (1 Peter 4:11 KJV).

8. Prayer

He said to them, "The Scriptures declare, 'My Temple will be called a house of prayer,' but you have turned it into a den of thieves!" (Matthew 21:13).

If He Were on Earth

For if he were on earth, he should not be a priest, seeing that there are priests that offer gifts according to the law:

Hebrews 8:4

Continuing with his powerful apostolic summation, the Apostle Paul makes a very staggering apostolic statement. He boldly declares that *if Christ Jesus were on earth, He would not be a priest*, since there is an "earthly priesthood" that offers sacrificial gifts according to the law. This earthly priesthood is none other than the Levitical priesthood that served the Jewish people for thousands of years. This statement explains why it was expedient for the Lord Jesus Christ to "return to Heaven" after the resurrection - so He could re-enact His heavenly Melchizedek priesthood here on earth. As our eternal High Priest, the Lord Jesus Christ had to change His physical address in order to initiate His heavenly priesthood. This is why it is critical for born again Christians to understand the Order of Melchizedek priesthood of Jesus Christ, and how it functions here on earth. Failure to do so has relegated the Church to operating under a Levitical system of ministry that has overly exaggerated the importance of "temple ministry" over "ministry in the marketplace."

A Shadow of Heavenly Things

Who serve unto the example and shadow of heavenly things, as Moses was admonished of God when he was about to make the tabernacle: for, See, saith he, that thou make all things according to the pattern shewed to thee in the mount.

Hebrews 8:5

No matter how much one may be enamored with the liturgical Leviticus system of worship, which dominated much of the Old Testament, it is at best only a "passing shadow" of things to come. Everything under the Old Covenant was merely an example and shadow of heavenly things. When God commissioned Moses to create the Tabernacle, God warned him to make sure that he created it in accordance with the pattern of heavenly things. There is a movement in the body of Christ seeking to make Christians become more "Jewish" by returning to Old Testament Levitical practices. While I hate anti-Semitism, going back to Old Covenant practices in order to secure

God's favor is a direct assault on the finished work of Jesus Christ on the cross. Please remember a Jew-loving, Jewish apostle wrote the book of Hebrews. But his message is clear. The Old Covenant (Mosaic Covenant) has been, "done away with," in order to establish a new and everlasting covenant, established on better promises. I am not implying that the teachings of the Old Testament have all been done away with. *It's an Old Covenant written on tablets of stone instead of hearts of flesh and the sacrificial laws that have been done away with. In the gospels Yeshua said that it was possible for heaven and earth to pass away but the true essence of the Torah would never pass away!*

A More Excellent Ministry

But now hath he obtained a more excellent ministry, by how much also he is the mediator of a better covenant, which was established upon better promises.

Hebrews 8:6

The New Testament Order of Melchizedek priesthood of Christ is also powerful because Jesus Christ has an *"excellent and superior ministry"* **to that of any other earthly high priest.** The most unique aspect of the Order of Melchizedek priesthood is that unlike the Levitical priestly Order, this eternal priestly Order is both a marketplace *and* priestly ministry. The High Priest of this eternal priestly Order is first and foremost a King who does priestly work. As a King, His influence extends beyond the boundaries of the temple, right into the marketplace. As a King-Priest, Jesus Christ has an ongoing dual influence over both the services of the temple and the activities of the marketplace. This is why Christ's priesthood has a more excellent and superior ministry than the Levitical priesthood.

In his final summations the Apostle Paul also gives us two other very important factors that contributes to the Melchizedek priesthood of Jesus Christ having a more excellent ministry than the Old Testament Levitical priesthood. These two factors are as follows:

1. The Melchizedek priesthood of Jesus Christ has a "more excellent ministry" because it is "mediated by a better Covenant."

2. The Melchizedek priesthood of Jesus Christ has a "more excellent ministry" because it is "established on better promises."

A Doomed Covenant

For if that first covenant had been faultless, then should no place have been sought for the second. 8 For finding fault with them, he saith, Behold, the days come, saith the Lord, when I will make a new covenant with the house of Israel and with the house of Judah: 9 Not according to the covenant that I made with their fathers in the day when I took them by the hand to lead them out of the land of Egypt; because they continued not in my covenant, and I regarded them not, saith the Lord.

Hebrews 8:7-9

Perhaps one of the most stunning statements in the apostle's summation of the revelation contained in the book of Hebrews is what he says about the Old Covenant. He makes a compelling argument that the "first covenant" that God made with the people of Israel failed because God found "faulty" in the people of Israel who failed to keep His perfect Law. Since the people that Moses led through the wilderness were not "faultless" there was dire need for God to establish a second covenant established on "better promises." The people of Israel failed to abide by the righteous but rigorous dictates of the Law; because the people were imperfect. *Scripture tells us that by the "works of the Law shall no man be justified."*

THE OLD COVENANT HAS BEEN "DONE AWAY WITH," IN ORDER TO ESTABLISH

A NEW AND EVERLASTING COVENANT, ESTABLISHED ON BETTER PROMISES.

The more the people tried to keep the Law of Moses, the more they failed miserably at it (Romans 7). Their sincere efforts to galvanize righteousness by their own good deeds only ended in dismal failure. The "Law" working through "Sin" within our members only managed to inflame the "sin nature" within. The people who lived under the Old Covenant ended up giving God lip service worship, while struggling with the dictates of sin within their members. But the Lord promised that He would make a New Covenant with the House of Israel. The New Covenant would be a covenant of the circumcision of the heart, which was not based upon external observances. The New Covenant would not be by *"might or by power but by His Spirit!"*

The New Covenant

For this is the covenant that I will make with the house of Israel after those days, saith the Lord; I will put my laws into their mind, and write them in their hearts: and I will be to them a God, and they shall be to me a people: 11 And they shall not teach every man his neighbour, and every man his brother, saying, Know the Lord: for all shall know me, from the least to the greatest.

Hebrews 8:10-11

The New Covenant is spoken about first in the book of Jeremiah. The Old Covenant that God had established with His people required obedience to the Old Testament Mosaic Law. Because the wages of sin is death (Romans 6:23), the law required that people perform rituals and sacrifices in order to please God and remain in His grace. The prophet Jeremiah predicted that there would be a time when God would make a new covenant with the nation of Israel.

"'The day will come,' says the Lord, 'when I will make a new covenant with the people of Israel and Judah. . . . But this is the new covenant I will make with the people of Israel on that day,' says the

Lord. 'I will put my law in their minds, and I will write them on their hearts. I will be their God, and they will be my people.'"

Jeremiah 31:31, 33

Jesus Christ came to fulfill the Law of Moses (Matthew 5:17) and create the New Covenant between God and His people. The Old Covenant was written in stone, but the New Covenant is written on our hearts, made possible only by faith in Christ, who shed His blood to atone for the sins of the whole world. Luke 22:20 says, *"After supper, [Jesus] took another cup of wine and said, 'This wine is the token of God's new covenant to save you – an agreement sealed with the blood I will pour out for you.'"* Now that we are under the New Covenant, we are not under the penalty of the law. We are now given the opportunity to receive salvation as a free gift (Ephesians 2:8-9). Through the life-giving Holy Spirit who lives in all believers (Romans 8:9-11), we can now share in the inheritance of Christ and enjoy a permanent, unbroken relationship with God.

Hebrews 9:15 declares,

"For this reason Christ is the mediator of a new covenant, that those who are called may receive the promised eternal inheritance—now that He has died as a ransom to set them free from the sins committed under the first covenant."

Their Sins Will I Remember No More

For I will be merciful to their unrighteousness, and their sins and their iniquities will I remember no more.

Hebrews 8:12

Hebrews 8:12 is a verse that stumbles and confuses many Christians who are very "Sin conscious." In the lives of some Christians and Messianic Jews, "Sin" seems to be a more powerful technology than "righteousness." This is why most Sunday morning sermons at most churches are aimed at convicting those in attendance of Sin. While conviction of Sin is appropriate in cases where it is the most appropriate response, there are churches that are so "evangelical in mindset" that in every service they hold, they treat all those in attendance as though many of them have not yet been made the righteousness of God in Christ Jesus. This would also explain why many Christians seem to have a lot of "grace for sinners" when they sin, but fail to lavish the same grace on members of the Body of Christ who fall into sin. I believe that without holiness no man shall see the LORD but the body of Christ can be a little more merciful and gracious to our fallen brothers and sisters.

God on the other hand is on the exact opposite spectrum of the legalistic "Sin conscious" Church. God so believes in the "finished work of Christ" that He boldly declares, "For I will be merciful to their unrighteousness, and their sins and their iniquities will I remember no more." God goes beyond a mere promise; He "vows" that "their sins" and "iniquities" will I remember no more. Wow! God vows not to remember our "sinful acts" and the "consequences of those sinful acts" when we repent of them and turn to Christ! The above statement is NOT a license to sin, but it is a larger blanket of grace than Christians give to each other in times of moral failure. The expression, "I will remember no more" is very powerful. It is easier for us to forgive someone for an offense against us but "choosing not to never remember" how they offended us is another matter. Forgiveness is hard enough for a lot of people but choosing not to remember what people did to us after we have forgiven them can be very challenging. But this is exactly what God has done to all born again believers (Jews and Gentiles), for Yeshua's sake.

IN THE LIVES OF SO MANY *Christians,* "SIN" SEEMS TO BE A MORE POWERFUL TECHNOLOGY THAN "RIGHTEOUSNESS."

Done Away with

In that he saith, A new covenant, he hath made the first old. Now that which decayeth and waxeth old is ready to vanish away.

Hebrews 8:13

But it is the last statement in the Apostle Paul's summation that deals the Old Covenant a final fatal blow. The writer of the book of Hebrews argues that once God declared that He would "establish a new covenant" with the house of Israel, He inevitably made the Old Covenant "obsolete." It was effectively "done away with." Once a contract becomes obsolete, it loses its 'enforceability" in all matters related to regulating human conduct. This is why Christians and Messianic Jews cannot mix the Old and New Covenants. The two covenants are completely different in the way they change our relationship to God. Drawing on one cancels the other, because they are mutually exclusive ever since the resurrection of Yeshua. This is why there is nothing more powerful in changing human life as the Grace of God. The Grace of God is the undying faithfulness and love of God superimposed on our humanity to help us become partakers of the divine nature. But please DO NOT confuse the "passing away" of the Old Covenant for the "passing away of the instructions of the TORAH," which is the only Bible that the early Church had before the apostles wrote the New Testament epistles and gospels.

What has been done way with because of our being born-again in Yeshua are the following:

- *The Penalties of disobedience to those Moral Codes listed in the book of Deuteronomy, because Christ became a curse for us on the Cross.*

- *The practice of sacrificing animals as a way to atone for our sins has been done away with, because Yeshua's blood is now the cleansing agent against the stain of sin.*

- *Strict adherence to the "Kosher Laws" has been done away with, even though God's wisdom and scientific findings prove that the foods, which God proclaims as unclean, are less healthy than the ones He proclaims clean.*

A CONTRAST OF COVENANTS

I HOPE and pray that journeying through the book of Hebrews has blessed you as much it has blessed me while writing about it. Perhaps there is no other chapter in this wonderful apologetic book that gives us a striking contrast between the Old and New Covenants like the ninth chapter of Hebrews.

- The Civil and Moral Code- that which God considers Holy and that which He says is sin.

- The Rewards for obeying the Torah (instruction).

- The Penalties for disobedience to those Moral Codes

- A Way for Grace and Atonement- the sacrificial system with its various offerings. The most important is the establishment of the need for the "shedding of blood" to make atonement.

- The Kosher Laws- eating foods that are healthy and those foods, which we shouldn't eat because the species was created by God not to be eaten and could lead to sickness and death. (There was NO penalty prescribed if you ate non-kosher foods, but you could wind up sick; realizing the wisdom of God.)

- The Prophecies (the Promise to Abraham, Isaac and Jacob) the promise of greater prophet than Moses (Messiah) and the future redemption of Israel and the nations of the World.

- The Appointed Times (Sabbath and Feasts, that speak to what the Messiah fulfilled and is yet to fulfill).

It goes without saying that without the foundation established by the Old Covenant there would be no New Covenant. Nevertheless the two Covenants while having some similarities are also very different.

A Worldly Sanctuary

Then verily the first covenant had also ordinances of divine service, and a worldly sanctuary. 2For there was a tabernacle made; the first, wherein was the candlestick, and the table, and the shewbread; which is called the sanctuary.

Hebrews 9:1-2

The writer of the book of Hebrews tells us that the first covenant had ordinances of divine worship and a worldly sanctuary (one made by human hands). This worldly or earthly sanctuary was made of two sections. The first section was known as that "holy place" and it consisted of the candlestick (the menorah) representative of the seven spirits of God. It also contained the table of showbread, which is a prophetic representation of God's manifested presence. This section prophetically correlates with the soul of man and the outer court correlates with the physical body. Under the Old Covenant, only the Levites could dare enter into the holy place. The rest of Israel could only go as far as the outer court. One of the main weaknesses of the Levitical priesthood is the fact it excluded eleven other tribes of Israel from participating in the priesthood. The Melchizedek priesthood on the other hand is very inclusive of all members of the Body of Christ.

The Holy of Holies

And after the second veil, the tabernacle which is called the Holiest of all;

Hebrews 9:3

After the first section there was a second section of the Tabernacle of Moses that was out of bounds for all Levites except for the High Priest. This second section was known as the holy of holies because it was the habitation of the Ark of the Covenant and the golden censer.

The Levitical High Priest spent a whole year sanctifying himself for the annual entrance into this most sacred but dreaded chamber. Whenever the High Priest broke through the veil of restriction to gaze upon the Ark of the Covenant, he did so with fear and trembling. Even his priestly garments could not be stained with sweat or he would risk divine retribution. Sweat (Genesis 3) is a symbol of "work" that is driven by the power of the flesh and God does not want the flesh to glory in His presence (1 Corinthians 1:29).

There was a thick veil of separation between the holy place and the holy of holies. This curtain of separation was split in two when the Lord Yeshua died on the cross. Through His death and resurrection, Jesus had opened up an ancient pathway into the very presence of God. The only difference is that while the Levitical High Priest entered the holy of holies in great fear and trembling, we can enter boldly because of the shed blood of the Messiah. While we reverence the presence of God, we are never afraid of being struck down by the power of God while we are in His presence.

The Ark of the Covenant

Which had the golden censer, and the ark of the covenant overlaid round about with gold, wherein was the golden pot that had manna, and Aaron's rod that budded, and the tables of the covenant;

Hebrews 9:4

The writer of the book of Hebrews tells us that under the Tabernacle of Moses, the Ark of the Covenant and the golden censer were located in the holy of holies. This means that none of the ordinary worshippers got to lay their eyes on the Ark of the Covenant, except in those rare moments when the children Israel were moving through the wilderness towards the Promised Land.

ONE OF THE MAIN WEAKNESSES OF THE
LEVITICAL PRIESTHOOD IS THE FACT THAT

CHRIST JESUS OUR ROYAL HIGH PRIEST

IT EXCLUDED ELEVEN OTHER TRIBES OF ISRAEL FROM PARTICIPATING IN THE PRIESTHOOD.

The Ark of the Covenant was overlaid with gold to represent divinity or God's divine nature. The insides of the Ark of the Covenant contained:

1. The golden pot that had "Manna." Manna is a prophetic representation of Christ the living Word of God.

2. Aaron's rod that "budded" supernaturally. Aaron's dead stick that budded supernaturally after it was left in the presence of God is a prophetic picture that true spiritual authority is the territory of those who have truly died to self. These men and women have tasted "the death of self" in His presence and have now been entrusted with "the power of the resurrection."

3. The Tablets of Stone containing the Ten Commandments. When Moses spent forty days and nights in the presence of God on Mount Sinai, God gave him a covenant written on stone. The tenets of this Covenant are what are known globally as the Ten Commandments. These Ten Commandments are an integral part of the judicial system and philosophy of most law-abiding nations. Nations that scoff at these laws have seen anarchy spread like a malignant cancer in the fabric of those nations. But under the New Covenant, God has written His laws on our hearts and minds, not on tablets of stone.

From Mercy Seat to Throne of Grace

And over it the cherubims of glory shadowing the mercyseat; of which we cannot now speak particularly. 6Now when these things were thus ordained, the priests went always into the first tabernacle, accomplishing the service of God.

Hebrews 9:5-6

The writer of the book of Hebrews now tells us that one of the most consequential things that the Lord Jesus Christ did through His death, resurrection and ascension was transform the mercy seat into the throne of Grace, permanently. This does not mean that there was no grace in the Old Testament. In the Old Covenant, the Levitical High Priest brought the blood of bulls and goats onto the mercy seat in the holy of holies to plead for the forgiveness of the nation of Israel. The reason the seat was known as the mercy seat is because "Mercy" is when God does not punish us for things we deserve punishment for. "Grace" is when God goes beyond "Mercy" and confers upon us innumerable blessings and favor that we do not deserve.

The Lord Jesus Christ went into the heavenly holy of holies and secured our eternal redemption. But the efficaciousness of His precious blood went beyond the mere act of acquiring God's mercy but also securing His everlasting "good will." In essence, the judgment seat became a seat overwhelmed by grace: the grace of our Lord Jesus Christ. Consequently, men and women from all walks of life can come boldly before God Most High to obtain grace in their time of need. My dear friend, this is the preciousness of the gospel of Jesus Christ.

A Terrifying once a year Appointment

But into the second went the high priest alone once every year, not without blood, which he offered for himself, and for the errors of the people:

Hebrews 9:7

Many of us have had appointments with certain people that meant more to us than others. But there was no appointment more sacred

143

and scary than the annual appointment between the Levitical High Priest and the glory of God. The High Priest would spend an entire year preparing for this one encounter with the presence of God in the holy of holies. If the High priest died in the presence of God because he entered with the stain of sin on him, the entire nation would be affected. The other Levites would in such a case pull his dead body out of the holy of holies. Thank God that the Lord Jesus Christ completely changed the spiritual technology for approaching the presence of God for people who place their faith in His finished work on the cross.

Operating in Shadows

The Holy Ghost this signifying, that the way into the holiest of all was not yet made manifest, while as the first tabernacle was yet standing: 9Which was a figure for the time then present, in which were offered both gifts and sacrifices, that could not make him that did the service perfect, as pertaining to the conscience;

Hebrews 10:8-9

The writer of the book of Hebrews finally gives us his most ferocious indictment of the inherent limitation of the Old Testament Levitical system of worship. He tells us that the entire Levitical priesthood was operating in the shadows of the good things to come. The writer of Hebrews tells us that the "veil or curtain" between the holy place and the holy of holies was indicative of the fact that the way into God's presence had not yet been secured. Consequently, the entire Levitical priesthood was relegated to ministering in the shadows of good things to come. The showbread was a shadow of the manifested presence of God. The golden laver was a shadow of Christ the living Word of God and so forth. But after Jesus died on the cross, the veil or curtain between the holy of holies and the holy place was split in two. Signifying that access to the very presence of God had been secured forever.

THE *Lord Jesus Christ* WENT INTO THE HEAVENLY HOLY OF HOLIES AND SECURED OUR ETERNAL REDEMPTION.

The Time of Reformation

Which stood only in meats and drinks, and divers washings, and carnal ordinances, imposed on them until the time of reformation.

Hebrews 9:10

The writer of the book of Hebrews tells us that all the sacrificial meats, drinks and divers ceremonial washings practiced under the Levitical priesthood were only shadows of good things to come. The writer of Hebrews tells us that God allowed or tolerated all of this religious system of sacrifice until the "Time of Reformation." The time of reformation started with the birth of the Lord Jesus Christ and will continue till the consummation of the ages in Christ Jesus. The word reformation simply means, "to return to the original form or formation." Consequently, reformation deals with returning the things of the spirit to their divine roots and origins. God is releasing the spirit of true reformation in the greater Body of Christ.

A High Priest of Good Things to Come

But Christ being come an high priest of good things to come, by a greater and more perfect tabernacle, not made with hands, that is to say, not of this building;

Hebrews 9:11

The writer of the book of Hebrews makes a very powerful proclamation. He tells us *"Christ has become a High Priest of good things to come!"* What does this mean? The proclamation means that Christ has become the High Priest who presides over all that is good that is contained in the New Covenant. What are the good things that are contained in the New Covenant? I am glad you asked me. The New Covenant is full of goodies, such as healing, deliverance from demons, prayer, prophecy, favor, righteousness, peace and financial prosperity, just to name a few. According to the writer of the book of Hebrews, whenever we pray for some to get healed and they get healed, the Lord Jesus Christ presides as High Priest over such a miracle. This also means that the Lord Jesus Christ is not opposed to His people enjoying the good things of this life. The religious church would have us think that the Lord Jesus Christ is opposed to Christians having a good time here on earth. But the book of Hebrews says that He is the High Priest over good things to come.

Enter through His Blood

Neither by the blood of goats and calves, but by his own blood he entered in once into the holy place, having obtained eternal redemption for us. 13For if the blood of bulls and of goats, and the ashes of an heifer sprinkling the unclean, sanctifieth to the purifying of the flesh:

Hebrews 9:12-13

The writer of the book of Hebrews shifts his focus to discussing the technology of entrance Jesus Christ used to access the holy of holies in the heavenly realm. We are told that Jesus entered the most holy place with His own precious blood. His precious blood was the access code into the very presence of God. Once a year, the Old Testament Levitical High Priest passed through the veil into the holy of holies in great fear and trembling. This is because the High Priest did not know whether he would come out dead or alive; even with the blood of a sacrificial animal mitigating his entrance.

On the other hand, the eternal High Priest of the Melchizedek Priesthood, the Lord Jesus Christ, entered the holy of holies with His own blood, which was shed on a rugged cross here on earth. As soon as the Heavenly Father accepted His shed blood as the ransom for the sins of mankind, the Messiah secured our eternal redemption. Since Christ secured our eternal redemption through His shed blood, the blood then becomes our key for accessing God's presence. We too can enter the holy of holies without fear through the blood of Christ.

A Conscience Free from Dead Works

How much more shall the blood of Christ, who through the eternal Spirit offered himself without spot to God, purge your conscience from dead works to serve the living God?

Hebrews 9:14

After the writer of the book of Hebrews makes a very powerful case for the efficacy of the blood of bulls and goats that was used in the Levitical temple, he moves to the case for the redeeming power of the blood of Jesus Christ. He tells us that the blood of sacrificial animals could sanctify the bodies of the priests who worked in the temple of God. He goes on to say that if such was the case for the blood of animals, what of the precious blood of Christ? In his rhetorical answer, he informs us that the precious blood of Christ goes much further in its ability to sanctify than the blood of animals.

The writer of the book of Hebrews tells us that the blood of Yeshua is so powerful and penetrating it can purge our conscience from "dead works" so that we can serve the living God. "Dead works" are works or acts of self-righteousness that stem from a guilty conscience. Christians with a guilty conscience will start beating themselves over faults and failures that they think make them unworthy of the love of God. These Christians and Messianic Jewish believers usually take a long time to forgive themselves over things that the Lord forgave them of the moment they sought His forgiveness. The Apostle Paul tells us that the blood of Christ can cleanse us from "dead works" produced by a guilty conscience.

The Mediator of the New Covenant

And for this cause he is the mediator of the New Testament, that by means of death, for the redemption of the transgressions that were under the first testament, they, which are called, might receive the promise of eternal inheritance.

Hebrews 9:15

The resurrection of Jesus Christ from the dead placed Him in a more powerful position than any other testator in human history. No person after having left a "Will" for his or her children has ever been able to "mediate" the execution of the signed "Will" after they died. When siblings start fighting over the estate of a dead parent, the deceased has no power to mediate the situation from beyond the grave. But Jesus Christ is in a very different category, because after His death he did not stay dead. He was resurrected!

The Bible says that Jesus Christ rose from the dead on the third day from the day of His execution on the cross. In His resurrected state, Jesus Christ was able to do something that no testator in human history has ever done. Jesus Christ became the first person to be both "testator" and "mediator" of a Testament that His death had eternally secured. By being both "testator" and "mediator", Jesus Christ ensures that every person who places their faith in Him and the New Covenant would never be cheated out of their spiritual inheritance. Could there be any greater compelling reason for faith? I do not know of any other!

The Death of the Testator

For where a testament is, there must also of necessity be the death of the testator. 17For a testament is of force after men are dead: otherwise it is of no strength at all while the testator liveth.

Hebrews 9:16-17

The expression, *"where a testament is, there must also be the death of the testator,"* behooves us to dig deeper. We need to understand the far-reaching implications of this weighty statement, because it holds the key to why Jesus's death was so necessary. We will begin by first defining two very important words that the writer of the book of Hebrews uses in the text: "Testament" and "Testator."

1. Testament: A Testament is a covenant, especially between God and humans.

2. Testator: A Testator is a person who has died leaving a valid will.

As soon as our eyes glance over the definitions of these two As soon as our eyes glance over the definitions of these two powerful words, the divine intent for the life and death of Jesus Christ becomes overwhelmingly obvious. Christ Jesus lived in a human body for thirty-three and a half years to explain and demonstrate His "Will" for all of mankind. In life, He wrote "His Will" for all who come under the New Covenant but He knew that no "Will" ever goes into effect while the person bequeathing the "Will" is alive. As a former life and health insurance salesman, I understand the powerful relationship between "Wills and Death Benefits." I wrote policies for loving parents who took out a life insurance on their lives and named their children as beneficiaries. But these beneficiaries got nothing until the death of the "testator."

People, who say that the death of Jesus Christ was either unnecessary or too barbaric, do not know what they are talking about. Jesus Christ like every wise testator knew that the tenets and benefits of the New Covenant (Testament) would not go into effect without His death. His death made the New Covenant or Testament legally enforceable. This is why when we stand on the power of the New Covenant (Testament) in the face of demonic opposition; victory will surely be ours because it is in Christ Jesus's "living Will."

Sanctified by the Blood

Whereupon neither the first testament was dedicated without blood. 19For when Moses had spoken every precept to all the people according to the law, he took the blood of calves and of goats, with water, and scarlet wool, and hyssop, and sprinkled both the book, and all the people, 20Saying, This is the blood of the testament which God hath enjoined unto you. 21Moreover he sprinkled with blood both the tabernacle, and all the vessels of the ministry.

Hebrews 9:18-21

The writer of the book of Hebrews now tells us that under God's holy Law "all things are sanctified by blood." The reason for this is due to the fact that the life of all flesh is in the blood. This means that the blood poured out symbolizes a life totally poured out or "surrendered" to God's purpose. Such a life is truly a sanctified life. The word sanctified simply means to be "set apart for a higher and holier purpose."

The writer of the book of Hebrews looks into biblical history to draw our attention to the dedication of the Tabernacle of Moses. He tells us that every article and person who had anything to do with the work of the temple was sprinkled with the blood of bulls and goats. This sprinkling of blood was to ceremoniously set apart all the persons and articles that were going to be used in the service of God. But while God allowed Moses to sanctify the persons and articles of the Levitical temple with the blood of animals, He sanctifies New Testament believers with the precious blood of Christ. This is why the level of sanctification God expects from New Testament believers must be higher than the sanctification of the earthly Levitical priesthood. It is a shame that in many Christian circles the absence of "true sanctification" is clearly visible and goes a long way to explain the absence of power in many Churches.

PEOPLE, WHO SAY THAT THE DEATH OF *Jesus Christ* WAS EITHER UNNECESSARY OR TOO BARBARIC, DO NOT

KNOW WHAT THEY ARE TALKING ABOUT.

Without the Shedding of Blood

And almost all things are by the law purged with blood; and without shedding of blood is no remission. 23It was therefore necessary that the patterns of things in the heavens should be purified with these; but the heavenly things themselves with better sacrifices than these.

Hebrews 9:22-23

The Bible is clear that all of mankind has fallen and has come short of the glory of God (Romans 3:23). This means that the "sin" virus infects all of mankind. But the Law of God declares, "The soul that sins shall die!" This means that the Law of God places the sentence of death on the soul of all sinners. Since the life of all flesh is in the blood (Leviticus 17:11), it is impossible to meet the righteous demands of the Law of God without the shedding of blood. The writer of the book of Hebrews tells us "without the shedding of blood there is no remission or forgiveness of sins."

It behooves us to understand the gravity of the statement made by the writer of Hebrews. Jesus Christ did not die on the cross to simply dramatize His mission here on earth. Death through the shedding of blood was exactly what was needed to satisfy the demands of the Old Covenant Law . Had Jesus shed His blood in an accidental death that was not directly connected to the sins of the whole world, or had He died of natural causes, His mission to our troubled planet would have been a total failure. This is why the Lord Jesus rebuked Peter sternly when he tried to stop Him from going to the cross. The cross was a well-known symbol and instrument of punishment within the Roman Empire, reserved for the worst kind of criminals. It was also the most painful and bloodiest way to die. Death by hanging on the cross was also the most humiliating, as it was a public execution where the criminal bled to death. The Heavenly Father in His unfathomable love for all of humanity chose His only begotten Son to die this way to ensure the remission of the sins of everyone who comes under the New Covenant.

An Advocate in the Presence of God

For Christ is not entered into the holy places made with hands, which are the figures of the true; but into heaven itself, now to appear in the presence of God for us:

Hebrews 9:24

In the American judicial system, the suspect of a crime has constitutional protection against self-incrimination. The suspect also has the unalienable right to invoke the services of a defense attorney to represent the same before a judge. This defense attorney will serve as the suspect's advocate. By definition an "advocate" is *a person who speaks or writes in support or defense of a person, in a court of law.*

The writer of the book of Hebrews tells us that we have a heavenly advocate who is loftier than the best attorney in the entire world. This heavenly advocate is the Lord Jesus Christ. When He rose from the dead, He entered the holy of holies with His precious blood and interceded for our complete forgiveness. Since the Law demands that the soul that sins must die to satisfy its righteous demands, Jesus died in our place. Consequently, the presence of His precious shed blood in the throne room and courtroom of heaven is our best ongoing advocacy.

A Perfect Sacrifice

Nor yet that he should offer himself often, as the high priest entereth into the holy place every year with blood of others; **26***For then must he often have suffered since the foundation of the world: but now once in the end of the world hath he appeared to put away sin by the sacrifice of himself.*

Hebrews 9:25-26

Apart from the Lord Jesus Christ, Adam and Eve were the only humans who enjoyed a flawless bloodline from the moment of creation. Unfortunately, when they fell into sin their bloodline became corrupted and the LORD rushed to the rescue. But only the LORD knew that the price of their redemption would cost Him everything, because He was the only one who knew their true value. As a temporary contingence, the LORD killed an innocent animal and then covered them in its blood-drenched skin. But the LORD knew that only another being with the same "flawless bloodline" could redeem mankind. This same premise is the reason the Old Testament sacrifices of bulls and goats failed to satisfy the penalty of sin.

The writer of the book of Hebrews tells us that the High Priests of the Levitical priesthood went into the holy of holies yearly to sprinkle the blood of bulls and goats on the mercy seat for the remission of the sins of the people. Nevertheless, the inferior blood of animals could only cover the sins of the people without removing them completely. This state of redemption left the burden of a guilty conscience upon all Old Testament worshippers who came to unload their burden of sin. However, in the fullness of time God sent His Son, born of a woman but not through the sexual union between a man and a woman. Consequently, the precious Lamb of God comes into the world with the same incorruptible and flawless bloodline as the first Adam. God had finally found His perfect sacrifice, whose shed blood could vanquish sin and restore all that was lost. This is why there is no person in human history that could compete with Yeshua.

Death and Judgment

And as it is appointed unto men once to die, but after this the judgment: 28So Christ was once offered to bear the sins of many; and unto them that look for him shall he appear the second time without sin unto salvation.

Hebrews 9:27-28

When God told Adam and Eve that in the day they ate of the tree of the knowledge of good and evil they would die, the first couple did not fully appreciate the far-reaching implications of disobedience to this divine edict. Since the historic fall of the first Kingdom ambassadors, death has been an unending menace in the history of mankind. The technology of death has not spared children, the rich or the famous in its wake. All the while, the inherent struggle for an eternal existence continues to rage on in the human soul.

The writer of the book of Hebrews tells us that it is divinely appointed for men to die followed by divine judgment. The fact that death is followed by eternal judgment implies that the soul of man lives on after the expiration of the physical body. For born again believers this judgment is a judgment of works and not sin, because their sins were judged on the cross in the body of the Lord Jesus Christ. The judgment of born-again Christians and Messianic Jews takes place at the Judgment seat of Christ. For unbelievers and Jews who rejected Yeshua as God's substitute while they were alive, this judgment is a judgment of eternal imprisonment.

GRACE HAS CONQUERED LEGALISM

W E are currently living in a time in which the collective consciousness of the Body of Christ is once again being awakened to the transforming power of the Grace of God. There seems to be a renaissance of the grace message all over the world. Years of legalistic traditions within the Universal church have finally taken their toll. Sincere followers of Christ who feel like they can never do enough to please God because of the legalistic culture of most Christian churches are gravitating towards the grace message like flies to a light bulb. For many believers who have lived a life driven more by guilt than faith because of the Church's lack of understanding of the Grace of God, this renaissance is like a thirsty man who discovers an Oasis in a dry desert.

While the renaissance of the grace message is to be welcomed by all followers of Christ who love freedom, they are those who have taken this message beyond its biblical boundaries. Some of these "grace message" extremists are rapidly transforming the grace of God into a cloak of unrighteousness. A dear friend of mine visited a grace message church in Tulsa, Oklahoma and what he heard grieved him greatly. The Pastor of this church made this comment while he was preaching on Grace, *"God never rebukes us, because we are no longer under the Law, we are all under grace."* With one unbiblical and careless statement from the pulpit, this Pastor made it difficult for his congregation to respond to the chastening of the Lord (Hebrews 12:7-9).

Perhaps the greatest lie that prophets of the "extreme grace message" purport is that the Old Covenant or Old Testament did not have "grace." Nothing could be further from the truth. The Old

Testament is full of scripture that show just how many times God offered "grace" to the people who lived under the Old Covenant. It may come as shock to some of you, but the roots and origins of "grace" is found in the Old Testament. Just check the following scriptures and you will be amazed how many times "grace" is mentioned in the Old Covenant. (Please read these scriptures, Gen 6:8, Ex 33:12, Ex 33:13, Ex 33:16, Ezra 2:17, Psalm 45:2, Pr 3:34, Pr 4:9, Jer 26:10, Jer 31:2, Zech 4:7 and Zech 12:10). The only major difference is that in the New Covenant, Yeshua became the physical embodiment of the grace of God to all mankind.

While it is true that Grace has conquered the Law, it's dangerous to disassociate the grace message from the person of Jesus Christ. This is because "Grace" is more than a message. Grace is a living person in the form of the Lord Jesus Christ (John 1:7-9). This means that what Christ the Person would not do, Grace as a message should not do either. What Christ the Person did and said while He was on earth, is what Grace must say and do in our lives. So if Christ the Person saw fit to rebuke Peter when the disciple was in dire need of the same, why would the Grace of God spare us from the Lord's rebuke when we are in desperate need of the same?

SOME OF THESE "GRACE MESSAGE" EXTREMISTS ARE RAPIDLY TRANSFORMING THE GRACE OF *God* INTO A CLOAK OF UNRIGHTEOUSNESS.

Perhaps one of the most powerful stories in the Gospels that best illustrates the relationship between Legalism and Grace and individual responsibility is the story of the woman caught in adultery. This story above all others is the best demonstration of the grace message as personified in how the Lord Jesus Christ responded to both the woman and her accusers. So let us peek at the nuances' of this powerful story. Any powerful story has key actors who all play a role that enhances the plot and objective of the story. In this case, below are the key players or actors.

1. The Lord Jesus Christ

2. The Religious Pharisees who caught the woman in Adultery

3. Satan the accuser of the Brethren

4. The Sinner (the woman caught in adultery)

5. The Mosaic Law (that decided the Woman's penalty for her sin)

6. The Sin Question

7. The Transforming Power of Grace

According to the gospels, the Pharisees with a holier than thou attitude, dragged the woman caught in adultery before Jesus Christ. These Pharisees did not even follow the Torah, which demanded that they bring both offenders, not just the woman. The woman was fearful, dreading perniciously her impending judgment. She knew that the sentence for a woman caught in adultery under the Mosaic Law was death by stoning. She quivered in absolute terror at the thought of such a gruesome death. Her accusers on one hand licked their lips in anticipation. To them the whole thing was one big religious show of piety that was also designed to test Yeshua's commitment to the Law of Moses. Their religious bigotry had already misrepresented the true spirit of the Torah; in the presence of the Man who embodied the true essence of the Torah. Yeshua was the Torah in a human body.

The woman's accusers chose one of their peers to be the group's spokesperson. Like a prosecutor who has smelled blood in the water, the man proceeded to lay out the merits of what he thought was a closed and shut case. The woman was guilty. She had been caught red handed, in the very act of adultery. What is of note here is that the woman's accuser never brought the man she was caught with for sentencing; even though the Torah also required this. The woman's accusers were quick to remind Yeshua (the Word) that according to the Law of Moses the penalty for the woman's crime was death by stoning. The woman's accuser made his final summations and waited for Jesus to dish out the verdict that they all thought was obvious.

Jesus did not speak for a while, as though he was spellbound by the woman's accuser's closing argument. I am sure the Pharisees were licking their lips with satisfaction sensing that they had pigeonholed Yeshua into a theological quagmire. Jesus bowed his head and wrote something in the sands of time that held his feet. When He finally spoke, they were dumbfounded because it was not the kind of comeback they had anticipated. But Yeshua's response would forever enshrine in the minds of men the difference between Legalism and Grace, as well as the true spirit of the Torah. *"Whosoever among you is without sin must be the first one to throw the first stone."*

I believe that the woman's heart almost stopped when she heard Yeshua's response. She trembled with fear unfeigned as she waited for the arrival of the first stone. But the stones of judgment never arrived. To her great relief, her bloodthirsty accusers began to flee the scene, from the oldest to the youngest of them. Her worst fears unrealized she waited to see what Jesus was going to do with her. When he finally spoke, he asked her a leading question. "Where are those who condemned you?" Her eyes searched for her accusers but found none. She answered, "They are gone." His eyes meeting hers, he proceeds to announce her release from prosecution. "Neither do I condemn you. Go and sin no more."

The woman sighed heavily in unfeigned relief. She was sure that she was guilty and deserving of death. Fortunately, the Grace of God had intercepted her in the face of Jesus Christ and her precious life had been spared. But the same Grace that saved her life from prosecution had also placed a righteous restriction on how she lived her life after the fact. This righteous restriction is contained in the statement, "Go and sin no more!" This instruction correlates with the moral code of the Torah. The prophetic principle stated here is a prevailing principle throughout the entire Bible. God's grace delivers us from sin so we can live in righteousness. Grace that releases us from sin, while failing to hold us accountable to living a life invested in godliness is NOT the redeeming Grace supported by Scripture.

FORTUNATELY, THE GRACE OF *God* HAD INTERCEPTED HER IN THE FACE OF *Jesus Christ* AND HER PRECIOUS LIFE WAS SPARED.

Types and Shadows

For the law having a shadow of good things to come, and not the very image of the things, can never with those sacrifices, which they offered year by year continually, make the comers thereunto perfect.

Hebrews 10:1

In the above passage of Scripture, the writer of the book of Hebrews made it adamantly clear that the "Old Covenant" was merely a shadow of good things to come. But it is important to note that this Scripture is referring to the sacrificial laws within the Mosaic Covenant. The writer of Hebrews is very clear that the 'shadow of good things to come' he was referring to was the *"sacrifices, which the Levites offered year by year"* to atone for the sins of the people. The sacrifices of bulls, goats and sheep were a passing shadow of the true sacrifice of Christ on the cross. This is why those inferior sacrifices could not release Old Testament worshippers from the burden of sin.

While it is true that much of the Old Testament contains types and shadows of New Testament realities, we would be amiss to ascribe redundancy to the entire Old Testament Scriptures. This is another extreme pro-New Testament theological position into which some Christians fall. But I want you to remember; all Scripture is inspired by God (1 Timothy 3:16), including the Old Testament section of the Bible. Unfortunately many Christians dismiss much of what is written in the Old Testament by the simple but unqualified statement, *"We are not under the Law we are under Grace."* While the statement is true, it leaves much to be desired because it assumes that the entire Old Testament is the LAW. This is far from the truth. The above statement by most Christians also leads many of them to disdain the Law of God; seeing it as an hindrance to faith. This internal disdain for the Law of God slowly breeds a contempt for the law of the Land that many of these Christians are domiciled in. Saint Paul tells us in Romans that the Law is good and spiritual. But what makes the grace of God so powerful, appealing and efficacious is that its the "power of God" for Christians and Messianic Jews to keep the Law of God through *"living out the life"* of the One (Yeshua) who fulfilled all the righteous demands of the Torah!

The Old Testament portion of the Bible is made up of the following:

1. The Pentateuch: (The first five books of the Old Testament, Genesis to Deuteronomy, written by the Prophet Moses. Much of what is written in the book of Genesis was before the Old Covenant of Law; making it extremely relevant to New Testament believers.)

2. The Prophets: (These are prophetic books like Isaiah and Ezekiel that were written by the prophets themselves. These prophetic books cover topics that directly impacted the nation of Israel during the prophet's era. But they also contain prophetic messages for New Testament believers, as well as messages about the consummation of the ages in Christ Jesus.)

3. The Psalms: King David wrote The Psalms. Much of the prophetic poetry, songs and redemptive themes written in the Psalms directly impacts New Testament believers. Its King David in Psalm 110 who tells us of the resurrected Christ seated in heavenly places

operating in His Melchizedek priesthood, while waiting for His enemies to be made His footstool.

4. The Wisdom books: King Solomon wrote the Wisdom books, which include Proverbs, Song of Songs and Ecclesiastes.

To suggest that all the aforementioned books are nothing but "Legalism" is both erroneous and theologically inaccurate. I have met many New Testament Kingdom businessmen and women who trace their success to their daily readings of the book of Proverbs.

The Root of Sin Consciousness

For then would they not have ceased to be offered because that the worshippers once purged should have had no more conscience of sins. 3But in those sacrifices there is a remembrance again made of sins every year.

Hebrews 10:2-3

A "dead or evil conscience" is the root of all sin consciousness. A "dead or evil conscience" does not in any way imply an absence of conscience it just points to a conscience that is more alive to Sin than to Righteousness. This is why such a conscience is in need of being purged of dead works by the blood of Christ. The writer of the book of Hebrews tells us that the Jewish nation that lived under the Old Covenant had a difficult time breaking free of "Sin Consciousness or the condemnation of the Law." The repetitive nature of the daily and yearly sacrifices for sin constantly reminded them of the sin nature residing within.

Even though the sacrifice of the Body of the Lord Jesus Christ on the cross has paid for our sin, many Christians constantly struggle with sin consciousness. This is in part due to a conscience that they have not yet allowed the Holy Spirit to purge from "dead works" through the blood of Christ. "Dead works" are works performed by religious people who want to earn God's unmerited favor through their supposedly good works. Consequently, these Christians get caught up in outward religious performance rather than in the internal dynamics of a relationship with the Heavenly Father driven by the grace of our Lord Jesus Christ. The other culprit responsible for much of the sin consciousness thousands of Christians wrestle with is a theology of legalism championed by many well-intentioned but misguided "fire and brimstone" preachers. This legalistic theology centers on God being more of an angry God in search of justice than a loving Heavenly Father who went to such great lengths to reconcile mankind to Himself in the Body of the Lord Jesus Christ. It's my prayer that as you read this anointed writing that you will find the power to break free from the burden of "Sin consciousness."

Imperfect Sacrifices

For it is not possible that the blood of bulls and of goats should take away sins. 6In burnt offerings and sacrifices for sin thou hast had no pleasure.

Hebrews 10:4

The writer of the book of Hebrews continues his dissertation and tells us that one of the many reasons Old Testament saints struggled with the issue of "Sin Consciousness" is due to the imperfect nature of the sacrifices used in the atonement. The Apostle tells us that the blood of bulls and goats could NOT take away the sin nature in man. The sacrifices of animal blood just managed to cover the sins of the people before God, but had zero power in removing the inherent sin nature in the worshippers. In actuality, God was never fully satisfied with the "atonement value" of these animal sacrifices but He tolerated them until He could reveal His perfect sacrifice in the fullness of time. God's answer to the ongoing Old Covenant dilemma of imperfect sacrifices came in the form of the Lord Jesus Christ.

The Incarnation Foretold

Wherefore when he cometh into the world, he saith, Sacrifice and offering thou wouldest not, but a body hast thou prepared me:

Hebrews 10:5

The incarnation of the Lord Jesus Christ is the most powerful and prolific event of the entire Bible. It is without a shadow of doubt the most important event in human history. While lying in a manger in swaddling clothes God had managed to become one of us. Since the fall of man, sin has exercised dominion on mankind, making it impossible for us to be like God. So He (Christ) became one of us so that He could provide us with a legitimate pathway for us to be like God once more.

The Incarnation of the Lord Jesus Christ was also God's ingenious answer to the dilemma of daily and yearly animal sacrifices that could not remove sin. When Christ pierces the veil of time and space to enshroud Himself in human form, He makes a startling announcement: *"In Sacrifice and offering (Heavenly Father) you have not been pleased but you have prepared me a body"* (Adapted by Author). Christ, the eternal and living Word was making it clear that His physical body crafted by the hand of God would become the true sacrifice for the sins of all mankind, past, present and future. This above all is the reason Christians and Jews alike must celebrate the incarnation of Yeshua the Messiah.

THE INCARNATION OF THE LORD *Jesus Christ* WAS ALSO *God's* INGENIOUS ANSWER TO THE DILEMMA OF DAILY AND YEARLY ANIMAL SACRIFICES THAT COULD NOT REMOVE SIN.

Power to Do His Will

Wherefore when he cometh into the world, he saith, Sacrifice and offering thou wouldest not, but a body hast thou prepared

---

me: 7Then said I, Lo, I come (in the volume of the book it is written of me,) to do thy will, O God.

Hebrews 10:5, 7

There is a very powerful hidden truth in the passage above that directly impacts our ability to do His will. The God we serve is a God who does everything according to the counsel of His will, making His will the central axis of all the predetermined purposes of God. Unfortunately, many Christians struggle to do God's will on a consistent basis. Spiritual warfare zealots lay the blame for this inadequacy directly onto the shoulders of the Devil. But in the above passage of Scripture, the writer of the book of Hebrews does include the Devil as a factor in the doing of God's will.

The writer of Hebrews makes a very startling statement that uncorks the mystery behind the power to do His will. He states, "With sacrifice and offering you were not pleased but a body hast thou prepared for me and I come in the volume of the book to do thy will, O God" (Adapted by author). In this passage, the Apostle makes it clear that one of the most important aspects to doing God's will consistently is to have a "body that is prepared" to do the will of God. The reality is that the regenerated spirit of a born again believer is always willing to do God's will. The Lord Jesus said it this way, "the spirit is willing but the flesh is weak." This is why I admonish Christians to include fasting in their spiritual arsenal so they can learn how to subdue the fleshly dictates of the body. For instance, if the Holy Spirit stirs the spirit of a believer to wake up and pray, the believer has a choice between obeying the prompting of the Holy Spirit or obeying the tiredness of their own body. This is why a "prepared body" is so critical to the doing of God's will.

Taking Away the First to Establish the Second

Above when he said, Sacrifice and offering and burnt offerings and offering for sin thou wouldest not, neither hadst pleasure therein; which are offered by the law; 9Then said he, Lo, I come to do thy will, O God. He taketh away the first, that he may establish the second.

Hebrews 10:8-9

The critical underlying difference between the Old and New Covenants lies in the quality and quantity of the sacrifice that was used in both covenants to satisfy the demands of a righteous God. Under the Old Covenant, the Levitical priests sacrificed animals in order to atone for the sin of the people of Israel. Since mankind was created of a higher pedigree than animals, it follows that man's blood is also superior in value to that of animals. This would explain why the endless sacrifices of the blood of bulls, goats and sheep could not remove the sin nature in mankind or separate him from the sins thereof. Instead the blood of these sacrificial animals could only "cover the sins" of the people of the Old Covenant. This would explain why the writer of the book of Hebrews informs us that God was not pleased with these animal sacrifices. When Christ makes the startling announcement that in the "volume of the book, I come to do thy will, O God;" He set aside the entire Old Testament Levitical sacrificial system. Christ the living Word was to become the Lamb of God who takes away the sin of the whole world.

Sanctified Once for All

By the which will we are sanctified through the offering of the body of Jesus Christ once for all.

Hebrews 10:10

Under the Old Testament Levitical sacrificial system, the worshipers were always going through sanctification because the blood of animals failed to excommunicate the sin nature in the worshippers. But under the New Covenant, we have a very different spiritual inheritance. The apostolic epistles tell us that when Christ was on the cross, he permanently crucified our old sin ravaged nature. He became sin on the cross (1 Corinthians 5:21) so that we might become the righteousness of God in Christ Jesus. The word sanctified means "to be set apart from." The Apostle Paul tells us here that

God sanctified us once and for all when He offered the body of Jesus Christ on the cross. We cannot pay for our sins beyond what Christ accomplished for us in the offering of His sinless body on the cross. This is why Christians who are failing to live sanctified lives are either ignorant of the merits of the finished work or have simply chosen to live after the dictates of their flesh nature. Sanctification under the New Covenant does not begin with our human effort; it begins with our ability to identify with the finished work of Christ.

The Perfect Sacrifice

And every priest standeth daily ministering and offering oftentimes the same sacrifices, which can never take away sins: 12But this man, after he had offered one sacrifice for sins for ever, sat down on the right hand of God;

Hebrews 10:11-12

Since the closure of the gates of the Garden of Eden, after the first couple committed high treason, God has been on a quest of unveiling His perfect sacrifice to answer the problem of sin in human life. Immediately after the fall of Adam and Eve, God killed an animal to atone for their sin and then clothed them in animal skin. Between the fall of Adam and the appearance of the last Adam in Mary's womb, thousands of animals were sacrificed in order to atone for the sins of the people of Israel. But no matter how much animal blood was shed, the blood of these precious animals was not sufficient enough to exorcise the sin nature that drives every human heart.

THE APOSTLE MAKES IT CLEAR THAT ONE OF THE MOST IMPORTANT ASPECTS TO DOING *God's* WILL CONSISTENTLY IS TO HAVE A "BODY THAT IS PREPARED TO DO THE WILL OF *God"*

Fortunately the appearance of Christ in the human body tipped the scales of redemption. God had finally found the most superior sacrifice to ever walk the earth. Yeshua the Lamb of God, child of Mary and Joseph, was the sinless, incorruptible man that every sinner on our troubled planet had been waiting on. In Him dwelt the very fullness of the Godhead bodily. His blood originated from the bosom of the Heavenly Father. Like the first Adam, he was truly the Son of God. Just as Adam's blood came from the Heavenly Father, Jesus Christ's blood came directly from the throne of God. It was the perfect, spotless blood sample to ever walk the earth since the Fall of the first couple. In Christ Jesus, God had found a sinless and spotless lamb that He could sacrifice in total obedience on the cross to atone for the sins of the whole world. This is why there is no other name under heaven given to men under which they can be saved, other than that of the Lord Jesus Christ (Acts 4:12).

His Enemies, His Footstool

From henceforth expecting till his enemies be made his footstool.
Hebrews 10:13

The writer of the book of Hebrews lets us know that the work the Messiah accomplished in His life, burial, resurrection and ascension is so complete that He sits on the right hand of God waiting for His enemies to be made His footstool. Since Christ is the head of the Church (the Body of Christ) it follows that we are His feet. Since we are His feet it follows that Christ will not return to the earth until the Body of Christ subdues His enemies under His feet. This passage is further confirmation that the Messiah is not returning for a bride that is wallowing in the dirt of defeat. He is returning to the adjuration of an overcoming Bride. He is not returning for a Church steeped in compromise and humanistic philosophies. He is coming back to a Bride that has come into the full stature of the Son of God. He is returning for a body of believers who are not easily carried away by every wind of doctrine (Ephesians 4:12-13).

We have been Perfected

For by one offering he hath perfected forever them that are sanctified.

Hebrews 10:14

From antiquity to the present times, the search for a perfect utopian society in the hearts of men rages on. This search for utopia is behind many of the world's "isms." The search for perfection and a perfect society is as old as the history of mankind. However this relentless search has yielded more frustrations than answers because such a search assumes that all the imperfections of mankind can be eradicated by more education or illumination. This assumption fails to acknowledge the fact that the search for utopia will fail if we fail to factor in man's inherent sinful condition and God's solution to this inherent corruption in man. This is where most new age spiritual transformation gurus fail, because they seem to believe that man's only problem is his lack of enlightenment. But the ancient Hebrew Scriptures are clear that "all have sinned and come short of God's glory (Romans 3:23)."

IN YESHUA, *God* FOUND A SINLESS AND SPOTLESS LAMB THAT HE COULD SACRIFICE IN TOTAL OBEDIENCE!

The Apostle Paul in the passage above makes a very startling announcement. He says that God has perfected in Christ all of them that are being sanctified. This might come as a shock to your religious sensitivities, but when God looks at a born again believer He sees you as both "perfected and sanctified." How can this be? The answer is staggeringly simple but deeply profound. Man is a spirit who has a soul and lives in a body (1 Thessalonians 5:23). Redemption therefore begins in the spirit of man, before it begins to penetrate the soul and the body. When a person is born again, their human spirit is regenerated into the very image and nature of God. This means that once a believer accepts Christ their spirit becomes instantly "perfected and sanctified." This is why a person who is truly born again can commit sin with their soul or body but never with their regenerated spirit. The regenerated spirit is made one spirit with the Lord in salvation and is incapable of practicing sin voluptuously. This explains why a true born again Christian can never live in sin and enjoy the experience. Most likely, they will be miserable throughout the whole process, because their "Conscience" which is the voice of their regenerated spirit will have them for breakfast until they change course. *This is not to say that a born again believer cannot choose over time to resist the voice of the Holy Spirit, even to the point of denying the Lord Jesus Christ.*

The New Covenant

Whereof the Holy Ghost also is a witness to us: for after that he had said before, 16This is the covenant that I will make with them after those days, saith the Lord, I will put my laws into their hearts, and in their minds will I write them; 17And their sins and iniquities will I remember no more.

Hebrews 10:15-17

There is a vast a difference between the Old and New Covenants even though the New Covenant builds upon what the LORD started with the nation of Israel. For a start, the New Covenant is established on better promises than the Old Covenant. One of the most powerful interesting features of the New Covenant is that the Holy Spirit plays the role of witness. The Holy Spirit is the most reliable witness you could ever have. The writer of the book of Hebrews tells us that the Holy Spirit stands ready to testify to the validity of the New Covenant, both to us and to the demonic powers in the heavenly realms.

Based upon the above passage of Scripture, the following are the critical features of the New Covenant.

❖ The Holy Ghost is a ready and reliable Witness to the power and benefits of the New Covenant.

❖ It is a Unilateral Covenant with God taking full responsibility for initiating it.

❖ God's holy laws are supernaturally engraved on our hearts and minds through the miracle of rebirth.

❖ God's promise of complete forgiveness of our sin and iniquity. The phrase, "their sins and iniquities will I remember no more," denotes God's deliberate intention to go beyond forgiving us to actually refusing to use our past against us. Nevertheless there is an ongoing need to confess our sins when we act contrary to the Word of God.

No More Offering for Sin

Now where remission of these is, there is no more offering for sin.
Hebrews 10:18

Hebrews 10:18 is perhaps the most important statement the Apostle Paul makes in this epistle to confirm the complete atonement for sin afforded to mankind through the offering of the body of the Lord Jesus Christ. He states...*Now where remission (forgiveness) of these (every kind of sin) is, there is no more offering (Sacrifice) for sin.* You just missed a place to stand up and shout! Once Jesus Christ sighed his last statement on the cross, "it is finished," sin was truly vanquished. It was rendered powerless in its ability to hold the soul in captivity of anyone who calls upon the name of the Lord. Since the offering of Christ Jesus extends to every known sin, no matter how depraved the sin, this is truly a life defining statement. *Sin in its every form, past, present and future was atoned for by the offering of the body of Jesus Christ on the cross. But this incredible blessing can only be accessed by the truly "repentant heart."*

Unfortunately, the spirit of legalism has tried to quench the life giving grace of God drenched in this one verse. Some legalistic minded theologians have used this passage to insinuate that this verse means that when a Christian sins "willfully" there is "no more offering for sin" left for such a person. Christians victimized by this flawed interpretation of this passage of Scripture have been stocked with unbearable guilt, robbing them of the joy of their salvation. Truthfully speaking, apart from generational iniquity all sin by humans is willful. You will be hard pressed to find sin, which does not involve the faculty of human will. However, Hebrews 10:18 is not a license to sin for anybody, but it is the basis for the promise of complete forgiveness for sins, past, present and future; when we come before God in true repentance. *Please remember that scriptural forgiveness from sin is always predicated on the sinner showing forth fruit worthy of repentance.*

Boldness to Enter His Presence

Having therefore, brethren, boldness to enter into the holiest by the blood of Jesus,

Hebrews 10:19

One of the critical differences between the Old and New Covenants is in the technology for entering the presence of God. Under the Old Testament, both the priests and laity had a fearful dread when they got too close to the presence of God. Even the High Priest took a whole year preparing himself meticulously for that one entrance into the Holy of Holies. When the Day of Atonement came, the High Priest entered the Holy of Holies with fear and trembling. This entrance was rarely with boldness.

Fortunately for us, under the New Covenant, the shed blood of the Lord Jesus Christ has forever opened the "way" into the I AM presence of God. New Testament believers unlike their Old Testament counterparts can access the presence of God at will and without the fear of divine retribution. This does not in any way give us the license not to reverence the presence of God. God's presence is the holiest and most priceless asset of creation. To take the presence of God lightly unmasks our lack of appreciation for the penalty the Messiah paid to give us access to the presence of God. Those who know and love Him the most are the ones who appreciate His presence the most.

A New and Living Way

By a new and living way, which he hath consecrated for us, through the veil, that is to say, his flesh; 21And having an high priest over the house of God;

Hebrews 10:20-21

The writer of the book of Hebrews tells us that through the offering of Jesus's body on the cross, God has opened up a "New and Living way" for born again believers. The Apostle goes on to describe the nomenclature of this new and living way as follows:

❖ This spiritual pathway is...New! This means that no man had ever walked on this pathway before Christ purchased it with His own blood.

❖ This spiritual pathway is...a Living pathway! This means that people who step on this pathway will be drenched with the life of God.

❖ This spiritual pathway has...been consecrated for us through the veil of the body of Christ, leading us into the Holy of Holies. This means that none of us can earn our way into the presence of God apart from appropriating the benefits of the finished work of the Messiah.

❖ This new and life giving spiritual pathway is... administered by the risen Lord, who is our redeemer and high priest.

Let us Draw Near

Let us draw near with a true heart in full assurance of faith, having our hearts sprinkled from an evil conscience, and our bodies washed with pure water.

Hebrews 10:22

Perhaps one of the most romantic transitions between the Old Testament and the New Testament can be summed up in one statement, "let us draw near!" In the Old Testament when God's fearsome glory descended on Mount Sinai, the people of Israel were terrified of drawing near. They were so terrified of coming closer to the glory of God that they interceded with Moses to stand between them and the glory of God. Even when they beheld the residue of God's glory on Moses's face, they asked him to wrap cloth around his face.

But after the death and resurrection of Jesus Christ both the technology and emotion for engaging the presence of God changes radically. Under the Old Covenant some of the people of Israel approached God in much the same way that a criminal approaches the judge's chambers - in unfeigned trepidation. But under the New Testament our relationship to God has changed radically. God treats us like sons and daughters for Yeshua's sake. In this sonship approach to the presence of God, we are charged to do the following:

- ❖ Draw near with a sincere heart.

- ❖ Draw near in full assurance of faith.

- ❖ Draw near free from an evil conscience. An evil conscience is a conscience that is burdened with guilt over our past sins and indiscretions that the Lord has washed away with His blood.

- ❖ Draw near in the power of a life sanctified by being washed in the water of the Word of God.

The Profession of our Faith

Let us hold fast the profession of our faith without wavering; (for he is faithful that promised;)

Hebrews 10:23

The writer of the book of Hebrews lets us know that our faith is a profession. Faith as a profession means that we have to work at being consistent in our "faith confessions" until the manifestation of what God has promised us. A profession is usually a career that we work at in order to earn an income. In the economy of the Kingdom, "Walking by Faith" is a real profession that can earn us an income within the economy of the Kingdom. One of the reasons why we have to stay the course in our faith confession is because God is faithful to complete what He promised.

Provoking Love and Good Works

And let us consider one another to provoke unto love and to good works:

Hebrews 10:24

The political divide in the United States is growing steadily, dividing the country into a collection of Red and Blue states. The animosity between the two political factions and their supporters has become toxic to the general welfare of the nation. This animosity plays out mainly through the News and media outlets, where there is stiff competition as to who can provoke the other side into a tantrum. Unfortunately, this same spirit has filtered into the lives of many Christians who have aligned themselves on the different sides of the political divide.

I believe that Christians going after each other's throat, whatever the case, grieves the Holy Spirit. Instead, we are admonished by the passage above to do the following:

❖ Consider one another...this means that we are careful to place the interests of our brothers and sisters above our own.

❖ Provoke each other into a lifestyle governed by the same agape love that took Christ to the cross.

❖ Provoke one another into a lifestyle driven by good works, especially to those of the household of faith. Our works must be a demonstration of our faith in God, not our self-righteousness.

The Power of Apostolic Community

Not forsaking the assembling of ourselves together, as the manner of some is; but exhorting one another: and so much the more, as ye see the day approaching.

Hebrews 10:25

We are living an age in which the advancement in both science and technology affords us the luxury of living a life completely isolated from other people. The boundaries of interpersonal fellowship have been in rapid decline around the nations, even in the Body of Christ. But the truth of the matter is that God created us for Community. We need community to properly develop as both spiritual and social beings. God has called every Christian to a life of divine interdependence; in the same way He designed the faculties of our body to function. The eye can never tell the nose or ears that I have no need of you.

The writer of the book of Hebrews is clear in the charge he gives to all citizens of the Kingdom of God. We need to be part of a functional apostolic community made of persons of like precious faith. This charge is contained in the expression, "Not forsaking the assembling of ourselves together!" The apostle then proceeds to tell us the reasons for being part of a robust apostolic community.

❖ For exhorting one another unto love and good works.

❖ For personal accountability, which some having abandoned fell into the trap of the enemy.

❖ For encouraging each other to stay the course even as the day of Christ's second coming rapidly approaches.

Willful Sin

For if we sin wilfully after that we have received the knowledge of the truth, there remaineth no more sacrifice for sins, 27But a certain fearful looking for of judgment and fiery indignation, which shall devour the adversaries. 28He that despised Moses' law died without mercy under two or three witnesses: 29Of how much sorer punishment, suppose ye, shall he be thought worthy, who hath trodden under foot the Son of God, and hath counted the blood of the covenant, wherewith he was sanctified, an unholy thing, and hath done despite unto the Spirit of grace? Hebrews 10:26-29

The above passage of Scripture has baffled many teachers of the grace message, while fueling the fire of the "fire and brimstone" messages of many legalistic minded theologians. Many of those who teach the grace message skirt around this passage of Scripture nervously, while legalistic theologians employ this passage to fuel the argument that a born-again Christian can easily lose their salvation because of "willful sin." The reality is that both sides have real stock in this passage. The passage is actually proof of both the awesome grace of God and His holy severity.

FAITH IS A REAL PROFESSION THAT CAN EARN US GREAT DIVIDENDS WITHIN THE ECONOMY OF THE KINGDOM.

The redeeming truths behind this passage are found in examining the passage as a whole instead of zeroing in on each individual verse. Legalistic theologians have used Hebrews 10:26-27 to prove that any Christian involved in "willful" sin can easily lose their salvation and go to hell instead of heaven when they die. But this argument is only a partial truth and must be treated in concert with the context of the whole passage.

First and foremost, almost all sin that a believer will ever commit is inherently "willful." If "willful" sin by a born again believer automatically robs them of their salvation, we would have to conclude that the majority of Christ following Christians who have ever sinned since they turned to the Lord are actually going to hell. But this is not the case. Peter's sin of denying Christ three times was certainly "willful" and yet the Lord completely restored and absolved him of his sin.

Closer examination of the passage as a whole quickly unravels the mystery of the entire passage. The passage is actually describing the drastic steps a born again Christian would have to take in order to renounce their salvation. The passage also unmasks the degree of willful sin that can lead a believer to renounce their salvation. These drastic steps are as follows:

❖ The Christian who renounces their salvation…is engaged in ongoing willful sin.

❖ The Christian who renounces their salvation…will ignore all biblical teaching on eternal judgment.

❖ The Christian who renounces their salvation…develops spiritual apathy towards the (Word) law of God.

❖ The Christian who renounces their salvation…develops an antagonistic and irreverent attitude towards the blood of Jesus Christ.

❖ The Christian who renounces their salvation…will also develop a resistant and irreverent attitude towards the Holy Spirit.

❖ The Christian who renounces their salvation…despises the grace of God by using the Grace of God as a cloak for unrighteousness.

I have been saved for over two decades and I can count on both of my hands born again Christians I have met who fit the above prognosis for a spiritually reprobate Christian. The underlying message of Hebrews 10:26-29 is simply this: a born again believer who chooses to consistently live in sin, against the conviction of both the Word and the Spirit has...no more sacrifice for sins left, except the same fearful judgment that awaits all of God's enemies!

Vengeance is the Lord's

For we know him that hath said, Vengeance belongeth unto me, I will recompense, saith the Lord. And again, The Lord shall judge his people. 31It is a fearful thing to fall into the hands of the living God.

Hebrews 10:30-31

We live in a world of cause and effect. This is why the Bible admonishes us to be careful what we sow. In a world driven by the engines of chaos through the Sin technology, it's not difficult to see why people hurt each other. Ever since the fall of Adam and Eve, sin and the self-centeredness that comes with it has resulted in multiple offenses. Jesus put it this way: "Offenses will come" and then proceeded to admonish us to forgive each other.

While desiring retribution for offenses we have suffered is human, it goes against the divine nature. This is why the Scripture warns us against seeking "vengeance." The Scriptures declare that vengeance is the Lord's. God literally owns this domain and this is why:

❖ God is the only one who can justly give us "recompense" for the offenses we have suffered in service of His Kingdom.

❖ God is the only one who can properly adjudicate our case without showing any partiality whatsoever.

❖ God is the only one who can properly dish out the appropriate measure of punishment for the offenses we have suffered in the service of His Kingdom.

Godly Persecution

But call to remembrance the former days, in which, after ye were illuminated, ye endured a great fight of afflictions; 33Partly, whilst ye were made a gazingstock both by reproaches and afflictions; and partly, whilst ye became companions of them that were so used. 34For ye had compassion of me in my bonds, and took joyfully the spoiling of your goods, knowing in yourselves that ye have in heaven a better and an enduring substance.

Hebrews 10:32-34

The global proliferation of the "seek-sensitive-feel-good-gospel" has given birth to Christians who cannot stay faithful to God under the pressure of persecution. But the Bible is very clear that if we suffer with Him (Christ) we shall also reign with him. The Apostle Paul in the book of Timothy admonishes belivers who aspire to live a godly life to be aware that such a lifestyle is never without persecution. The reason for the persecution is staggeringly simple. We live in a world where much of the populace is under the dominion of sin. In a world dominated by sin, it is easy to see why those who live a godly life find themselves in opposition to the lack of morality in our culture.

The famous Sprite commercial tagline is "Obey your thirst!" This tagline is a perfect description for how the sin nature in mankind operates. In a world where everyone is more concerned about obeying his or her thirst than the Word of God, it does not take much imagination to see why this world is filled with so much suffering. But those of us who have chosen to live a godly life in a world of ever evolving morality are on a collision course with our culture of loose morals. Church history has proven that the gospel of the Kingdom flourishes much more rapidly in cultures where Christians and Messianic Jews suffer for their faith. This is not to imply that Christian growth can never be experienced apart from persecution. But it does explain why God allows the godly to suffer persecution from time to time. Nevertheless we are more than conquerors through Christ our Lord.

The Power of Confidence

Cast not away therefore your confidence, which hath great recompense of reward.

Hebrews 10:35

The writer of the book of Hebrews now admonishes us not to "Cast, or throw away" our confidence in the Lord. He tells us that our "Confidence in the Lord" carries with it "great recompense of reward." The word "recompense" means to pay or give compensation for; make restitution or requital for (damage, injury, or the like). God intends to make good on our behalf all the trouble we have suffered for His name's sake. This is why the Apostle Paul is emphatic that we do not allow life circumstances to rob us of our confidence in the Lord. We have good reason to approach God with confident expectation of a great recompense.

The Power of Patience

For ye have need of patience, that, after ye have done the will of God, ye might receive the promise. 37For yet a little while, and he that shall come will come, and will not tarry.

Hebrews 10:36-37

Perhaps there is nothing that many Christians struggle to maintain like patience. We all know that patience is a very powerful virtue, but this does not necessarily make walking in patience easier. But patience as a virtue becomes much easier to grapple with when we remember that faith and patience are two sides of the same coin. While our faith gives us the supernatural capacity to reach for the unknown, it is patience that will keep us steadfast until the object of our faith manifests itself. Many Christians have aborted their own breakthrough because they were too impatient.

Based upon the above passage of Scripture there is a two-fold reason we need patience.

❖ To help us obtain the promise after we have done or completed the will of God.

❖ To help us endure and stay the course while the promise is yet to manifest.

The Just Shall Live by Faith

Now the just shall live by faith: but if any man draw back, my soul shall have no pleasure in him. 39But we are not of them who draw back unto perdition; but of them that believe to the saving of the soul.

Hebrews 10:38-39

The tenth chapter of the book of Hebrews closes on a very powerful note. The writer of the book of Hebrews unmasks the secret to living a victorious life of faith within the economy of the Kingdom of God. He declares, "The Just shall live by faith!" This one statement suddenly hinges the entire Christian experience on the shoulders of "faith." History shows that the entire protestant reformation that rescued the Church from the dark ages under the monk, Martin Luther, was based upon this one Scripture. While the Roman Catholic Church was amassing wealth from commoners by selling indulgences, Luther discovered by searching the Scriptures that only faith can absolve a man of sin before God.

Martin Luther became so convinced that sinners could only be justified by faith alone that he strongly disputed the claim that freedom from God's punishment for sin could be purchased with money. He confronted indulgence salesman, Johann Tetzel, with his Ninety-Five Theses in 1517. The writer of the book of Hebrews makes it staggeringly clear: we are justified by faith but we also are called to live by faith once we are forgiven. Based upon the above passage of Scripture, below is a summary of why the just must live by faith.

❖ Sinful men can only be justified by faith in the face of a holy God.

❖ Faith is the only thing that can keep us from sliding back into our old sinful nature.

❖ Faith is the only way to please God.

❖ Faith is the only way we can navigate through the storms of life.

FAITH, THE CURRENCY OF THE KINGDOM

PERHAPS, there is no chapter in the Holy Bible more widely used by Christ's universal Body like the eleventh chapter of the book of Hebrews. This chapter is rightly named the "Faith Chapter of the Bible." Thousands of faith messages have been preached from this famous chapter on "Faith." But unfortunately, this famous faith chapter is often treated as a stand-alone chapter independent of the Apostle Paul's primary intent for penning the book of Hebrews. But this approach only robs the chapter and those who read it of its deeper meaning. This chapter in its proper context was intended to emphasize the fact that living under the New Covenant and the Order of Melchizedek priesthood of the Lord Jesus Christ is an ongoing act of faith. This is because the Order of Melchizedek is an eternal, spiritual and heavenly priesthood, which cannot be discerned with the physical senses. Functioning in this divine priesthood requires that we *"Walk by Faith and not by Sight!" Exacting the spiritual benefits of the New Covenant also requires that we walk by faith and not by sight.*

Now, Faith is…

> *Now faith is the substance of things hoped for, the evidence of things not seen.*
>
> Hebrews 11:1

The first thing that the great apostle to the Church teaches us about faith is that:

1. ***Faith only functions in the moment called "NOW!"***
   In other words, "Faith" functions best when we allow

ourselves to become captivated by all that the LORD has made readily available to us, within the confines of His eternal NOW! Faith cannot be relegated to the "Past" and neither can it be postponed for sometime in the "Future!" The moment we do so, it is no longer the "God-kind of Faith." Such a "Faith" is actually "Unbelief" in reverse, because it supposes that God is NOT all sufficient to meet our needs the moment we present them to Him..

2. ***Faith is the substance of things hoped for!*** This means that contrary to those who a make mockery of people of faith, real faith can be substantiated. Faith is both tangible and scalable. It is as tangible as the Law of Gravity even though both are invisible Laws of the Kingdom of God that govern certain aspects of God's creation. But Faith as a governing principle transcends the Law of Gravity because it can impact spiritual beings and substances that operate beyond the parameters of time and space as we know it. This is why a person who is "rich in Faith" is rich indeed!

3. ***Faith gains substance the moment hope springs out of the fountains of the human heart!*** This is why "Hope" is critical to "Faith." There can be no faith where the embers of hope have been quenched. This is why every demonic technology is ultimately designed to rob the human heart of its sparkle of hope. When any person believes that their situation is "hopeless", they separate themselves from the spiritual benefits that God has made available to people who have faith in His Word. This is why I loathe legalistic minded pastors who preach and teach condemnation into the hearts of their listeners. Such teachings can only aid the enemy in stealing hope from the hearts and minds of people who desperately need to see a move of God in

their lives. But when the life giving Word of God is preached, "hope" rises in the hearts of the hearers, and faith gains its spiritual substance and begins substantiating itself in time.

4. This final quality of "Faith" is what makes it quite revolutionary. *Not only is Faith, the substance of things hoped for, it is also the evidence of the very things that make up its substance.* The word evidence is very telling. It removes true biblical faith from the grey areas of presumption that plague the career gambler at the Casino. The gambler relies on unsubstantiated "chance" but has no real evidence to support his chances at the gambling table. The Webster dictionary defines "Evidence" as follows... *"Data presented to a court or jury in proof of the facts in issue and which may include the testimony of witnesses, records, documents, or objects."* It is clear that a person who walks by "Faith" does not at any given moment relegate his or her life to "Chance." The evidence that his or her faith offers in substantiating all that is "hoped for" is the "undying faithfulness of God" to His Word. In this regard, Faith, can then reach into the portals of history and point at everything God did in the past for people who placed their faith in Him and in His Word. This aspect of "Faith" is the reason the Apostle Paul includes the testimonies of dead saints who proved for themselves the undying faithfulness of God to His Word.

FAITH CANNOT BE RELEGATED TO THE "PAST" AND NEITHER CAN IT BE POSTPONED FOR SOMETIME IN THE "FUTURE!"

Faith's Report

For by it the elders obtained a good report.

Hebrews 11:2

The second thing that the Apostle Paul tells us about "Faith" is that faith creates a "good report" in the lives of people who have it. This means that "Faith" is the only thing necessary to pass any spiritual "Test" that comes our way. When I was in high school, I would become very anxious before the results of the last class test were announced. I knew that I had studied hard, but I just never knew if the answers I gave were exactly what my class teacher was looking for. My happiness knew no bounds once I discovered that my report card was quite impressive. This was mostly because I knew that my very strict father did not take kindly to me bringing a bad report card on my schoolwork. Once, he gave me a much-needed butt whipping for bringing home a very bad school report card. I never did it again.

Fortunately we do not have to worry about how our report card will look like if we *"Walk by Faith and not by sight!"* Faith always guarantees us a good report before God. When everyone around is saying, "I am sick," we say, "I am healed by His stripes." Faith does not bring an evil report. An evil report is any report that diminishes the power of God in the eyes of His people. The ten spies who went to spy out the Promised Land with Caleb and Joshua brought an evil report and caused the people of Israel to stumble (Numbers 13). These ten spies shifted the eyes of the children of Israel from the "power of God" to the "size and power of their enemies." As a result, that entire generation of Israelites who came out of Egypt died in the wilderness. God only spared Joshua and Caleb who never lost their faith in God.

Faith Brings Understanding

Through faith we understand that the worlds were framed by the word of God, so that things which are seen were not made of things which do appear.

Hebrews 11:3

The third thing that the Apostle Paul tells us about "Faith" is that "Faith" brings us into the understanding of the invisible elements of creation. Faith helps us to understand the spiritual connection between "invisible spiritual elements" and "visible elements of matter." Faith helps us to understand that whatever is "visible" is the brainchild of an invisible spiritual entity or formation. When we see "love" demonstrated on earth it is because "Love" does exist as a spiritual substance of real value, even though it cannot be discerned with the naked eye.

Furthermore, "Faith" helps us to understand that everything visible was created by invisible spiritual raw materials. This is due to the fact that God is a Spirit and He existed as "Himself" before He created our physical planet. Secondarily, God created the Heavens before He created our physical planet. This is why heavenly things have a profound influence on our world of matter than the other way round. Unfortunately, this kind of understanding of Creation can never be found by looking into a "Test tube" inside our highly advanced laboratories.

If we agree with the Apostle's conclusion that all visible matter is lower forms of much higher spiritual elements, our agreement begs the following important questions.

1. If this principle truly holds, what heavenly priesthood did the earthly Levitical priesthood imitate?

2. How can there be a lower earthly priestly Order here on earth unless it is preceded by a "higher spiritual priestly Order?"

It is now abundantly clear why the Apostle Paul devotes much of his time in the book of Hebrews contrasting the two priesthoods. In his apostolic dissertations, he makes it abundantly clear that one of the two priesthoods (Levi) is earthly, while the other (the Melchizedek priesthood) is heavenly. Consequently only by "Faith" can we truly come to understand and accept this powerful eternal priesthood.

CHRIST JESUS OUR ROYAL HIGH PRIEST

Faith Frames Our World

Through faith we understand that the worlds were framed by the word of God, so that things, which are seen, were not made of things, which do appear.

Hebrews 11:3

The fourth thing that the Apostle Paul tells us about "Faith" is "Faith Frames our World!" This is a very important statement. Misunderstanding the spiritual implications of this statement can sentence believers to a life outside our "full inheritance in Christ." We will find ourselves "Surviving instead of Thriving!" We have all been in homes and offices with framed pictures hanging on walls. In each case, the parameter of the picture is contained with the dimensions of the "Picture Frame." In other words, the "Picture" is trapped with dimensions of the "Frame" that contains it.

When it comes to the quality of life we are living in the economy of the Kingdom of God, the dimensions of our spiritual inheritance are determined and governed by the size and quality of our "Faith." When it comes to "Faith" God is not a respecter of persons. I know of Christians who are living like kings in Africa, while I also know of Christians in America who are living in poverty-infested shelters. In many instances, "Faith" is the "Frame" that has framed the world that they live in. This statement might sound arrogant, but it is an undeniable biblical truth. "We can change the picture of our world when we change and expand our Faith-frame."

Faith Defines Giving

By faith Abel offered unto God a more excellent sacrifice than Cain, by which he obtained witness that he was righteous, God testifying of his gifts: and by it he being dead yet speaketh.

Hebrews 11:4

The writer of Hebrews now moves further into explaining how "Faith" affects the different aspects of the life of a believer. The first aspect in the believer's life that will experience a radical shift once the believer begins to operate by "Faith" is how they give. Giving is a very important spiritual activity and technology for securing the future destiny. The absence of "Giving" will doom any marriage, friendship or business partnership.

Giving is such an important spiritual technology of the Kingdom of God that it is intrinsically built into the very nature of God. God is "Love" and love cannot exist without "Giving," just like "Faith without works is dead." But ever since the fall of Adam and Eve, giving has been a struggle for most humans. The sin nature is bent on "self centeredness" which is contrary to the selfless and generous nature of God. In order to facilitate "Giving" after the fall of man, "Faith" is a must and not an option. Faith allows us to give beyond the dictates of our fallen nature and enjoy the spiritual benefits of giving from a heart inflamed with the Love of God.

Faith for Translations

By faith Enoch was translated that he should not see death; and was not found, because God had translated him: for before his translation he had this testimony, that he pleased God.

Hebrews 11:5

The writer of the book of Hebrews goes further in his faith dissertation and introduces us to another very fascinating aspect of "Faith": "Faith for Translations." We are told that by faith Enoch the servant of the Lord was "translated that he should not see death!" This statement gives us a clue as to the spiritual nature of translations. "Translations" involve supernatural travel through "spiritual portals" that defy and transcend both "time and space." Dying is the natural way of leaving planet earth and entering into the heavenly realm; but Enoch bypassed this natural process, because he had faith that God could translate him.

WHEN IT COMES TO "FAITH" *God* IS NOT A RESPECTER OF PERSONS.

I believe that as the global Body of Christ enters into the spiritual benefits and covenantal realities of the New Covenant and Christ's Melchizedek Priesthood, many more believers will be translated through the portals of time and space. This prophetic company of breakthrough believers will know their God and do exploits. Air travel is not the only way to travel from the United States to India to preach the Gospel of the Kingdom. God can translate His people from one nation to the next, if He so chooses. This is exactly what happened to Philip, the evangelist, in Acts chapter 8.

And when they came up out of the water, the Spirit of the Lord [suddenly] caught away Philip; and the eunuch saw him no more, and he went on his way rejoicing. 40But Philip was found at Azotus, and passing on he preached the good news (Gospel) to all the towns until he reached Caesarea.

Acts 8:39-40 (AMP)

Without Faith

But without faith it is impossible to please him: for he that cometh to God must believe that he is, and that he is a rewarder of them that diligently seek him.

Hebrews 11:6

The great apostle to the Church finally introduces us to the apex of faith. He presents a fundamentally different view of faith that will surprise many proponents of the "Word of the faith movement." Faith in its primary construct is not about getting things from God. True biblical faith is not rooted in the desire to possess more material possessions, but in pleasing God. Faith then has as its primary objective: the quest to please God. Too much of the faith messages that are taught in many Christian circles leave one feeling as if faith absolves the believer from having to truly trust God. I have met many well-meaning Christians who have more faith in their faith than they do in God himself. True faith according to the writer of the book of Hebrews is always towards God. Pleasing God is the objective of true biblical faith. So we must strive to use our faith, not to possess God's promises, but to possess the God of the promises.

What the apostle Paul is proposing here is a radically different view of faith than that for which we are accustomed. We teach faith from a perspective that makes man the center of operation, but what Paul is suggesting here is a view of faith that makes God the axis of the entire operation. This radical view of faith will force us to know God intimately before we ask Him for things. The expression, "for he that cometh to God must believe that he is" presents us with another radically different view of faith. True biblical faith brings us to God and convinces us of the fact of His eternal existence without requiring physical proof of the existence of the divine essence in all that is in nature. Faith's secondary objective is to persuade us that God "IS." The word "IS" in the verse implies that God is the life force behind all living things. In Him, we truly live, move and have our being.

Unfortunately, in many predominantly Word of Faith circles, the expression, "for he that cometh to God must believe that He is", has morphed into, for he that cometh to God must believe that He HAS. This unfortunate transition has caused many proponents of faith to look at a God as a divine "Sugar Daddy" who exists for the sole purpose of meeting our endless needs and fantasies. While the exercise of faith as a means of pleasing God can bring us into a place of great material prosperity, the use of faith to acquire material prosperity has never been the primary objective of God. It goes without saying that God rewards the sacrifice of obedience with the supernatural provision necessary to satisfy the demands of His kingdom assignment upon our lives. This does NOT in any way mean that we cannot use our faith to believe for material things. But so many of God's children are caught up in such fleshly pursuits, that pleasing God is no longer the primary motivation fueling their faith. The true exercise of faith is supposed to bring us closer to God rather than things.

TRUE BIBLICAL FAITH IS NOT ROOTED IN THE DESIRE TO POSSESS MORE MATERIAL POSSESSIONS, BUT IN PLEASING *God.*

Faith Leads to Salvation

By faith Noah, being warned of God of things not seen as yet, moved with fear, prepared an ark to the saving of his house; by the which he condemned the world, and became heir of the righteousness which is by faith.

Hebrews 11:7

The writer of the book of Hebrews now tells us that faith leads to salvation. By faith Noah saved his family from a devastating global flood that destroyed all living things (Genesis 7) by finding shelter in a larger than life Ark. Noah's ark was a prophetic representation of Christ, the Ark of our salvation. Paul's statement connecting salvation to faith was a revolutionary idea for the Hebrews who had lived for centuries under a Covenant that promised salvation by works. The concept of salvation by faith is also revolutionary for fallen mankind who is inherently attracted to salvation through the power of his good deeds. This is why God raises men like Martin Luther to pull the Church out of the dark ages. The Church entered the dark ages when man's inherent desire to engineer his own plan of salvation took center stage.

"**Martin Luther** born November 10, 1483 was a German monk, priest, professor of theology and iconic figure of the Protestant Reformation.[1] He strongly disputed the claim that freedom from God's punishment for sin could be purchased with money.

He confronted the indulgent salesman, Johann Tetzel, with his Ninety-Five Theses in 1517. His refusal to retract all of his writings at the demand of Pope Leo X in 1520 and the Holy Roman Emperor Charles V at the Diet of Worms in 1521 resulted in his excommunication by the pope and condemnation as an outlaw by the Emperor.

Luther taught that <u>salvation</u> is not earned by good deeds, but received only as a free gift of God's grace through <u>faith</u> in <u>Jesus Christ</u> as our redeemer from sin. <u>His theology</u> challenged the authority of the <u>Pope</u> of the <u>Roman Catholic Church</u> by teaching that the <u>Bible</u> is the <u>only source</u> of <u>divinely</u> revealed knowledge and opposed <u>sacerdotalism</u> by considering <u>all baptized Christians to be a holy priesthood.</u>" *Sacerdotalism is the belief that propitiatory sacrifices for sin require the intervention of a priest. That is, it is the belief that a special, segregated order of men, called the priesthood, are the only ones who can commune directly with God or the gods. This system of the priesthood is exemplified by the priests in the Old Testament.[1] (Quote from Wikipedia)*

"Salvation by grace through faith", is the simple revolutionary truth that Martin Luther restored back to the church's collective consciousness, which resulted in the greatest protestant reformation since the day of Pentecost. Millions of people across Europe and Asia were swept into the Kingdom of God by this one readjustment to the theology of the church. But this was to be expected. A holy stamped ensued once lost souls, who were unduly burdened by the legalistic traditions of men, realized that salvation from sin relied solely on having faith in the finished work of Christ on the cross. Paul uses the story of Noah, a well-known historical figure, as an example to the people of Israel to demonstrate that even for Noah, salvation from the flood was by faith and not by his own works.

Faith to Answer the Call of God

By faith Abraham, when he was called to go out into a place, which he should after receive for an inheritance, obeyed; and he went out, not knowing whither he went.

Hebrews 11:8

The writer of the book of Hebrews now introduces us to another very important aspect to the believer's walk of faith. *Faith is for answering the <u>Call of God</u> upon our lives.* Since the Apostle Paul uses Abraham to demonstrate this dynamic aspect of faith, we will mine Abraham's life for nuggets that are related to this aspect of faith.

By examining Abraham's life and the above passage of Scripture, we come up with the following:

- The Call of God: is always directed towards an individual even though the call itself has far reaching corporate ramifications. This aspect of faith means that no other human being can answer the call of God upon our lives if we refuse to respond. Since the Call of God is private, it truly requires faith to launch out.

- The Call of God: requires a corresponding action on our part. This is why faith is an essential ingredient in this whole process. The "action" to obey the call of God may involve quitting a job that pays well in order to move to a different state or country to which the Spirit is leading us. The legendary healing evangelist, John G. Lake, gave up a very lucrative Chicago law firm in order to move to South Africa.

- The Call of God: is always to a place and the people who are domiciled in that space of real estate. God never calls us to "things", but He always calls us to people and the land that those people live in. This is why people who treasure "things" more than God's purpose never fulfill the totality of their God given assignment. They develop a spiritual paralysis over time.

- The Call of God: unfolds over time, revealing many aspects of the Call that we were not fully aware of when we got started. Details such as how God is going to provide for us once we jump into our call, as well as how people will respond to our God given assignment. These important, but missing details can cause stress in the carnal mind that requires physical proof before responding in total obedience. This is why faith is such a critical factor during this process. In the absence of these critical details, our faith in God becomes the substance that we can hold onto, until the time of total manifestation of what God has promised us.

The Sojourner's Faith

*By faith he sojourned in the land of promise, as in a strange country, dwelling in tabernacles with Isaac and Jacob, the heirs with him of the same promise: **10**For he looked for a city which hath foundations, whose builder and maker is God.*

Hebrews 11:9-10

The writer of the book of Hebrews now introduces us to another important aspect of the believer's walk of faith. We are told that even though Abraham was the custodian of the Covenant of promise, he sojourned in the land of the promise as though he was in a strange country. Abraham was a "sojourner" in the land of promise. A sojourner is a person who knows that he is in a particular place for a temporary stay. Even though we live here on earth, our citizenship is heavenly. Living in this world, surrounded by both its luxuries and its struggles requires that we have the faith of a sojourner. A sojourner never gets so entangled with the affairs of the place he or she is in, to the degree that they forget their country of origin.

Abraham was living in great wealth and luxury in the land of promise but never lost sight of the fact that he was in the world but not of this world. Many of today's believers do not have the sojourner's faith, so they are failing to escape the entrapments of this temporal world order. There is absolutely nothing wrong with prospering in this world, provided we do not fall in love with the things and spirit of this world. Joseph lived in great luxury and affluence in Egypt, but he never forgot the upward call towards the God of his forefathers, Abraham, Isaac and Jacob. Everything Egypt had to offer paled in comparison to the things that God has stored in heaven for all those who love Him. After many years of apostolic service to the Lord, I am convinced that every born again believer needs an ample amount of the "sojourner's faith."

SACERDOTALISM IS THE BELIEF THAT PROPITIATORY SACRIFICES FOR SIN REQUIRE THE INTERVENTION OF A PRIEST.

Faith for Conception

Through faith also Sara herself received strength to conceive seed, and was delivered of a child when she was past age, because she judged him faithful who had promised. 12Therefore sprang there even of one, and him as good as dead, so many as the stars of the sky in multitude, and as the sand which is by the sea shore innumerable.

Hebrews 11:11-12

Generations have been captivated by the story of Abraham and Sarah, who engaged an extra-ordinary God in the spirit of total obedience. A central issue in God's promise to Abraham was the promise of the birth of a child of promise through the womb of a woman who was many years past menopause. When the Lord visited Abraham's tent (Genesis 18) on his way to visit Sodom, He promised that He would bless Abraham with a child who would be conceived in Sarah's womb. The promise that God gave them seemed to be so far-fetched that both recipients struggled to receive the promise. Sarah laughed hysterically while Abraham interceded before God for Ishmael to take the place of Isaac.

Abraham and Sarah's initial response of unbelief did not dissuade the Lord from His eternal purpose. He proceeded to make a decree that within a year, Sarah would be nursing a baby boy. Within the year specified by the Lord's promise, something supernatural happened to Sarah. She received strength to conceive seed by faith. A transforming governmental type of faith rushed into her spirit and body and quickened her mortal body. This transformative fusion of faith reversed the sentence of time on her womb. My dear friend, Dr. Gordon Bradshaw, has a very scholastic explanation of what happened to Sarah's womb in his bestselling book, *"Authority for Assignment: Releasing God's Government in the Marketplace."*

> "Sarah, Abraham's wife, is known for the supernatural comeback she experienced at an extremely old age. She believed God that she would bear a child and provide Abraham with an heir. The odds were against her ever conceiving and bearing a child but because of the prevailing power of God in her life, she accomplished the purpose of God and gave birth to Isaac. She created a powerful supernatural down-line for the economy of the kingdom."

I am convinced that the closer the church gets to the consummation of the ages in Christ Jesus, millions of born again believers are going to receive a supernatural infusion of faith to "conceive whatever the Lord wants to birth through them." I am convinced that the best ideas have not yet been conceived. But the time of supernatural conception of God ideas is now upon us. God is going to impregnate the Body of Christ with multi-billion dollar ideas and witty inventions that will transform the economies of nations overnight.

Died in Faith

These all died in faith, not having received the promises, but having seen them afar off, and were persuaded of them, and embraced them, and confessed that they were strangers and pilgrims on the earth .14For they that say such things declare plainly that they seek a country.

Hebrews 11:13-14

Ever since the fall of man in the Garden of Eden, the fear of death has terrorized man's consciousness. The inherent desire in all humans to live forever, coupled with the uncertainty of the nature of life after death, has caused millions to dread the very thought of death. Nothing can unmask the inherent fear of death that most humans share than at the funeral of loved ones. The tear drenched faces of the mourners and the somberness of funerals tell it all. Man hates death, but it is nevertheless an inconvenient truth that he has to deal with in his search for immortality.

But God in His creative and redemptive genius finds ways to use even our mistakes to accentuate His eternal purpose in our lives. The writer of the book of Hebrews in the above passage introduces us to a very powerful concept of "dying by faith." It would seem like a contradiction of sorts, for death and faith to be mentioned in the same sentence. The age-old tension between "Faith" and "death" has been duly noted in the corridors of human history. But the Apostle Paul seemingly ignores this perplexing tension and offers us a side of the believer's walk of faith that can harmonize with the finality of the death technology.

In the above passage of Scripture, the writer of the book of Hebrews seems to suggest two kinds of "dying by faith."

1. In its first embassy, *the concept of dying by faith* refers to the attitude that all followers of Christ should have when death comes to retire them from planet earth. This attitude is not an attitude of fear and despondency. It is an attitude driven by the living hope that those who die in Christ (1 Corinthians 15) will also be resurrected unto life eternal at the consummation of the ages in Christ. It is an attitude of dealing with death that affirms the fact that this mortal body shall soon put on immortality. The writer of Hebrews makes it quite clear that all the Patriarchs died in faith, not having received all the promises. But they died believing that what God promised them would be completed in them beyond the reach of the grave. This is why I believe that the death of any one of His saints is NOT a funeral; it is a glorious celebration of a glorious homegoing. To be absent in the body is to be present with the Lord.

2. In its second embassy, the *concept of dying by faith* denotes the *death to self* that we all need to go through

in order to embrace the will of God. It takes faith for us to embrace the crucifixion of our old selfish nature on the Cross of Christ. Carrying the cross of self-denial will test and stretch the limits of our faith. Perhaps this would explain why many Christian churches are no longer preaching the message of the cross. Telling Christians who are obsessed with self that they need to crucify self is not a very sexy message. But true biblical faith will introduce us to the sanctification that comes by *"dying by faith to our own agenda." Christians who embrace this process will discover the joy of living a life free of the dictates of the inflaming passions of the flesh.*

The Point of No Return

And truly, if they had been mindful of that country from whence they came out, they might have had opportunity to have returned .15But now they desire a better country, that is, an heavenly: wherefore God is not ashamed to be called their God: for he hath prepared for them a city.

Hebrews 11:15-16

While we vigorously celebrate the triumph of the Christ over sin, death and the Devil, we yet live in a fallen world. Living for God in a world driven by the engines of chaos and the fallen demonic powers is no cakewalk. Sometimes the journey of faith, in an environment that is hostile to faith, has caused some Christians to renegotiate their destiny.

A Test of Faith

By faith Abraham, when he was tried, offered up Isaac: and he that had received the promises offered up his only begotten son, 18Of whom it was said, That in Isaac shall thy seed be called: 19Accounting that God was able to raise him up, even from the dead; from whence also he received him in a figure.

Hebrews 11:17-19

Since every believer is called by God to walk by faith and not by sight, the Lord will initiate, or allow, circumstances to test the credibility of our faith. But great teachers do not give their students a test on a subject that he or she never taught them. Since faith is the true spiritual currency of the Kingdom of God, God will go to great lengths to ensure the authenticity of our faith.

BUT *God* IN HIS CREATIVE AND REDEMPTIVE GENIUS FINDS WAYS TO USE EVEN OUR MISTAKES TO ACCENTUATE HIS ETERNAL PURPOSE IN OUR LIVES.

God knows that we can never accomplish anything significant in His Kingdom without faith. God was not going to let Abraham wear the title of "father of faith" without earning the title through a series of God orchestrated faith based trials. Perhaps the biggest test of faith that Abraham ever went through was the offering of Isaac. Abraham and Sarah had waited for a child of their own for decades before Sarah received the strength to conceive seed in her old age. No doubt, they were both deeply attached to their new born, especially Sarah, since Isaac was her one and only pregnancy. So when God told Abraham to sacrifice Isaac on Mount Moriah, the divine request pushed his faith to its very limit. God's request was so unusual that Abraham could not bring himself to tell his wife, Sarah. When he left his house to head towards the place of the sacrifice, he left his wife with the impression that they were just going to worship. How many of us would have gone through with it? Each step Abraham took towards the Mountains of Moriah, the heavier the steps became and yet he pressed on.

Why would God place him in such a predicament? The answer is painfully obvious. God wanted to make sure that Abraham did not love the promise more than he loved the promise giver. Unfortunately, humans have a tendency of loving the promise more than the one who gave it. God will never place second to something that He gave us. But the million-dollar question is why did Abraham go through with it? The passage in Hebrews 11:17 contains the reason Abraham went through with it. According to the passage, Abraham made two very important assumptions that helped him stay the course. These life-giving assumptions must be incorporated into the spiritual life of every believer who desires to walk with God.

❖ He knew that whatever happened, God had already promised him that he would bless the nations through his son, Isaac.

❖ He reasoned that since Isaac was a child of promise, God would raise him from the dead if he killed him on the altar of obedience.

Faith to Bless

By faith Isaac blessed Jacob and Esau concerning things to come. 21By faith Jacob, when he was a dying, blessed both the sons of Joseph; and worshipped, leaning upon the top of his staff.

Hebrews 11:20-21

We live in a culture that is attracted to negativity. Even in the news media misfortune sells faster than good news. Stories involving sexual scandals dominate the news cycle more than stories of fidelity. In such an environment, it is no wonder it is easier for us to curse people than to bless them. But the Scriptures are clear that "blessing someone" is a higher spiritual technology than cursing a person. However, blessing anyone requires faith. The reason is staggeringly simple but deeply profound.

Pronouncing a blessing on another person requires us to invoke the participation of a higher being who can confer the desired blessing. This higher being is the Lord of creation Himself.

The passage above tells us that when Isaac blessed his sons, Jacob and Esau, concerning things that had not yet manifested, he did it by faith. Isaac told Jacob in the pronounced blessing that God would sustain him with plenty of corn and wine years before this event actually manifested. Such an act truly requires that the pronouncer of the blessing has faith that God will back up what he or she is pronouncing.

Since Jacob had been the recipient of a blessing that had been conferred by faith, he knew firsthand the power of a pronounced blessing by a man of faith. When Jacob knew that he was dying, he summoned his favorite son, Joseph, to his bedside. Joseph brought his two sons, Manasseh and Ephraim with him. Jacob asked Joseph to bring the two boys closer so he could pronounce a blessing upon them. Joseph made sure that his firstborn son, Manasseh was positioned next to his father's right hand, while the younger son, Ephraim was dutifully positioned on Jacob's left side. This is because the blessing of the right-hand was normally conferred on the firstborn son. Even though Jacob was now practically blind, he crossed his hands into an X formation, so that his right-hand was placed on Ephraim and his left on Manasseh. Joseph was very displeased with his father's formation and tried to change it. But the dying patriarch refused and declared that the Ephraim will be greater in blessedness than his older brother. Jacob never lived to see the fulfillment of his pronounced blessing; but history shows that the tribe of Ephraim became greater in both stature and blessing in the nation of Israel than the tribe of Manasseh. This proves that blessing people by the Spirit requires us to have faith especially when we are pronouncing a special blessing on people that we would normally sidestep.

Faith Filled Bones

By faith Joseph, when he died, made mention of the departing of the children of Israel; and gave commandment concerning his bones. Hebrews 11:22

Perhaps the greatest act of faith that the patriarch Joseph ever demonstrated during his divinely inspired life was his last official business. When he knew that the technology of death was knocking on his door, he gathered the elders of Israel and bound them to a solemn oath. This oath was the most sacred covenant that came out of the people of Israel's time in Egypt. Joseph looked the elders in the eye and told them that God was coming for them as a people. God was going to take the children of Israel out of Egypt, back to the land of promise.

Joseph was so sure of this prophetic future event that he made the elders of the children of Israel promise to take his bones with them to the Promise Land. What was even more dramatic about Joseph's unusual request is that Joseph, as the second most important person in Egypt, was buried in the same pyramids that the Egyptian Pharaohs were buried in. How was a nation of slaves going to get access to the tombs of the Pharaohs in order to meet their obligation? This in itself was mission impossible. But after ten nation-shaking plagues, the Egyptians were left so dispirited that they were more than willing to break years of established royal protocol. They willingly allowed Moses to access the revered tombs of the Pharaohs to take out the bones of Joseph. I have Goosebumps just thinking about this. When the children of Israel walked out of Egypt, they had in their possession the "faith filled bones" of Joseph with them. Wow!

Faith for Divine Protection

By faith Moses, when he was born, was hid three months of his parents, because they saw he was a proper child; and they were not afraid of the king's commandment. 24By faith Moses, when he was come to years, refused to be called the son of Pharaoh's daughter;

Hebrews 11:23-24

From the closure of the gates of Eden to the opening of the gates of the New Jerusalem, the world has had more than its fair share of tyrants, bullies, villains and devils. When Cain rose and killed his brother in the fields, it was clear that the post-Edenic world that we now live in is also a very dangerous world. One glimpse at most headline news alerts will quickly unmask just how dangerous our world has become. The righteous in many instances are like tilapia swimming in a pond full of sharks.

It does not take a rocket scientist to figure out that in such a volatile environment we stand in dire need of divine protection. The Bible tells us that He (God) who watches over Israel neither sleeps nor slumbers. The writer of Hebrews tells us that nothing is hidden from His sight. This is why when He is our shield and protector we can sleep peacefully. We can also navigate the Shark tank in relative peace and safety. The writer of the book of Hebrews tells us that the great lawgiver, Moses, was born into a very hostile environment. The Pharaoh at the time of his birth had ordered his subjects to kill every Jewish baby boy. The consequence of disobeying the decree of the Pharaoh was instant death.

Moses was born when thousands of male Jewish babies had been slaughtered at birth despite the screaming protests of the infant's mothers. The writer of Hebrews tells us that when Moses was born his mother had faith that God would supernaturally protect her new infant from the King's irrevocable decree. Moses's mother, and his sister, Miriam, had faith for divine protection in a very bloody environment. The Lord did not disappoint the faith of these two daring Jewish women. God supernaturally protected Moses from sure death when he was born. The Lord also protected the young infant from drowning in the Nile or worse, being eaten by crocodiles, while the baby was sailing the treacherous river in a papyrus basket. When the infant's papyrus basket washed up ashore in front of Pharaoh's daughter, God protected the infant from suffering the fury of the Pharaoh. To the contrary, divine providence made it possible for Moses to be raised in the Palace of the same man who was the author of the treacherous satanic law. Glory to God in the highest! Like Moses's mother, God wants born again believers to have faith in His ability to protect them in this dangerous world.

Faith to Bear the Reproach of Christ

Choosing rather to suffer affliction with the people of God, than to enjoy the pleasures of sin for a season; 26Esteeming the reproach of Christ greater riches than the treasures in Egypt: for he had respect unto the recompence of the reward. Hebrews 11:25-26

The eleventh chapter of the book of Hebrews is truly the "Faith Chapter" of the Holy writ. We finally tread upon the type of faith that is sadly lacking in so many Christian circles around the world, especially in First world nations. This faith is the faith to "bear the reproach of Christ." We are living in the age of the Church of Laodicea. It is a Church that worships fame and fortune at the expense of complete abandonment to the cause and person of Christ.

The writer of the book of Hebrews tells us that by faith, Moses, even though he was brought up in the immense luxuries of the Palace, chose to suffer shame with the people of God rather than to enjoy the pleasures of sin for a season. Unfortunately, many of today's Christians who are obsessed with living a life of faith without conflict would fail this test miserably. But Moses believed that the reproach of Christ is of far greater riches than anything this world could offer him in terms of worldly comforts. I am convinced that as many born again Christians rediscover the Melchizedek priesthood of Jesus Christ there will be many more Christians who will choose to suffer with the godly in their generation instead of having their names on man's billboards.

Faith that Overcomes Fear

By faith he forsook Egypt, not fearing the wrath of the king: for he endured, as seeing him who is invisible.

Hebrews 11:27

Since the fall of man, we live in a world of conflicting and competing philosophies. It is a world of conflicting opposites. Light versus darkness, good versus evil and so forth, but one of the first evils to enter our world after the fall of Adam and Eve is fear. This unholy emotion is one of the first things that Adam and Eve experienced. This fear was so overpowering that it deepened the separation between Adam and the Lord. While faith is undoubtedly the currency of the Kingdom of Heaven, fear is truly the currency of that fallen demonic kingdom.

> MOSES BELIEVED THAT THE REPROACH OF CHRIST IS OF FAR GREATER RICHES THAN ANYTHING THIS WORLD COULD OFFER HIM IN TERMS OF WORLDLY COMFORTS.

Fear has kept many from obeying God. Fear has kept many from their God-given destinies. Fear has kept many from the mate that the Lord has or had for them. The writer of Proverbs tells us that the fear of man is a snare to the soul. But as the demonic machinery gathers momentum through time-continuum, mankind has been assaulted by more fears, both real and imagined. But do not despair because the writer of the book of Hebrews tells us that there is a faith that overcomes all fear. We can triumph in the face of insurmountable odds. This fear conquering faith gathers its strength by keeping us focused on the immeasurable power of Him (God) who governs the invisible or spiritual world. We will quickly realize that greater is He who is in us than He (Sin and the Devil) who is the world.

Redeeming Faith

Through faith he kept the passover, and the sprinkling of blood, lest he that destroyed the firstborn should touch them. 31By faith the harlot Rahab perished not with them that believed not, when she had received the spies with peace.

Hebrews 11:28, 31

The writer of the book of Hebrews now engages us in a faith conversation that was the sole engine behind Martin Luther's reformation. After the Church fell into the dark ages, the question of how one acquired salvation for the soul was sold to the highest bidder. In order to raise money to build some monstrous Papal edifices, the Catholic church of that era began to sell indulgences to those who could afford to pay for them. As with everything controlled by money, the poor got the short end of the stick. While the rich and powerful could afford to buy highly priced indulgences that guaranteed them a sure path into Abraham's bosom, the poor dreaded the afterlife.

A monk by the name of Martin Luther became infused with a divine revelation concerning the salvation of the soul. He discovered that salvation of the soul could never be achieved by works or by the buying of useless indulgences. He discovered that all sinners are justified by faith alone, in the finished work of Christ. Martin Luther's revolutionary revelation brought much persecution on his person but it also brought the Church out of the dark ages. The writer of the book of Hebrews tells us of "redeeming faith." He shows us that the children of Israel kept the Passover by faith when they sprinkled the blood on their doorposts to avoid the death angel. It was faith in God and the sprinkled blood that saved their homes from suffering the death of the firstborn, while all of Egypt mourned the loss of the same. For Christians today redemption from sin is still a matter of having faith in Christ and His shed blood. We cannot secure the blessings of redemption through our own human effort.

Faith to do Exploits

By faith they passed through the Red sea as by dry land: which the Egyptians assaying to do were drowned. 30By faith the walls of Jericho fell down, after they were compassed about seven days.

Hebrews 11:29-30

Without a doubt, the Bible would have been like many of the boring and lifeless sacred texts of many other world religions had it not been for the recorded exploits of faith of men and women who dared to take God at His Word. The Holy Bible is written around the faith journey of ordinary men and women who were intercepted by an extraordinary God. The faith and obedience, or lack thereof, of these ordinary men and women spawns the pages of the Holy Scriptures. I truly believe that it is difficult, if not impossible, for a believer to operate under the Order of Melchizedek if he or she struggles with the concept of approaching God by faith. The Melchizedek priesthood of Jesus Christ is a heavenly priesthood, hidden from the naked eye's view. Without faith we will struggle to believe that we are truly kings and priests unto God in the Spirit even though in the natural we are not dressed in attire that would suggest the same.

The writer of the book of Hebrews has already told us in Hebrews 11:6 that without faith, it is impossible to please God, making "faith" the true currency of the Kingdom of God. The writer of the book of Hebrews is quick to attribute the great miracles of the Bible to the faith of the men and women that were so used by God. He has us take note that the crossing of the Red Sea by the children of Israel was accomplished by faith. Over one million Israelites crossed the Red Sea as though they were walking on dry land. The writer of the book of Hebrews also tells us that the impregnable walls of the ancient City of Jericho fell into smothering rumbles because of the faith of Joshua and the children of Israel. The great scientific minds of our time grapple with the challenge of believing the stories of the Bible in light of scientific data that would suggest otherwise. But faith transcends the realm of human reasoning that all sciences are based on. If we are to do great exploits in the Kingdom of God, we need to loose our faith in God's limitless ability.

Heroes of Faith

And what shall I more say? for the time would fail me to tell of Gedeon, and of Barak, and of Samson, and of Jephthae; of David also, and Samuel, and of the prophets:

Hebrews 11:32

We made mention previously that the Bible is spawned around the lives of men and women of faith who engaged an extraordinary God in the spirit of total obedience. I call these men and women around which the

Bible was spawned, "Heroes of Faith." Like all heroes, these men touched the lives of the people around them and the age they lived in. The writer of the book of Hebrews lists the names of some of these Heroes of faith.

❖ He mentions Gideon, who defeated 120,000 Philistine soldiers with only 300 men who were handpicked by God.

❖ He mentions Samson, the man who was born with super human strength, the likes of which can only be found in an animated movie.

❖ He mentions the beloved King of Israel, David, the man after God's own heart. The story of David killing the Philistine giant, Goliath, with a slingshot is renowned around the nations of the world.

❖ The Bible is full of other heroes of faith, who also subdued nations, conquered kingdoms and overcame incredible odds through faith.

The Different Administrations of Faith

Who through faith subdued kingdoms, wrought righteousness, obtained promises, stopped the mouths of lions. 34Quenched the violence of fire, escaped the edge of the sword, out of weakness were made strong, waxed valiant in fight, turned to flight the armies of the aliens. 35Women received their dead raised to life again: and others were tortured, not accepting deliverance; that they might obtain a better resurrection: 36And others had trial of cruel mockings and scourgings, yea, moreover of bonds and I imprisonment: 37They were stoned, they were sawn asunder, were tempted, were slain with the sword: they wandered about in sheepskins and goatskins; being destitute, afflicted, tormented; 38(Of whom the world was not worthy:) they wandered in deserts, and in mountains, and in dens and caves of the earth.

Hebrews 11:33-38

Before wrapping up his dissertation on faith, the writer of the book of Hebrews lists the different, but essential, administrations of faith. I will list some of them below. This is by no means an exhaustive concordance on the different administrations of faith.

❖ Faith to subdue kingdoms

❖ Faith to plant the righteousness of God into a worldly Culture

❖ Faith to obtain the promises of God

❖ Faith to conceive Seed

❖ Faith to Prevail against all odds

❖ Faith to Stand strong in the face of imminent death

❖ Faith to escape demonic entrapments

Obtaining a Good Report through Faith

And these all, having obtained a good report through faith, received not the promise: 40God having provided some better thing for us, that they without us should not be made perfect.
Hebrews 11:39-40

Those of us who have ever been through formal education know the immense value of obtaining a good report. In school, a good report means that the student has mastered the teacher's lessons. A student who obtains a good report automatically qualifies to move on to higher things. A student who obtains a good report is also the delight and joy of his or her teacher. The writer of Hebrews tells us that one of the important uses of faith is for helping the believer obtain a "good report" before God. The good report obtained by our faith walk is our guarantee of also inheriting the promise.

As we come to the end of this chapter, I want to ask you a couple of questions:

❖ How is your faith walk?

❖ Are you using your faith to obtain a good report before God or are you using your faith to simply acquire stuff? Selah.

MANIFEST SONS IN THE HANDS OF A LOVING FATHER

A Great Cloud of Witnesses

Wherefore seeing we also are compassed about with so great a cloud of witnesses, let us lay aside every weight, and the sin which doth so easily beset us, and let us run with patience the race that is set before us.

Hebrews 12:1

AFTER concluding a dynamic biographical discourse on the faith heroes of the Bible in the previous chapter, the writer of the book of Hebrews shifts his focus to the "great cloud of witnesses." This great cloud of witnesses consists of all the heroes of faith who have died in the Lord and moved on to heaven, as well as living saints here on earth. The great apostle paints a portrait of a believer who is in essence living out his or her faith in front of a very interested audience of other members of the Body of Christ. For this reason, the writer of the book of Hebrews admonishes a follower of Christ to do three things, namely:

❖ **Laying aside every weight** A spiritual weight is anything that is not necessarily sinful but has the power to weigh us down and slow our movement towards the God given destiny. For instance, watching football or basketball is not necessarily sinful but if the pursuits of these activities are hindering our ability to spend time with God in prayer, then they are in effect weighing us down. In such a case we have to make a conscious decision of laying these weights down.

❖ **Laying aside besetting Sins** On the other hand, besetting sins are habitual sins that easily ensnare us. For example: it is so easy for some believers to get ensnared in outbursts of rage over the most minor of offences. For many Christians overeating is a very common besetting sin. The writer of the book of Hebrews admonishes us to take inventory of these besetting sins and lay them down at the foot of the cross.

❖ **Run the race set before us with patience.** The cumulative reason as to why followers of Christ must lay aside weights and besetting sins is because we have a race that has been set before us by the Lord Jesus Christ. We must run the race to fulfill our God given destiny but our pursuit needs to be undergirded by the force of patience. The reason we have to run the race set before us with patience is due to the fact that actualizing our God given destiny requires both time and effort. *Running our race with patience is part of the process of living out our salvation and sanctification.*

Author and Finisher of our Faith

Looking unto Jesus the author and finisher of our faith; who for the joy that was set before him endured the cross, despising the shame, and is set down at the right hand of the throne of God.

Hebrews 12:2

Perhaps one of the most profound faith statements in the book of Hebrews is the expression, "looking unto Jesus the author and finisher of our faith." As an author I profoundly appreciate the spiritual implications of this statement. Every time I write a book I first decide its purpose, which in turn determines its destiny.

Then I decide how I am going to write it, who is going to read it and how long the book will be. I also decide the content that will go into the book.

A SPIRITUAL WEIGHT IS ANYTHING THAT IS NOT NECESSARILY SINFUL BUT HAS THE POWER TO WEIGH US DOWN AND SLOW OUR MOVEMENT TOWARDS THE *God* GIVEN DESTINY.

By calling Jesus the author and finisher of our faith, the writer of the book of Hebrews is suggesting that the burden of the believer's walk of faith rests primarily on the Lord's shoulders. Just as an author of a book is largely responsible for authoring and finishing his or her work, we are the Lord's epistles read of all men. The Lord Jesus Christ who has begun a good work in us will bring it to its glorious conclusion (Philippians 1:6). Many Christians get into a "rut" when they begin to believe that the work of perfecting themselves is dependent on their religious striving. Before they know it, they become prisoners of a self-imposed legalistic approach to faith. Such an approach to faith is both spiritually toxic and emotionally draining. It makes "self" the center of our faith instead of Christ. The problem with making "self" the center of our faith is that "self" is already under the sentence of death. A life of faith driven by self will lead us into great disillusionment. This is the reason the Apostle Paul admonishes us in the above passage to look to Jesus who is the author and finisher of our faith. Looking to others or ourselves will only serve to strengthen the technology of sin and death in our lives.

Consider Him

For consider him that endured such contradiction of sinners against himself, lest ye be wearied and faint in your minds. 4Ye have not yet resisted unto blood, striving against sin.

Hebrews 12:3

The third verse of the twelfth chapter of the book of Hebrews begins with a very interesting phrase: "Consider him!" We are admonished to "consider Him!" The word consider in this phrase denotes a "thorough and thoughtful investigation" of His person and how He handled the constant opposition to His ministry from the world. The apostle uses the word "endure" in the text, which implies that Jesus did not enjoy the constant barrage of criticism that came against Him, but He still rose above it all.

I am glad the writer of the book of Hebrews uses the word "endure" because it lets me know that I do not have to enjoy the opposition of sinners against the Christ in me. But I can still live in victory over opposition from the world. The primary reason we are admonished to "Consider Him" is because it is so easy to become "weary and faint" in our minds when we face an onslaught of demonically engineered opposition from the world. Sometimes this distressing contradiction against us can come from carnal Christians who have allowed themselves to be used as tools of the enemy.

When we feel overwhelmed by demonically engineered opposition from sinners, the Apostle Paul bids us to remember that many of us have never fought with sin to the point of shedding our own blood. But the Lord Jesus Christ fought and resisted sin to the point of shedding His own blood on the cross in defense of righteousness. Since we are members of the Body of Christ, we share in His glorious victory over Sin on the cross. This means that every born again believer under the right circumstances carries the grace to resist sin unto the shedding of their own blood. The History of Christian martyrdom proves this to be the case. Thousands of born again believers were offered to food-starved lions in Roman Coliseums in plain view of pagans hungry for the sight of blood. These followers of Christ chose death over the alternative of denying their Lord and Savior. Whenever I begin to feel overwhelmed by the spiritual opposition against me, I remind myself of the sacrifice of these martyrs. When I meditate on the sacrifice of these martyrs, I am quickly reminded of how my sacrifice pales compared to theirs. I thank God that many Christians who live in developed nations like the United States will never know the horror of having to resist sin unto the shedding of their own blood. The religious and civil liberties we enjoy exclude us from facing such a fate; even though our brothers and sisters in the Middle East and China face many occasions in which resisting sin requires the shedding of their own blood.

The Chastening of the Lord

And ye have forgotten the exhortation which speaketh unto you as unto children, My son, despise not thou the chastening of the Lord, nor faint when thou art rebuked of him: 6For whom the Lord loveth he chasteneth, and scourgeth every son whom he receiveth.

Hebrews 12:5-6

The proliferation of the "User-friendly Gospel" in Christendom has left in its wake a generation of Christians who despise the chastening of the Lord: the very thing we are admonished not to do by the writer of the book of Hebrews. I have talked to pastors who are terrified of confronting their people in righteousness lest they become "offended" and leave the church. In America, new church plants are mushrooming everywhere. Many of these so-called church plants are rooted in a spirit of offense towards a former pastor. It's not difficult to imagine why Christians birthed in an atmosphere of offense have very little tolerance for the "Chastening of the Lord."

But even in church plants that have a righteous root, the apostles or pastors over these congregations are walking on eggshells when it comes to challenging sin in the lives of their church members. Unfortunately, the Lord Jesus Christ and the Holy Spirit do not walk on eggshells for anybody, especially when those eggshells concern His dear children. God will chastise or discipline any of His children at any given moment regardless of the level of fame and influence they have in the Body of Christ. *So if we walk in holiness we will not need the chastisement.*

The writer of the book of Hebrews is quick to point out that the reason God chastises or disciplines His children is because He loves us with an everlasting love. True love, especially the Agape kind of love, cannot stand silent in the face of wrong. But the Lord's chastisement is not a harsh judgment of an adversarial judge. It's the all-consuming righteous judgment of a Heavenly Father oozing with unbridled affection for His children. When I lived in South Africa, I befriended an African brother who worked for the South African Air force. His eighteen year-old son committed suicide in his house. Next to the dead body was a note that deepened the grief of the grieving father. In the suicide note, the boy stated that he had killed himself because he was convinced his father did not love him, because he never chastised him when he was doing wrong. This experience opened my eyes to the wisdom of Hebrews 12:5-6.

Spiritual Bastards versus Spiritual Sons

If ye endure chastening, God dealeth with you as with sons; for what son is he whom the father chasteneth not? 8But if ye be without chastisement, whereof all are partakers, then are ye bastards, and not sons.

Hebrews 12:7-8

The writer of the book of Hebrews tells us that when God is "chastening" us, He is dealing with us as sons and daughters. This being the case we are admonished to endure the chastening of the Lord. But it's what he says next that caused the hairs on my skin to stand up. The Apostle Paul says that if the Lord does not chastise us then we are "bastards" and not "sons." This is a very serious state of affairs.

A "bastard" is a person without a father. It's a person disconnected from the loving and nurturing affection of a father. Worse still, a bastard is a person who has been disowned as a son by a father because of systemic rebellion to the father's authority. In ancient Greek and Roman mythology, the people believed that a person who did not have a god who could claim him or her was "cursed by the gods." To be parentless as it pertained to the gods was deeply frowned upon. If people who worshipped worthless idols believed in the importance of belonging to a deity, we have much to be excited about. We are serving the true and living God, who treats us as sons and daughters.

The Father of Spirits

Furthermore we have had fathers of our flesh, which corrected us, and we gave them reverence: shall we not much rather be in subjection unto the Father of spirits, and live?

Hebrews 12:9

Life's greatest tragedy is that many nations, corporations, families and even churches are led by orphans. How many nations, corporations, families, and even churches are led by a man or woman who never knew their father? How many nations, corporations, families, and even churches are led by a man or woman who has never experienced the constant and unwavering companionship of a loving, caring, and responsible father? How many nations, corporations, families, and even churches are led by a man or woman who endured the devastating pain of seeing their father walk out on them? How many nations, corporations, families, and even churches are led by a man or woman who came home from school to hear their tear-drenched mom say, "Dad has left us! He's not coming back home." (Excerpt from the Order of Melchizedek)

When I was hosting a school of ministry in the United Kingdom, one of my students was a 67year old man who had been raised in an orphanage. He had been married for over 40 years but he struggled, expressing any form of physical affection towards his wife even though his actions belied the fact that he truly loved her. On the second night of our school of ministry he walked up to me and started bemoaning the fact that he couldn't show his dear wife any meaningful emotional response because, as an orphan, he always felt unworthy and unwanted. I placed both of my hands on his shoulders and looked him in the eye and said, "Who told you that you are an orphan?"

He was shocked by my response. I told him that he was not an orphan; he had a very loving heavenly Father who fathered his human spirit. I told him that his reference point for being an orphan was the wrong starting point because it eliminated the role of the all-powerful Heavenly Father in his life. Suddenly a light bulb of revelation flashed through his spirit and he started crying with ecstasy. The following morning this man wore the most dazzling smile you have ever seen. His wife was also happy. She told us that he was finally flooding her with kisses, hugs and words full of heartfelt emotional warmth. The writer of the book of Hebrews admonishes us never to forget that God is our primary Father, long before our natural parents come into the picture as a distant second. This revelation is capable of transforming the lives of millions of Christians and Messianic believers worldwide.

The Purpose of Spiritual Fathering

For they verily for a few days chastened us after their own pleasure; but he for our profit, that we might be partakers of his holiness.

Hebrews 12:10

Malachi 4:5-6 is, in my opinion, one of the most profound Scripture passages in the whole of the Bible. This one verse captures the heartbeat of Kingdom living. It captures the very heartbeat of God. What is even more striking about this Scripture passage is that it is a forerunner to the Messiah's Order of Melchizedek priesthood. It is also the last verse in the Old Testament. Just imagine: the last thing that God talked about and mandated Himself to in the entire Old Testament involves the supernatural infusion of a fathering spirit into the earth. (Excerpt from the Order of Melchizedek)

The primary purpose of spiritual fathering is to make us become partakers of His holiness. Holiness is the eternal condition of God. It is His divine essence and nature. This is why we are commanded to be holy even as He is holy. Making us holy is one of the main reasons why the Lord chastises or scourges His children. There are a lot of men of God in the Body of Christ who act like the purpose of spiritual fathering is to fatten their wallets and increase their followership. But nothing could be further from the truth. Spiritual fathering is an extension of the heartbeat of the Heavenly Father for His dear children. This divine heartbeat when supernaturally deposited into the hearts of mature ministers in the Lord creates the dynamic known as "spiritual fathering." But since God does not work against Himself, true spiritual fathers carry the same desire to see God's children become partakers of His holiness. Once the greater Body of Christ comes into an accurate understanding of the Melchizedek priesthood of the Lord Jesus Christ, the Holy Spirit will raise many bona fide spiritual fathers and mothers. This prophetic company of spiritual fathers and mothers will take ownership of the task of discipling the next generation into the purposes of God. Before the close of this present age into the millennial reign of Christ on earth, the Holy Spirit will baptize many mature ministers in the Body of Christ with the purest form of spiritual fathering and mothering that this planet has ever seen, void of ego, self-promoting agendas and greed.

The Peaceable Fruit of Righteousness

Now no chastening for the present seemeth to be joyous, but grievous: nevertheless afterward it yieldeth the peaceable fruit of righteousness unto them, which are exercised thereby. 12Wherefore lift up the hands, which hang down, and the feeble knees; 13And make straight paths for your feet, lest that which is lame be turned out of the way; but let it rather be healed.

Hebrews 12:11-12

The writer of the book of Hebrews now unravels God's ultimate intent for chastening and scourging those He loves. Like any responsible natural fathers, God knows that "foolishness" is bound up in the heart of a child. A natural child who is left to grow without any sort of correction grows up into a spoiled and self-centered adult. This is perhaps the reason King Solomon declares from the holy writ, "foolishness is bound up in the heart of a child but the rod of correction will drive it far from him." If the above scenario is true of a natural child it's even more so for spiritual children.

If God never corrects or scourges us when we act contrary to His Word and divine nature, we would morph into spoiled and self-loving Christians. Without divine chastening our "outer man" would completely rule our "regenerated inner man." Unfortunately, this is the primary condition of many Christians. The powerful shell of their outer man has never been broken by the dealings of God so as to release the Spirit who resides in their born-again spirit. But Paul the Apostle tells us in the above passage that when we endure the chastening of the Lord it produces the "peaceable fruit of righteousness", even though divine chastening does not feel exciting when we are going through it. But once the Lord is finished dealing with us, we immediately fall in love with the person we have suddenly become. I have never met any Christ loving Christian who went through the chastening of the Lord who regretted having gone through it. Every Christian who has ever been disciplined by the Lord was eternally grateful to the Lord for doing so.

In the final analysis, the writer of the book of Hebrews shows us that divine chastening also has the added "benefit" of strengthening areas of weakness in our lives. Every person born of a woman after the fall of Adam and Eve apart from the Lord Jesus has inherent character flaws. These character flaws, or unhealed soul conditions, can open doors for the enemy to attack us. For example, some Christians have the weakness of being easily offended. If the Lord does not chasten them into a place of deliverance in this vunerable area of their life, the Devil will take advantage of them.

The Pathway of Peace and Holiness

Follow peace with all men, and holiness, without which no man shall see the Lord:

Hebrews 12:14

There is a path that every member of the Body of Christ has to travel if they desire a closer walk with God. God seekers such as Enoch, who walked with God until he was raptured, have stepped on this pathway. Moses, the lawgiver, whose face sparkled with the radiance of God's glory after spending forty days in the presence of God, also traveled on this pathway. What pathway am I referring to? It is the "pathway of Peace and Holiness."

The writer of the book of Hebrews sternly admonishes to "follow" the "way of peace and holiness." He ends his serious admonition by declaring that without walking on the pathway of peace and holiness there is no man who will ever see the Lord. Wow, this is serious business. This stern warning of the Apostle Paul flies against the message of "greasy grace" that is permeating many Christian churches in the Western world. I am a strong believer in the grace of the Lord Jesus Christ. But I shudder when "Grace" is used as a license for living a life that is less than honoring to the Lord. I hate religious legalism, too. But I find the "extreme grace message" just as unsettling. Child of God, let nothing and no one steal your peace and condition of holiness.

The Root of Bitterness

Looking diligently lest any man fail of the grace of God; lest any root of bitterness springing up trouble you, and thereby many be defiled;

Hebrews 12:15

I have been saved for over twenty years. I have yet to come across any spiritual condition that is more poisonous than a heart filled with the "root of bitterness." The root of bitterness is a very dangerous root. It is the breeding ground of an avalanche of demonic activity. I have seen this root destroy marriages, destinies, businesses and churches.

The writer of the book of Hebrews gives us a powerful glossary list of what happens once the "root of bitterness" is sown in our hearts or the people close to us.

1. The root of bitterness will cause the one who has it to fall short of the Grace of the Lord Jesus Christ. This means that when a person has a root of bitterness in his or her heart, he or she automatically disqualifies him or herself from receiving the grace of the Lord Jesus Christ.

2. Christians who carry the root of bitterness will stir up trouble wherever they are. This is because their heart is already embittered. An embittered heart is a heart driven by a demonically engineered desire for revenge. A bitter person has no room in their heart that wishes for the well-being of others.

3. The root of bitterness quickly establishes itself in the spiritual climate of those closest to it, until they are also infected by it. I have seen great churches that were torn to shreds when one of the staff members became embittered and then went on a warpath. This is because the "root of bitterness" in the heart opens the door for the spirit of bitterness to spread in the camp like a malignant cancer. This is why the Lord Jesus Christ resists His children who allow themselves to be influenced by this demonic spirit.

Watch out for people, especially professing Christians, who carry the root of bitterness in their heart. They are easy to recognize because their favorite subject is demeaning or undermining other fellow Christians. Whenever you come across such a person, run for your dear life, unless you are mature enough in Christ to negotiate their complete deliverance. If you stick around you will be recruited to serve a demonic agenda. It has been said, "misery loves company;" so does bitterness. Bitterness is actually the mother of misery. If you are struggling with the root of bitterness run to a mature believer and confess your faults that you may be healed. Tell on yourself before the Devil destroys you with it.

The Proliferation of the "User-Friendly Gospel" in Christendom has Left in its Wake a Generation of *Christians* who Despise the Chastening of the *Lord*

Don't Sell your Birthright

Lest there be any fornicator, or profane person, as Esau, who for one morsel of meat sold his birthright. 17For ye know how that afterward, when he would have inherited the blessing, he was rejected: for he found no place of repentance, though he sought it carefully with tears.

Hebrews 12:16-17

When Rebecca was pregnant, she became bothered by the tag of war in her womb and sought the Lord for the meaning behind it. The Lord responded by telling her that she was pregnant with two nations. Two baby boys were going to come out of her womb. They would have diametrically different destinies and callings. The younger one was called to a higher destiny than the older one. As told to her by the Lord, on the day of delivery, two boys came out of her womb. The firstborn was named Esau and the second child came out of the womb with his hand holding on to the heel of his elder brother - a prophetic sign for a life long struggle for preeminence between the two brothers.

Esau quickly grew into an outdoor man, who loved to hunt wild animals. He would have been a zealous member of the NRA had he been an American. Esau also established himself as his father Isaac's favorite son. Jacob on the other hand was a domesticated sort of guy who spent more time in the kitchen with his mother and tending to his father's flock. Rebecca, who was privy to the prophetic word that came out of the mouth of God that the younger son would be the most preeminent in heaven's economy, invested her deepest affection for her younger son, Jacob.

No doubt, Rebecca must have shared the heavenly edict with her adoring son, who became hungrier for the blessing of God as time clocked on. Jacob was more attuned to the things of the Spirit than his worldly-life-loving elder brother. In the process of time, Esau returned from an exhausting hunting trip. He was starving. His hunger-glazed eyes fell upon the lentils that Jacob had meticulously cooked to perfection. He begged his brother for the bowl of lentils. His brother sensing an opportunity for a one-sided negotiation grinned. Jacob told his elder brother that he was willing to offer his starving brother the bowl of lentils if he gave up his "firstborn right."

> *Esau said to Jacob, "I'm starved! Give me some of that red stew!" (This is how Esau got his other name, Edom, which means "red.") 31"All right," Jacob replied, "but trade me your rights as the firstborn son." 32"Look, I'm dying of starvation!" said Esau. "What good is my birthright to me now?" 33But Jacob said, "First you must swear that your birthright is mine." So Esau swore an oath, thereby selling all his rights as the firstborn to his brother, Jacob.*
>
> (Genesis 25:30-33).

This Bible passage contains one of the most tragic renunciations of the blessing of God by a human being void of spiritual understanding. His love of "self" spit in the face of God. Faced with the opportunity to choose between a natural product of sustenance and a supernatural one; he chose an inferior, ever diminishing natural element. He chose food over destiny. He chose ego over purpose. He chose a bowl of lentils over his God given spiritual birthright!

Heaven noted his catastrophic decision with a sigh of finality. The Holy Spirit wrote in heaven's minutes, "Esau's birthright sold on earth for a bowl of lentils. Heaven duly acknowledges this earthly transaction. All angels assigned to Esau's birthright are duly reassigned. Amen." The transaction between Esau and Jacob here on earth is living proof that "what we do here on earth echoes in eternity!" The writer of the book of Hebrews tells us that after Esau realized the far-reaching implications of what he had done, he tried desperately to reverse the transaction. But heaven was not listening. His decision was final. Esau would die as an insignificant progenitor in the economy of the Kingdom here on earth. History would remember him only to reference him as the fool who sold his God given birthright for a bowl of lentils.

Unfortunately, there has been many Esau's since. The Body of Christ is full of men and women who internally despise who they are and what they were created to be in order to be someone else. They seem to forget that in God's eyes they are God's firstborn, because there is no other person in human history that carries their distinctive DNA and destiny. The spirit of Esau is the primary technology behind the spirit of jealousy and competition that has destroyed so many spiritual alliances for Kingdom advancement. May the good Lord deliver us from this demonic insidious nature.

Mount Zion

For ye are not come unto the mount that might be touched, and that burned with fire, nor unto blackness, and darkness, and tempest, 19And the sound of a trumpet, and the voice of words; which voice they that heard intreated that the word should not be spoken to them any more: 20(For they could not endure that which was commanded, And if so much as a beast touch the mountain, it shall be stoned, or thrust through with a dart: 21And so terrible was the sight, that Moses said, I exceedingly fear and quake:) 22But ye are come unto mount Sion, and unto the city of the living God, the heavenly Jerusalem, and to an innumerable company of angels, 23To the general assembly and church of the firstborn, which are written in heaven, and to God the Judge of all, and to the spirits of just men made perfect.

Hebrews 12:18-23

The writer of the book of Hebrews finally introduces us to Mount Zion, the City of the Living God. This is the same City of God that is responsible for demonstrating the eternal power of the Melchizedek

Priesthood of Yeshua to a lost and dying world (Psalm 110:1-4). Jesus Christ, the Unchanging Person and His Unshakeable Kingdom are the spiritual architectural composition of Mount Zion. Mount Zion is the Mountain Kingdom of God's Holy habitation. The prophet Daniel told a dumbfounded King Nebuchadnezzar that this holy Mountain would displace all the kingdoms of this world through a "stone cut" without human hands (Daniel 2:37-46). The stone cut without human hands is the blessed Lord Jesus Christ who was born outside the confines of the sexual union of a man and a woman.

What I love about the book of Hebrews is that it goes further than any other book of the Bible to describe the spiritual composition of this eternal City of the Living God. We will now take an introspective look at the spiritual and architectural composition of Mount Zion.

❖ Mount Zion is the City of the Living God. This means that this City is the Spiritual habitation of the IAM presence of God.

❖ Mount Zion is the heavenly and spiritual Jerusalem, which is the mother of us all - Jew and Gentile (Galatians 4:26).

❖ Mount Zion is the true City of Angels and not the fictional imagination of Hollywood movie producers. The number of angels who live and are employed in the service of God in Mount Zion is innumerable. A calculator from our world cannot calculate the number of angels stationed in Mount Zion! This also means that there are far more angels in the universe than there are demons. This is why born again Christians have no reason to live in fear.

❖ Mount Zion houses "the general assembly." The General Assembly are the larger majority in the crowd of witnesses alluded to in the twelfth chapter of the book of Hebrews. The "General Assembly" consist of all born again believers who came to the saving knowledge of the Lord Jesus Christ while they were on earth but "never really paid the price" to be overcomers in this life the same way He (Yeshua) overcame (Revelation 3:21).

❖ Mount Zion also houses the "Church of the firstborn." The *Church of the Firstborn* consist of all born again believers who came to the saving knowledge of the Lord Jesus Christ while they were on earth and "paid the price" for the higher calling of God in Christ Jesus (Philippians 3:10-20). They became overcomers in this life in much the same way Yeshua overcame to become the firstborn from the dead (Revelation 3:21). Members of the Church of the Firstborn earned the right through their walk of obedience to God here on earth to be eternally enthroned with Christ. These are the "kings" He is King of. These are the ones who crucified self for Christ's sake and loved not their own lives unto death (Revelation 12:11). Christ's millennial Kingdom will be full of multiplied millions of blood-washed redeemed followers of the Messiah, but as individuals not all of them will be enthroned in Mount Zion. Nevertheless, all the redeemed as members of the corporate Body of Christ will reign with Christ forever and ever. Even as I write this book, I pray with fear and trembling that the Holy Spirit would help me to live a life here on earth that will qualify me to be included in the *Church of the Firstborn.*

❖ Mount Zion houses all "the written records" of all the redeemed of the Lord. These written records also contain the foreordained destinies and righteous works of the redeemed in heaven and on earth. These written records also contain the eternal, immutable counsel of God for His creation from before the foundation of the world. These written records also contain the redeeming work of Jesus Christ as the Lamb of God slain before the foundation of the world (Revelation

13:8). These written records also contain information on the all actions of the wicked from the beginning of time. These written records also contain the knowledge of "witty inventions, scientific discoveries and technologies" that will rapidly advance the Kingdom of God, while improving the standard of living here on earth.

❖ Mount Zion is also the spiritual location of the "Highest Court of Appeal" in all of creation. It's the location of God, the righteous Judge of all of creation. This is why Jesus said, *"when the Son of man sets you free, you are free indeed."* This is because when Yeshua sets a person free, the Highest Court of Appeal places its seal of approval on the acquittal. Since Mount Zion is also the spiritual location of the "Highest Court of Appeal" there is no demonic activity here on earth ambassadors of Christ cannot place under His feet (Psalm 110:1-2).

❖ Mount Zion also houses the "spirits of just men made perfect." This spiritual company includes all the righteous Old Testament Jewish believers, before the Mosaic Law and after who lived before the shedding of Jesus's blood on Calvary but served God whole-heartedly with complete abandonment. Abraham, Isaac, Jacob, King David, Queen Esther and many others belong to this group of the "spirits of just men made perfect." Some in this group also belong to *the Church of the Firstborn*. This group of the "spirits of just men made perfect" is the same group of Old Testament saints that came out of their graves when Jesus Christ rose from the dead (Matthew 27:52-53). This is the same group of saints that Christ Jesus led "captive" when He ascended to heaven (Ephesians 4:10).

❖ **Disclaimer:** *I do not believe in the gospel of inclusion or ultimate reconciliation where each soul who has* *ever lived ultimately ends up in heaven, reconciled to God. The Bible does teach that there are people who will be resurrected unto eternal damnation because they completely rejected Yeshua as their Messiah and continuously violated their conscience. However only God knows for sure who will ultimately end up in heaven or hell. But His indispensable and everlasting sense of justice will make sure that those who end up in hell have cemented their decision to be there!*

The Blood Speaks

And to Jesus the mediator of the new covenant, and to the blood of sprinkling, that speaketh better things than that of Abel.

Hebrews 12:24

Mount Zion is also the eternal habitation of Yeshua, the mediator of the New Covenant, as well as His precious blood. According to the writer of the book of Hebrews, the predominant voice or sound in Mount Zion is the voice of the precious blood of Jesus Christ. When the devious and envious Cain murdered his righteous brother; Abel's shed blood began to cry out for vengeance as soon as it touched the ground. God's courtroom was bombarded by cries for justice from the blood of Abel that had seeped into the ground (Genesis 4). Consequently, God approached defiant Cain in judgment. The judgment of God that fell upon Cain in order to execute justice drove Cain from the presence of the Lord, turning him into a vagabond here on earth.

Fast forward. Four thousand years later the Lord sent His only begotten Son (Yeshua) born of a woman under the Law to redeem mankind (Galatians 4). When Jesus Christ's time came to die for the sins of all mankind, He started shedding His blood in the Garden of Gethsemane all the way to the Cross. When a Roman soldier pierced His side (rib), blood and water came out. Thus, His bride, the Church, was born through the power of the precious blood and water.

When Jesus rose from the dead, His first assignment was to take the "shed blood" to the throne room of the Heavenly Father. When He entered the heavenly holy of holies like the Old Testament Levitical High Priest, it was with his precious blood. The blood was poured on the Throne of God transforming it immediately into the "Throne of Grace and Mercy." Since then the blood of Jesus has been "speaking of better things" than the blood of Abel. Instead of crying for vengeance, the precious blood of Christ cries for mercy, healing, deliverance, forgiveness and restoration.

The Shaking of Heaven and Earth

See that ye refuse not him that speaketh. For if they escaped not who refused him that spake on earth, much more shall not we escape, if we turn away from him that speaketh from heaven: 26Whose voice then shook the earth: but now he hath promised, saying, Yet once more I shake not the earth only, but also heaven. 27And this word, Yet once more, signifieth the removing of those things that are shaken, as of things that are made, that those things which cannot be shaken may remain.

Hebrews 12:25-27

The writer of the book of Hebrews now warns us to tread carefully and remain sensitive to the voice of the Holy Spirit. As the Church and the nations of the world approach the consummation of the ages in Christ Jesus, the Lord has initiated a divinely orchestrated "shaking." Many Christians and Messianic Jews who are not spiritually attuned to the frequency of heaven will misconstrue this shaking as the work of the Devil. In so doing, many will resist the dealings of the Lord and suffer more in their spiritual walk for failing to discern His mighty hand. God has promised to shake heaven and earth, targeting only those things that can be shaken. The "things" that can be shaken lack the composition of His Kingdom, which cannot be shaken.

What are the "things that will be shaken?" This is a very important question for us to ask ourselves, lest we are found holding onto "things" scheduled for shaking. The book of Romans contains the category of the "things" that will be shaken (Romans 1:20-32). 1 Corinthians 15:28 is clear that some of the "things" that must be shaken are the demonic principalities of this present age of darkness. These demonic powers have blinded the spiritual eyes of generations from seeing the glorious Gospel of the Lord Jesus Christ. God is shaking, and will shake, more of these evil entities from their place of power over the affairs of the nations of this present age.

The Unshakable Kingdom

Wherefore we are receiving a kingdom, which cannot be moved, let us have grace, whereby we may serve God acceptably with reverence and godly fear. 29For our God is a consuming fire.

Hebrews 12:28-29

The writer of the book of Hebrews finally unveils God's primary intent behind the universal shaking of all that can be shaken. The divine intent is three-fold. Firstly, the shaking of all things is to clearly distinguish the "things" that belong to His Kingdom against the "things" of this present age that are passing away. If the thing you are holding to is "shaking" under the rumblings of God's glory, it's a sure sign that you really do not need it to fulfill your spiritual assignment. The spirit of materialism that has gripped many Christians like a malignant cancer has caused many people of faith to be married to "things" that do not really matter. The shaking will deliver many Christians from this cancer, while devastating others. We will learn how to hold onto material things "loosely."

Secondly, the divine intent behind the shaking is to demonstrate to His blood washed children the power and immutability of the Kingdom that we have received. God wants to show us that we have received a "Kingdom," which cannot be shaken, through the shaking. We will discover that areas of our lives that used to shake us no longer move us. Some of us are shaking in our boots at the prospect of rejection from our peers. But when God is finished with the shaking we will be as emotionally stable as Mount Zion. We will come to know firsthand that there is nothing in the demonic kingdom that can "shake the Kingdom" within us.

> IF THE THING YOU ARE HOLDING IS "SHAKING" UNDER THE RUMBLINGS OF *God's* GLORY, IT'S A SURE SIGN THAT YOU REALLY DO NOT NEED IT TO FULFILL YOUR SPIRITUAL ASSIGNMENT.

Finally, the divine intent behind the shaking is to give us the grace to serve God acceptably, in the fear of the Lord. The fear of man is suffocating the lives of multiplied thousands in the Body of Christ who are in servitude to the whims of other people's opinions. But thank God, the shaking has already started. *Many children of the kingdom will be delivered from the fear of men to the fear of the Lord.* The fear of the Lord will soon become a very common spiritual technology within the greater Body of Christ. It is my humble opinion that it's impossible to serve God acceptably without the fear of the Lord. It is the fear of the Lord that makes a married person refuse to cheat on their spouse. It is the fear of the Lord that keeps a pastor from fleecing his sheep. Without the fear of the Lord, spiritual mayhem will reign in the lives of the people of God.

KINGDOM CULTURE & MORAL VALUES

D R. BEN CARSON, divisional director of Pediatric Neurosurgery at the world famous Johns Hopkins Hospital, in his dazzling speech at the 2012 National Prayer Breakfast in Washington DC made some very powerful observations. His compelling speech was addressed to a room full of movers and shakers, including President Barack Obama and Vice President Joe Biden. You can watch this moving speech anytime on YouTube. Here is one of the statements that he made that struck a nerve in my spirit and I quote:

> *"I think particularly about ancient Rome. Very powerful - nobody could even challenge them militarily...they destroyed themselves from within," Carson continued. "Moral decay. Fiscal irresponsibility."*

Kingdom Moral Values

Let brotherly love continue. 2Be not forgetful to entertain strangers: for thereby some have entertained angels unawares. 3Remember them that are in bonds, as bound with them; and them which suffer adversity, as being yourselves also in the body.

Hebrews 13:1-3

Dr. Ben Carson's argument is that enemies from without did not destroy one of the most powerful kingdoms in human history- the Roman Empire. It destroyed itself over the decline in moral values and fiscal responsibility. This is why the Lord Jesus Christ in his famous Sermon on the Mount focused on the subject of Kingdom moral values. No kingdom, no matter how strong, is unable to survive without a set of immutable moral values that all citizens have to adhere to. Adherence of citizens to these moral values creates the powerful social phenomenon known as "Culture."

In the above passage of Scripture, the writer of the book of Hebrews joins Dr. Ben Carson in declaring the importance of a set of immutable, changeless moral values to the survival of kingdoms. In the passage above, the Apostle Paul only lists three of those immutable moral values that all Kingdom citizens are expected to emulate. To get more immutable Kingdom moral values, please refer to the Sermon on the Mount in the fifth chapter of the gospel according to Matthew. Nevertheless, I will quickly list the three that the writer of Hebrews alludes to in the above passage.

1. **Brotherly Love:** Brotherly love is one of the most important Kingdom moral values, because faith works through love and love covers a multitude of sins. Unfortunately, the absence of this Kingdom moral value is responsible for the carnage of godly relationships within the Body of Christ. Life's greatest cancer is "self-love" but God's antidote to this spiritual disease is brotherly love.

2. **Hospitality:** Even ancient Israel was admonished by God to be hospitable to strangers at all times because they (Israelites) had also been strangers in a foreign land (Egypt) that had treated them harshly. The writer of the book of Hebrews tells us that many Kingdom citizens are unaware that they entertaining angels because they lack the spirit of hospitality. Christians need to be more hospitable to one another and not be married to "material stuff." There are Christians who have vacation homes they hardly live in who will not lift a finger to accommodate a brother or sister in Christ whose home was just foreclosed on. Heaven weeps as the absence of genuine hospitality continues

to compromise the moral code of God's unshakable Kingdom. Even our immigration policy must never be so difficult to meander that it makes it impossible for countries to be hospitable to immigrants who are in "true" need of shelter from mortal danger, as well as those who have a God given heavenly calling to the nations in question.

3. **Charity:** The third Kingdom moral value that the writer of Hebrews touches on is quickly entering the dinosaur age in most Western nations and is being replaced by a more egregious spirit, a spirit of entitlement! History will quickly show that one of the main characteristics that defined past generations of Americans was their deep commitment to charity. Everybody worked hard so they could be a blessing to someone else. Giving to the poor and the less fortunate defined American exceptional-ism. But the spirit that made this country great is being replaced by a spirit of entitlement that teaches the citizenry to master the art of receiving while crushing the spirit of innovation and giving. Consequently, giving to charitable organizations is now the lowest it has ever been in American History when the percentage of giving is adjusted for inflation. The Body of Christ needs to recapture this important Kingdom moral value. God's people must be the best people at helping the poor and less fortunate.

Marriage is an Honorable Institution

Marriage is honorable in all, and the bed undefiled: but whoremongers and adulterers God will judge.

Hebrews 13:4

The institution of Marriage is under tremendous assault all over the world, most especially in the liberal nations of the West. Prophets of political correctness and propagators of liberal ideology would have us believe the lie that the enduring definition of marriage being between a man and a woman is outdated. Nothing could be further from the truth.

NO KINGDOM NO MATTER HOW STRONG, CAN SURVIVE WITHOUT A SET OF IMMUTABLE MORAL VALUES THAT ALL CITIZENS HAVE TO ADHERE TO.

The writer of the book of Hebrews tells us that marriage is honorable in all, and the bed undefiled. This expression has far reaching spiritual and natural implications. The expression carries the following implications:

❖ Marriage is honorable. This means that marriage is something every male and female person should aspire to get into. It's not a prison like some liberal thinkers would have us believe.

❖ Marriage is honorable in all. This means that the honor God has placed on marriage has an enduring quality to it that transcends the shifting sands of time and human thought. It also means that marriages are both honorable and applicable to all cultures. How one culture celebrates the marriage of a man and a woman may differ, but God honors each ceremony with His presence. The only marriage that God does not honor is the marriage between partners of the same sex (Romans 1:24-26); even though the Lord loves and died for the people who are caught up in these situations.

❖ Marriage is the only relationship between a man and a woman, which does not bring a spirit of defilement into the bedroom during the act of sexual intercourse. There are a lot of Christians in the Western Hemisphere who are engaged in active sexual activity with their so-called live-in boyfriend and girlfriend. Most justify this behavior by saying they intend to get married anyway! But the intent to get married is not marriage. This "shacking up" (having sex before marriage) culture has become a breeding ground for demonic powers and technologies that have crept into the Church. When you have preachers siring babies out-of-wedlock you know that this is certainly an epidemic!

❖ Whoremongers (fornicators, sexual perverts) and adulterers (cheating spouses), God Almighty will judge. This expression in the verse expresses just how passionate God is about defending the honorable institution of marriage.

A New Breed without Greed

Let your conversation be without covetousness; and be content with such things as ye have: for he hath said, I will never leave thee, nor forsake thee.

Hebrews 13:5

The writer of the book of Hebrews now tells us that God wants His people to be a *"new breed without greed"* in the earth; in a world that is rampant with systemic financial corruption and greed. God's people are admonished to let their walk of faith be without "covetousness," instead we are to be content with whatever worldly possessions we currently have. This is not to suggest that God is advocating that Christians who find themselves in impoverished stations in life are not to make efforts to better their station in life. But it is to say that God does not want either our lack of money or our abundance to cause us to be so restless that we walk out of the peace of God. Jesus already told us in the gospels that a man's life does not consist of the things that he or she owns. God, and not material possessions, is to be the center of our lives.

Many of the problems that *Christians and Messianic Jews have can be traced back to a soul infected by the spirit of materialism.* We live in a world that is largely influenced by the pseudo lifestyles of most Hollywood icons, who spend money on frivolous pleasures like there is no tomorrow. It's easy to see why the Church has been bought into the same spirit of materialism. Unfortunately, materialism only opens the door to the cancer of greed. This green-eyed monster has destroyed many business alliances in the marketplace between many Christian businessmen and women. The writer of Hebrews finally presents the main reason why Christians need to be content in whatever financial station they find themselves. They need to live in contentment because God has already given them something that money cannot buy in a billion years: the abiding presence of God.

Breaking the Fear of Man

So that we may boldly say, The Lord is my helper, and I will not fear what man shall do unto me.

Hebrews 13:6

One of the main reasons the founding fathers of the United States of America left Europe and traveled thousands of miles across the treacherous seas was to build a nation under God where they could have freedom of worship. Intricately tied to freedom of worship is the freedom of speech; a right that they fought for and bled to defend. But this unalienable right is currently under siege in American society by proponents of "Political Correctness." Consequently, many Americans are afraid to speak up in fear of the repercussions from those who would take offense to their words.

But why would many Americans give up on a right that the founding fathers proudly died to defend? The reason for this is hidden in an ancient story of both deception and treason. In the Garden of Eden after Adam and Eve heeded the voice of the Serpent and committed high treason against the government of God, the spirit of fear suddenly came upon them when they heard the voice of God walking in the cool of the day. Since then engines of fear have not stop turning. This demonic factory churns out all kinds of fears. But the most common and the most lethal is the "fear of man."

HOW ONE CULTURE CELEBRATES THE MARRIAGE OF A MAN AND WOMAN MAY DIFFER, BUT *God* HONORS EACH CEREMONY WITH HIS PRESENCE.

The fear of man is the most common and the most lethal because ever since the Fall, human kind has been plagued with the worst case of identity crisis. People who have an identity crisis are terrified of any kind of rejection from their peers, especially from people whose favor they desperately covet. The fear of rejection is essentially what opens the door to the fear of man. The graveyards are filled with the skeletons of men and women who were buried with dreams and destinies that were never realized because they failed to break the "fear of man" over their lives. The writer of Hebrews tells us that the antidote to this cancer is to become conscious that the LORD is our helper. In the book of Romans, the great apostle declares, "if God be for us, who can be against us?" Answering this question will deliver many people of faith from the fear of man.

A Culture of Honor

Remember them, which have the rule over you, who have spoken unto you the word of God: whose faith follow, considering the end of their conversation. 17Obey them that have the rule over you, and submit yourselves: for they watch for your souls, as they that must give account, that they may do it with joy, and not with grief: for that is unprofitable for you.

Hebrews 13:7, 17

The writer of the book of Hebrews now moves his apologetic discourse to one of the most important ingredients of Kingdom Culture. It is the subject of honor. The corridors of human history testify to the power of this one ingredient in sustaining kingdoms and relationships.

There is nothing more powerful and life giving than the bestowment of honor upon those to whom honor is due. The primary Being who deserves to be honored by all of His creation is God. Honor is one of the most important principles of the Kingdom of God. It is the cornerstone of kingdom living; without it kingdoms go into a state of decline. No spiritual culture can ever be referred to as a "Kingdom culture" which does not have this principle of honor deeply imbedded in it. Honor quickly establishes itself as a divine life-giving principle whenever it is instituted into any relationship. Marriages, governments, friendships, covenants, and business relationships flourish whenever the principle of honor is engrafted into them. (Excerpt from the Order of Melchizedek by Dr. Francis Myles)

The Unchanging Person

Jesus Christ the same yesterday, and to day, and forever.

Hebrews 13:8

In a world of ever shifting moral standards and ideologies, it's quite reassuring to know that Jesus Christ will never change. His passion for his people, his principles, love and mission will never suffer the decay of time and space. Who He is does not depend on the changing of the sands of time or on how good or bad His people behave. We can expect Yeshua to remain faithful to what He promised even when we are unfaithful as ancient Israel was at times.

It excites my heart greatly when I contemplate the fact that born-again Christians have been given citizenship in an unshakeable Kingdom governed by an Unchanging Person. The "unshakeable Kingdom" (Hebrews 10:31) is actually ruled by an "Unchanging Person." Election after election many politicians make grandeurous promises on the campaign trail that most never intend to keep. The person on the campaign, who offered the populace so much hope of a better tomorrow, usually turns out to be a ghost created by political pundits to win an election. Inevitably, once the election is over, the real person shows up, while the voters wonder what happened to their candidate.

This would explain why trust in government and politicians in America and around the world is at an all-time low. But glory be to God that we can trust everything that the Lord Jesus says and has ever said. He is truly the same yesterday, today and forever. What a wonderful feeling. If He performed miracles yesterday or fed the hungry, he will do it again and again. You can be sure of it.

A Heart Established in Grace

Be not carried about with divers and strange doctrines. For it is a good thing that the heart be established with grace; not with meats, which have not profited them that have been occupied therein.

Hebrews 13:9

We live in a world of endless competing political ideologies and religious philosophies. In a spiritual climate such as this, it's easy to see why some Christians are so spiritually tuned out. But the writer of the book of Hebrews tells us that we can enter a place in God where we will not be carried about by "false doctrines." The Apostle Paul offers the solution to the aforementioned dilemma. The man of God tells us that the Holy Spirit will give us the "grace" to live above both man-made and demonically engineered doctrines. "Grace" is divine enablement. God will flood our hearts with the grace to discern between true and false doctrines. Even as you read this book, I challenge you to ask the Lord to give you the grace to live above every wind of doctrine and establish your heart in grace.

Take the Flesh out of the Sanctuary

For the bodies of those beasts, whose blood is brought into the sanctuary by the high priest for sin, are burned without the camp. 12Wherefore Jesus also, that he might sanctify the people with his own blood, suffered without the gate.

Hebrews 13:11-12

The writer of the book of Hebrews now addresses the number one enemy of the Church. This enemy is the "flesh." This flesh is also referred to by the Bible as "our old man" who was put to death on the cross by the Lord Jesus Christ. In the fifth chapter of the book of Galatians the Apostle Paul gives us an excellent discourse about the tag of war between the Spirit and the flesh. The writer of Galatians goes as far as describing in great detail the "works or fruits" of the flesh. He surmises his argument against the "flesh" by declaring that those who do the bidding of the flesh will not inherit the Kingdom of God.

The "flesh" (our carnal nature) is such an enemy of God that even in the Old Testament liturgical system of worship and sacrifices, the Lord instructed the High Priest to burn the body of the scapegoat on the outskirts of the City. God did not want His people (Israelites) to even smell the burning of the bodies of sacrificial animals. Prophetically speaking the Lord despises the stench of the flesh in His Church, because God does not want the flesh to glory in His presence.

In keeping with the Old Testament prophetic pattern, the Lord Jesus Christ was crucified outside the City of Jerusalem because He was about to become sin on the cross. On that rugged cross outside the camp, the Lord Jesus took our "old man" (flesh) and crucified him. As His blood dropped to the ground, our victory against living a life driven by the flesh was secured. I believe that the rallying cry of the Spirit to the body of Christ is: "take the flesh out of my sanctuary!" Recent sexual scandals by very famous preachers once again shook the global Church but the scandals only served to show how the smell of the flesh is defiling the temple of God. There is a prevailing generation of Christians rising across the nations of the world, who will not tolerate anything spotted by the flesh.

Bearing the Reproach of Christ

Let us go forth therefore unto him without the camp, bearing his reproach.

Hebrews 13:13

I believe in the gospel of prosperity. I believe that from antiquity it has always been God's desire to prosper His people. This would explain why He created man and placed him in a garden of abundance. But unfortunately, there are some, in the "faith or prosperity camp," who teach that Christians who do not have money do not have enough faith in God. Material prosperity quickly became the treasured seal of the godly. If a Christian seemed to be going through prolonged financial challenges, there are those who are quick to point out that such Christians must be living in sin.

Fortunately, the writer of the book of Hebrews disagrees with this misguided thesis, by declaring that followers of Christ have been called to *"bear the reproach of Christ."* This expression means that God's people are called to "suffer" the shame that the world confers on people who, like Jesus, call it back to repentance. Unfortunately, many Christians just want to share in the charisma of Christ but shun incidences that will make them share in the reproach of Christ. This is why so many Christians are failing to pay the price for the higher calling of God in Christ Jesus (Philippians 3:10-16). On the other hand, when the apostles were arrested and punished by the Sanhedrin council (Acts 4) for preaching in the name of Jesus, they left their captors rejoicing at the fact that they had been counted worthy to share in the reproach of Christ. God is raising a prevailing Bride that will gladly embrace both the charisma of Christ as well as the reproach of Christ.

Waiting for the New Jerusalem

For here have we no continuing city, but we seek one to come.

Hebrews 13:14

We were created to live in a City. This is because we have a God given desire to live in community. In the famous faith chapter (Hebrews 11) the writer of Hebrews gives us an interesting glimpse into the driving passion of the patriarchs. He tells us that if these men and women had been mindful of the country of origin they would have returned to it. But instead, they persisted through life's trials because they were looking for a "City" whose maker and builder is God. This expression lets me know that God had somehow given them a glimpse of the "New Jerusalem."

The Apostle Paul in the fourth chapter of Galatians tells us that the New Jerusalem is the mother of us all (followers of Christ). This City is a City of freedom. There is no one who is bound in this City because it is Mount Zion, the City of the Living God. In the book of Revelation (chapter 22), John the revelator saw the New Jerusalem descending from heaven to dwell among men here on earth. This will be a glorious time indeed. This is why no Christian should be living on Prozac; because we have so much to look forward to now and then.

The Sacrifice of Praise

By him therefore let us offer the sacrifice of praise to God continually, that is, the fruit of our lips giving thanks to his name.

Hebrews 13:15

The writer of the book of Hebrews tells us, that post Calvary, the highest sacrifice we can give to God is the "sacrifice of praise." Praise must be the fruit of our lips. Instead of complaining and feeling sorry for ourselves, we are commanded to praise the Lord. Saint Paul also shows us the primary purpose of "praise" in the final expression of the verse *"giving thanks to His name." This expression contains the essence of true Spirit driven praise. Praise is about giving thanks to His name for who He is and what He has already done.*

But why does the apostle of God call the giving of thanks to His name "the sacrifice of Praise?" I am glad you asked me. The reason the writer of Hebrews calls it the sacrifice of praise is because more often than not God wants His children to bless His name even when our circumstances contradict the Word and goodness of God. Instead of being paralyzed by the giants in front of us, we must open our mouth and give thanks to His holy name. This is the secret of King Jehoshaphat, when the nation of Israel was challenged by a formidable enemy hell bent on destroying them (2 Chronicles 20). The King placed singers in front of his army as they walked towards the frontlines of the battlefield. The singers were praising God while the armies of Israel trailed behind. When they arrived at the front lines of the battlefield they discovered carnage of historical proportions. The army of the Syrians had turned on each other and every one lay dead on the ground. Its time the body of Christ took the weapon of praise seriously.

Kingdom Philanthropy

But to do good and to communicate forget not: for with such sacrifices God is well pleased.

Hebrews 13:16

As the Body of Christ comes into a consecrated place of spiritual maturity concerning its understanding of the gospel of the Kingdom and the Melchizedek priesthood of Jesus Christ, we are going to see an increase in Kingdom driven philanthropy. The writer of the book of Hebrews admonishes us not to forget to do "good and give generously". He also informs us that God is well pleased with such sacrifices.

It is a shame that for the longest time the world has been the global leader in community changing philanthropy while the Christians obsessed about going to heaven. This is in stark contrast to the early Church who pioneered Spirit led philanthropy for the purpose of advancing the Kingdom of God. The reason so many Christian churches are lagging behind the world in the area of philanthropy is due to the Church's obsession with the gospel of salvation instead of the gospel of the Kingdom.

The difference between the gospel of salvation and the gospel of Kingdom is staggering. The gospel of salvation focuses on the salvation of an individual and then preparing the same to go to heaven. While the gospel of the Kingdom, which Jesus taught while He was on earth, focuses on the salvation and transformation of nations. Since the gospel of the Kingdom is about the healing of nations, it refocuses our attention onto replanting the culture and values of heaven here on earth instead of just waiting on the rapture train, while nations crumble under the power of the enemy.

The Power of a Good Conscience

Pray for us: for we trust we have a good conscience, in all things willing to live honestly. 19But I beseech you the rather to do this, that I may be restored to you the sooner.
Hebrews 13:18-19

The Bible declares that some followers of Christ have made shipwreck of their faith because they learned the bad habit of violating their conscience. The conscience is the voice of the regenerated spirit of a born again believer. It is difficult to walk in a high level of spiritual authority over the demonic powers when we are violating our conscience. The writer of the book of Hebrews admonishes citizens of the Kingdom of God to have a good conscience by doing their best to live an honest life. This does not mean that we will never make a mistake but it does mean that we are to strive to live with a good conscience before God.

I believe that all famous men and women of God who have ever been publicly exposed in a sexual scandal were given multiple chances by the Holy Spirit to listen to their conscience. But I believe that after years of resisting their conscience, the Lord stepped aside and allowed the enemy to have his way. Over the years I have discovered that one of the ways we can live with a good conscience is to be quick to repent and forgive people who hurt us. The Lord who is faithful will cleanse us from all unrighteousness (1 John 1:9). The apostolic prophecy concerning the last days is that a generation will rise whose conscience (1 Timothy 4:2) is "seared with a hot iron." This must never become our spiritual state.

The God of Peace

Now the God of peace, that brought again from the dead our Lord Jesus, that great shepherd of the sheep, through the blood of the everlasting covenant,

Hebrews 13:20

In the United States of America men and women seeking peace in their shattered lives spend millions of dollars a year on psychiatry. Many of these precious people become hooked on their psychiatrist, but the peace they long for never comes. The writer of the book of Hebrews tells us that the Father of the Lord Jesus Christ is the God of Peace. This means that every soul starved of peace here on earth can come to Him through His beloved Son to acquire the much-needed peace of heart and mind.

IT IS A SHAME THAT FOR THE LONGEST THE WORLD HAS BEEN THE GLOBAL LEADER IN COMMUNITY CHANGING PHILANTHROPY, WHILE CHRISTIANS OBSESS ABOUT GOING TO HEAVEN.

The writer of Hebrews also shows us how the God of Peace transfers His peace to the people that desperately need it. The peace of the God of Peace was secured by the death of the Lord Jesus Christ on the cross. Consequently, the blood that Jesus shed on the cross became an everlasting symbol of the price that was paid by the great Shepherd of our soul to secure the peace of the God of Peace. In South Africa, a woman who had been insane for over fifteen years was instantly set free when I had a word of knowledge that Jesus was pouring a bucket of blood over a woman in the service. She instantly recovered the use of her mind and was gloriously saved.

The Grace to Do His Will

Make you perfect in every good work to do his will, working in you that which is well pleasing in his sight, through Jesus Christ; to whom be glory for ever and ever. Amen.

Hebrews 13:21

We were not saved to warm the pews of the Church until the return of Jesus. But sadly, this is the testimony of so many followers of Christ. Other than regular church attendance, many Christians are mere passengers on the bus of destiny. The writer of the book of Hebrews tells us that God wants to perfect or mature us so that we can "do His will!" We were created to do His will. Anything else is a complete waste of time and energy.

God wants to give us the "grace to do His will!" This means that obeying the call of God upon our lives does not have to be a struggle whatsoever. According to the writer of the book of Hebrews, this "grace" will work in us that which is pleasing in His eyes. This means that we will be instinctively drawn to doing things that are pleasing to the Lord. This grace to do His will is the same grace that was upon the Lord Jesus Christ when he was on earth. When the grace to do His will comes upon us, doing His will become first nature.

Suffering for the Word

And I beseech you, brethren, suffer the word of exhortation: for I have written a letter unto you in few words. 23Know ye that our brother Timothy is set at liberty; with whom, if he come shortly, I will see you. 24Salute all them that have the rule over you, and all the saints. They of Italy salute you.

Hebrews 13:22-24

God is raising Timothies (young ministers of the gospel) all over the world who are not afraid to suffer for preaching the Word of God. They are willing to suffer for the Word. Persecution for the sake of the Word does not seem to bother them. The church world is full of plastic Christians who melt easily in the heat of battle. The writer of Hebrews tells us of young Timothy who had been jailed for his faith in Christ. The Apostle Paul informs his audience of the fact that Timothy had just been released from jail, after having suffered for the Word. I believe that before the consummation of the ages in Christ there will be some Kingdom citizens who will be given the privilege of suffering for the Word of God.

All Believers Need Grace

Grace be with you all. Amen.

Hebrews 13:25

The Apostle's final salutation is probably just as important a truth as the rest of the chapter. He closes his dissertation by saying, "grace be with you ALL!" By this one statement the writer of the book of Hebrews makes it adamantly clear that all born again believers (followers of Christ) need grace. None of us can do what God has called us to do, let alone walk in the life of the One New man without the grace of the Lord Jesus Christ. It takes grace to do anything meaningful for God. I always tell people *"where there is no grace there is always disgrace."*

IS JESUS CHRIST MELCHIZEDEK?

SINCE writing and publishing my book, "The Order of Melchizedek," there is one question I am frequently asked by many Christians: *"Doctor Myles, is Jesus, Melchizedek?"* I know why this question above all others pops up frequently, as more Christians and Messianic Jews around the world are beginning to "awaken to the New Testament realities of the Melchizedek priesthood." Many born again and God-fearing Christians want the "Truth", but they do not want to be misled into following "another gospel."

I could not agree more as one who has seen the spiritual damage that can be caused by false doctrines. There are many pastors scared to even address the subject of "Melchizedek" because they do not know how to effectively answer the question, "Is Jesus Melchizedek?" These pastors nervously skirt around the subject of Melchizedek, each time they read the book of Hebrews, wondering why the Apostle Paul would spend so much time discussing a priesthood that they do not fully understand. Some pastors even believe that the subject on Melchizedek is either a Mormon doctrine, or at worst, a new age philosophy. This has caused them to get very defensive when you mention the Order of Melchizedek. Notwithstanding, the answer to the proverbial question, *"Is Jesus Melchizedek",* is a resounding, "YES!" But just saying, "Yes" trivializes one of the most important subjects in the Bible. So I will systematically and theologically answer this very important question, depending entirely upon the authority of the Holy Scriptures.

In doing so, I will be relying on what the Holy Spirit has personally revealed to me about the Order of Melchizedek. I will also be quoting from an unnamed author, who has a very scriptural exposé of this question on his website (www. http://www.near-death.com/ experiences/origen042.html). Any additions that I will be adding to the unknown author's original writing will be in italics. The Scripture tells us that the "Truth" is established upon the testimony of two or three witnesses, most especially if that witness is the witness of complementing scriptural passages.

According to John 1:1, Christ, the Living Word is the very essence of all of creation. So it must not surprise us that there are several "incarnations of Christ (Jesus), the Living Word through the shifting sands of time and space." Some theologians prefer to call these incarnations of the Living Word as "Theophany's." For instance, Christ was the Light that entered this world when God decreed, *"Let there be light" in Genesis 1:4!*

> *In Him was Life, and the Life was the Light of men.*
>
> John 1:4 (AB)

Christ was the Ladder reaching up to heaven that allows the holy angels to ascend and descend between heaven and earth.

And he dreamed that there was a ladder set upon the earth, and the top of it reached to heaven; and the angels of God were ascending and descending on it! 13And behold, the Lord stood over and beside him and said, I am the Lord, the God of Abraham your father [forefather] and the God of Isaac;

Genesis 28:12-13 (AB)

Christ was the Angel of the Lord, who met with Jacob at the river Jabok and changed his name from Jacob to Israel.

> *[The Man] asked him, What is your name? And [in shock of realization, whispering] he said, Jacob [supplanter, schemer, trickster, swindler]! 28And He said, Your name shall be called no more Jacob [supplanter], but Israel [contender with God]; for*

you have contended and have power with God and with men and have prevailed.

Genesis 32:27-28 (AB)

Christ was the Cloud by day and Fire by night that led the Children of Israel to the Promised Land.

And the Lord went before them by day in a pillar of a cloud, to lead them the way; and by night in a pillar of fire, to give them light; to go by day and night:

Exodus 13:21

Christ was the Rock that Moses struck twice, causing water to issue from the Rock so the children of Israel could quench their thirst. Christ had so incarnated into the Rock that when Moses struck the Rock twice in anger, God immediately judged him for his grievous sin. The Bible tells us that this was like crucifying Jesus Christ twice! The sin of striking the Rock twice was the reason God did not allow Moses to enter into the Promised Land. Divine judgment came upon his physical body even though his soul was spared. This is why the Devil came to fight with the archangel Michael, over the body of Moses.

Behold, I will stand before you there on the rock at [Mount] Horeb; and you shall strike the rock, and water shall come out of it, that the people may drink. And Moses did so in the sight of the elders of Israel.

Exodus 17:6

And they all drank the same spiritual (supernaturally given) drink. For they drank from a spiritual Rock which followed them [produced by the sole power of God Himself without natural instrumentality], and the Rock was Christ. I Corinthians 10:4

But when [even] the archangel Michael, contending with the devil, judicially argued (disputed) about the body of Moses, he dared not [presume to] bring an abusive condemnation against him, but [simply] said, The Lord rebuke you!

Jude 1:9

Another incarnation of Jesus or Yeshua is the Old Testament figure known as Melchizedek, the High Priest and King of Salem. It is clear from the Book of Hebrews that Melchizedek was not an ordinary man, assuming he even was a man. A careful examination of the evidence concerning the existence of Melchizedek reveals him to be a previous reincarnation of Jesus. There are strong parallels between Melchizedek and Jesus: both are the Son of God, priest of the Order of Melchizedek, King of Righteous, King of Peace, the Messiah, appointed by God, eternal priesthood, and preexistent. Besides the biblical evidence, there exists evidence from the discoveries of early Christian texts in 1945 and the Dead Sea Scrolls in 1947. There are also extra-biblical revelations that support this Melchizedek-Jesus connection.

Identical Characteristics between Jesus and Melchizedek

We will now examine identical characteristics between Jesus and Melchizedek that will help us greatly in answering the question "Is Jesus, Melchizedek?" These identical characteristics are not based upon my personal opinion but on comparing Scripture with Scripture. The Bible is one of the best books at the art of self-interpretation.

Both *Melchizedek and Jesus Christ* are:

1. *Sons of God*

2. *High Priests of God*

3. *Kings of Righteousness*

4. *Kings of Peace*

5. *Associated with Abraham*

6. *Anointed Ones*

7. *Appointed by God*

8. *Eternal ones*

9. *Have holy rituals of Bread and Wine*

10. *Both have a Royal Priesthood*

11. *Both collect tithes from their subjects*

12. *Priesthood of both is based upon personality not legality*

Identical Sonship: "Son of God"

•   In the Bible, the only individuals who have the title of the "Son of God" are Jesus, Adam and Melchizedek.

Adam: *"the son of Seth, the son of Adam, the son of God."* (Luke 3:38)

Melchizedek: *"Without father or mother, without genealogy, without beginning of days or end of life, like the Son of God he remains a priest forever."* (Hebrews 7:3)

Jesus: *"The beginning of the Gospel about Jesus Christ, the Son of God."* (Mark 1:1)

A. The Bible also states that Melchizedek was made in the image or likeness of the Son of God. This could be taken as the image of the Son of God (the second in the trinity) or as the image of the begotten Son of God, when the Lord took on a fleshly body. But they are one and the same.

Jesus: *"the glory of Christ, who is the image of God."* (2 Corinthians 4:4)

Jesus: *"You are a priest forever, in the Order of Melchizedek."* (Hebrews 5:6)

Definition of "order": *Greek "aphomoioo" (a) A facsimile (b) An exact copy or exact reproduction (c) A duplicate*

Jesus: *"And what we have said is even more clear if another priest like Melchizedek appears."* (Hebrews 7:15)

Definition of "another priest like": *Greek "kata ten homoioteta" (a) in every respect (b) after the similitude of (c) according to the likeness of (d) a thing so like another as to be indistinguishable from it.*

Identical Order of Priesthood: Priest of the God Most High of the Order of Melchizedek

A. Melchizedek and Jesus have identical priesthoods.

Melchizedek: *"He was priest of God Most High."* (Genesis 14:18)

Messiah: *"You are a priest forever according to the Order of Melchizedek."* (Psalm 110:4)

Jesus: *"You are a priest forever, in the order [facsimile] of Melchizedek."* (Hebrews 5:6)

Definition of "facsimile": *(a) an exact copy or exact reproduction (b) duplicate.*

Identical Age: Pre-existent

A. Both Melchizedek and Jesus are pre-existent (i.e. they existed before birth).

Melchizedek: *"Without father or mother, without genealogy, without beginning of days or end of life, like the Son of God he remains a priest forever."* (Hebrews 7:3)

Jesus: *"But you, Bethlehem Ephrathah, though you are small among the clans of Judah, out of you will come for me one who will be ruler over Israel, whose origins are from of old, from ancient times."* (Micah 5:2)

Identical Symbol of Rule: "King of Righteousness"

A. Melchizedek as the King of Righteousness:

- *"To whom Abraham gave a tenth part of all, first being by interpretation King of Righteousness and after that also King of Salem, whi0ch is King of Peace.* (Hebrews 7:2)

B. Jesus as the King of Righteousness:

- *"The days are coming," declares the Lord, "when I will raise up to David a righteous Branch, a King who will reign wisely and do what is just and right in the land."* (Jeremiah 23:5)

Identical Right to Rule: Appointed by God

A. Jesus' and Melchizedek's priesthoods are similar because they did not depend upon genealogy as the Aaronic priesthood did. The human lineage of Jesus was from Judah - a tribe that Moses did not associate with the priesthood.

- *"For it is clear that our Lord descended from Judah, and in regard to that tribe Moses said nothing about priests."* (Hebrews 7:14)

B. Jesus Christ is a priest after the order of Melchizedek, not because he came from the right line, but because he comes as one who has indestructible life - the only one who can be an eternal priest! The priesthood of both is a royal priesthood. The priesthood of both is based on personality, not legality. Both are universal priesthoods, for Gentile and Jew, because the priesthood of Melchizedek existed before the Law was given. Melchizedek illustrates an eternal priesthood of which Jesus is the reality.

Identical Title: "King of Peace"

A. Melchizedek and Jesus are the Kings of Peace.

Melchizedek: *"First, his name means "King of Righteousness"; then also, "King of Salem" means "King of Peace."* (Hebrews 7:2)

Jesus: *"And he will be called Wonderful Counselor, Mighty God, Everlasting Father, Prince of Peace."* (Isaiah 9:6)

B. Melchizedek is the "King of Peace" and Jesus is the "Prince of Peace." Who could be King of Peace over Jesus? *The answer is staggeringly simple. No human being, whether present or historical would be King of Peace over Jesus, unless the two personalities are actually the same person - the Lord Jesus Christ.*

Identical Term of Priesthood: Eternal

A. Melchizedek and Jesus are eternal priests.

Melchizedek: *"like the Son of God he remains a priest forever."* (Hebrews 7:3)

Jesus: *"You are a priest forever, in the Order of Melchizedek."* (Hebrews. 5:6)

B. Melchizedek and Jesus are priests forever with an unchangeable priesthood. This indicates they are the same priest - just different times.

Identical Association with: Abraham

A. Both Melchizedek and Jesus were both associated with Abraham:

Melchizedek: *"Then Melchizedek king of Salem brought out bread and wine. He was priest of God Most High, and he blessed Abraham, saying, "Blessed be Abraham by God Most High, Creator of heaven and Earth."* (Genesis 14:18-19)

Jesus: *"Your father Abraham rejoiced at the thought of seeing my day; he saw it and was glad. "You are not yet fifty years old,"* the Jews said to him, "and you have seen Abraham?" "I tell you the truth," Jesus answered, "before Abraham was born, I am!"* (John 8:56-59)

A. Melchizedek and Jesus are one spirit who incarnated many times and who transcended death.

B. They could enter and leave the world at will without having to go through birth and death.

"Now there have been many of those priests, since death prevented them from continuing in office; but because Jesus lives forever, he has a permanent priesthood."

Hebrews 7:23

Identical Use of Ritualistic Symbols: Bread and Wine

A. Melchizedek's offering of bread and wine to Abraham is the first incidence where bread and wine appear in the Scripture. Melchizedek provided a priesthood, which gave the symbols of bread and wine. Jesus also provided a priesthood, which gave the symbols of bread and wine.

Melchizedek: *"And Melchizedek King of Salem brought forth bread and wine..."* (Genesis 14:18)

Jesus: *"While they were eating, Jesus took bread, gave thanks and broke it, and gave it to his disciples, saying, "Take and eat; this is my body." Then he took the cup, gave thanks and offered it to them, saying, "Drink from it, all of you. This is my blood of the covenant, which is poured out for many for the forgiveness of sins. I tell you, I will not drink of this fruit of the vine from now on until that day when I drink it anew with you in my Father's kingdom."* (Matthew 26:26-9)

Identical in Likeness: Priest

A. Melchizedek and Jesus are priests of God.

Melchizedek: *"He was priest of God Most High."* (Genesis 14:18)

Jesus: *"And it is yet far more evident if, in the likeness of Melchizedek, there arises another priest who has come."* (Hebrews 7:15-16)

The word "likeness" is translated homoios: (a) "after the similitude of

Note: Heb. 7:15-16 does not mean Jesus is "similar to Melchizedek." In context, it means

"Jesus is Melchizedek."

Proof: Another Biblical example of "homoios" meaning "likeness.

Who, being in very nature God, did not consider equality with God something to be grasped, but made himself nothing, taking the very nature of a servant, being made in human likeness."

Philippians 2:6-7

Point 1: Jesus was human: *The Word became flesh.* (John 1:14)

Point 2: And Jesus had a human nature: *"The gospel he promised beforehand through his prophets in the Holy Scriptures regarding his Son, who as to his human nature was a descendant of David."* (Romans 1:2-4)

Conclusion: Jesus was more than just the likeness of Melchizedek

Jesus was Melchizedek!

B. Why would Jesus be compared to Melchizedek if his status was not equal to or greater than Jesus? He certainly would not be compared to anyone lesser than himself. This suggests that both Melchizedek and Jesus were of the same nature and of similar purpose and, therefore, the same person.

Dead Sea Scroll Discovery of 1947 revealed the Messiah to be a Reincarnation of Melchizedek:

In 1947, scrolls from the Jewish Essenes were discovered which affirmed that they believed Melchizedek would reincarnate as the Messiah.

These ancient scrolls of profound importance were discovered by young Bedouin shepherds, searching for a stray goat around the Dead Sea in Israel. They entered an undiscovered cave and found jars filled with ancient scrolls. The Dead Sea Scrolls were scrolls from a monastic group known as the Essenes, dated to be about two thousand years old. The Essenes were an apocalyptic Jewish sect who withdrew from society and established a monastery on the shores of the Dead Sea. It is believed that sometime during the Roman-Jewish war of 66-70 A.D., the Essenes hid their sacred writings.

The Essenes believed in the doctrine of pre-existence and reincarnation and appeared to have been influenced by Gnosticism. The Dead Sea Scrolls prove that the Jewish mystical tradition of divine union went back to the first, perhaps even the third, century B.C. Biblical scholars were not disturbed by what they found in the Dead Sea Scrolls because they had known all along that the origin of Christianity was not what was commonly supposed to have been.

The first-century Jewish historian Flavius Josephus stated that the Pharisees were believers in reincarnation. Josephus has several long passages dealing with the reincarnation beliefs of both the Essenes and the Pharisees. Josephus writes that the Jews in their secret or esoteric doctrines called the Kabbalah taught reincarnation openly.

The caves where the Dead Sea Scrolls were found yielded a series of thirteen fragments on Melchizedek which identifies Melchizedek as the one who will carry out the vengeance of God's judgments and the one who delivers the people from the hand of Belial and the spirits of his lot.

The belief that Melchizedek was the Messiah was a strongly held conviction among the Qumran community, as well as among some other Jewish and Gnostic sects in the first century A.D. This becomes apparent in the text entitled "The Last Jubilee" (Dead Sea Scroll: 11Q13, Column 2) about the coming of Melchizedek as the Messiah. "The Last Jubilee" is a sermon within the "Melchizedek Texts" (also known as "I IQ Melchizedek Text" or "I I Q Melchizedek"). The following is a summary of this sermon:

The Last Jubilee text refers in messianic terms to a future King of Righteousness. In the text, this King of Righteousness is described as passing judgment on Belial [Satan] and his followers. After the judgment in heaven comes the destruction of those who have followed Belial rather than God. The text states that "the one designed, by God's favor, for the King of Righteousness (which is what, by his very name, Melchizedek prefigures) will come into his dominion." The time of his coming "into his dominion" is identified as the period, which Isaiah termed the year of favor or "acceptable year of the Lord"

The Biblical reference for this can be found in Isaiah 61:1-2:

"The Spirit of the Lord God is upon me; because the Lord has anointed me to bring good tidings to the afflicted, he has sent me to bind up the brokenhearted, to proclaim liberty to the captive, and the opening of the prison to those who are bound; to proclaim the year of the Lord's favor, and the day of vengeance of our God; to comfort all that mourn ..."

Isaiah 61:1-2

Final Thoughts on the Priesthood of the Believer

Now, that we have answered conclusively the question of "Is Jesus Melchizedek?" We MUST now ask another equally important question. *"If Melchizedek is the Lord Jesus Christ, how does this reality impact the priesthood of the believer?"* The answer to this second question is also staggeringly simple, but revolutionary in nature. Since Jesus Christ is the Head of the New Testament Church, it goes without saying that the priesthood that flows through Him also flows through us, because we are His body. This means that all born again Christians or followers of Christ have a present day priestly ministry patterned after the Order of Melchizedek. This is the bona fide truth whether they know it or not. Pretending or denying the fact that the moon exists does not, in any way, negate this immutable fact.

As is the earthy, such are they also that are earthy: and as is the heavenly, such are they also that are heavenly.

I Corinthians 15:48

In the epistle to the Corinthians, the Apostle Paul declares that "as He (Jesus) is in Heaven" so are we (Kingdom Citizens) here on earth.

The book of Hebrews is adamantly clear that Jesus is currently seated in the third heaven on the right hand of God as an eternal High Priest after the Order of Melchizedek (Hebrews 5:4-10). Since this is the case, it means that born again Christians here on earth have a priestly ministry in accordance with the Order of Melchizedek.

> *But ye are a chosen generation, a royal priesthood, an holy nation, a peculiar people; that ye should shew forth the praises of him who hath called you out of darkness into his marvellous light;*
>
> I Peter 2:9

Any orthodox Jew who understood the Torah and the Talmud knew immediately that the Apostle Peter was not referring to the Aaronic or Levitical priesthood when he calls born again believers a "royal priesthood." Those deeply invested in Judaism knew that even though the Tribe of Levi was the priestly tribe of Israel, it was not a royal tribe. There was no royal lineage running through the priestly line. The only God ordained priesthood that the people of Israel had ever been exposed to, that allowed for a priest to also function in the kingly anointing, was the Melchizedek priesthood. It is thus clear that the Apostle Peter's usage of the term, "royal priesthood" was both deliberate and purposeful. It was meant to infer the Melchizedek priesthood in the minds of the Jewish believers who had just turned to the Lord Jesus Christ.

The Holy Spirit has already shown me the radical transformation that the global Church will come into once many of its members begin to rediscover the Melchizedek priesthood of Jesus Christ. ***The priesthood of the believer in the temple and the marketplace will become a universal reality that will greatly advance the Kingdom of God here on earth.*** The day will soon come and I believe that it's already upon us, when the "Order of Melchizedek Chronicles" of books that I have published, will become the blueprints for moving the Body of Christ into its final thrust of ministry to a lost and dying world. It is inevitable and necessary for the *"restoration of the Melchizedek Priesthood"* to precede the return of the Lord Jesus Christ and the consummation of the ages in Christ.

Whom heaven must receive until the times of restoration of all things, which God has spoken by the mouth of all His holy prophets since the world began.

Acts 3:21

The apostolic decree of Peter the apostle echoes throughout eternity that the "heavens must hold Jesus until the restoration of all things!" The understanding of the Order of Melchizedek by the Body of Christ is one of the key pillars of truth that needs to be restored to the Church's consciousness. Revelation 1:6 which states, *"He has made us a Kingdom of kings and priests unto God"* can never be realized without the Church entering into the Melchizedek priesthood of Jesus Christ.

REFERENCES

Laying the Foundation Vol 1 © 1986 — Derek Prince Ministries International Page 40, http://en.wikipedia.org/wiki/Martin_Luther Page 84

Authority for Assignment: *Releasing God's Government in the Marketplace,* by Dr. Gordon Bradshaw Page 86,

Is Jesus Melchizedek www.near-death.com/experiences/origen042.html, Page 178

OTHER LIFE CHANGING BOOKS BY DR. MYLES

(Please visit www.themarketplaceapostle.net or francismyles.com to order these dynamic books, DVDs, CDs and MP3)

To BOOK Dr. Francis Myles for your EVENT please email "themarketplaceapostle@gmail.com."

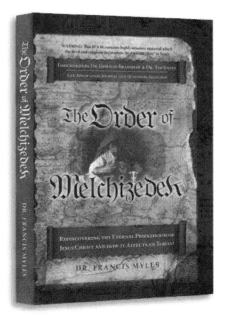

In this life-changing message Dr. Francis Myles wants to take this opportunity to "Introduce You" to one of the most powerful "Spiritual Orders" that God has ever instituted to service the spiritual needs of "Kingdom citizens" during their "Pilgrimage" here on earth The "ORDER" of "MELCHIZEDEK." *In this explosive teaching Dr. Francis Myles will show you:*

- God's enduring agenda to station on earth a functional body of Kings and Priests who can represent the Kingdom of God accurately.

- How the Order of Melchizedek will unleash a "Fathering spirit" in the church and the marketplace, for community transformation.

- Plus MUCH MORE…

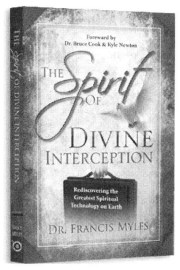

In this life-changing book, Dr. Francis Myles introduces the reader to one of the most powerful spiritual technologies in all of creation. God instituted this technology to govern the spiritual, social and financial affairs of Kingdom citizens during their pilgrimage here on earth. At the heart of all informed spiritual or scientific research is a body of questions that fuel the whole investigation. In the spirit of informed investigation, this book will seek to answer the following questions:

- Why are these stories of disaster and regret concentrated in the Marketplace?

- Why do Kingdom entrepreneurs lose millions of dollars in bad business deals?

- Is there a "fail-proof" technology for "intercepting" much of the evil that is visited upon humans before it actually happens?

- Plus MUCH MORE...

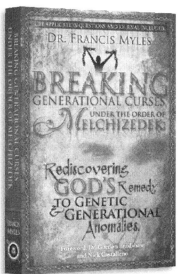

IN THIS "TRANSFORMATIVE" BOOK, Dr. Francis Myles wants to take this opportunity to introduce you to one of the most powerful "Spiritual technologies" for "Breaking Generational Curses and Healing all types of Genetic Anomalies" that God instituted to service the spiritual needs of "Kingdom citizens" who operate under the "Order of Melchizedek."

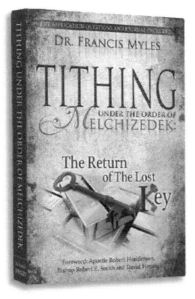

In this explosive book bestselling author Dr. Francis Myles confronts head on, inaccurate patterns of tithing within the global Body of Christ. This book is a MUST read for those who have given up on tithing and those who tithe regularly. Dr. Francis Myles will show the reader why Malachi 3:8-12 tithing model is NOT God's best tithing system for New Testament believers, while simultaneously uncovering the Abrahamic tithing model, which is based on "honor instead of legalism." A breakthrough-tithing model that the devil and religious tradition have tried to COVER-UP until NOW!

25388697R30152

Made in the USA
Charleston, SC
27 December 2013